VOLUME 22   NUMBER 2   2016

Area Impossible:
The Geopolitics of Queer Studies

Edited by Anjali Arondekar and Geeta Patel

Introduction

AREA IMPOSSIBLE

Notes toward an Introduction

Anjali Arondekar and Geeta Patel

I. Orientations

"Let me cry out in the void, say it as I can. I write on that void: Kash-
mir, Kaschmir, Cashmere, Qashmir, Cashmir, Cashmire, Kashmere,
Cachemire, Cushmeer, Cachmiere, Casmir. Or *Cauchemar* in a sea
of stories? Or: Kacmir, Kaschemir, Kasmere, Kachmire, Kasmir.
Kerseymere?"
—Agha Shahid Ali, *The Country without a Post Office*

$\mathcal{W}$hen a journal (such as *GLQ*) does a special issue on a topic as hoary as
area studies, there may well be cause for alarm, curiosity, even consternation.
One could ask, what is the novelty in such an engagement? Have we not already
been there and done that? Isn't area studies precisely the "void" we want to avoid?
After all, the past decade or so has seen the publication of a veritable cottage
industry of special issues, omnibus reviews, anthologies, and collections engaging
the nexus of geopolitics and sexuality. Variously articulated through the language
of transnationalism(s), regions, hemispheres, or more directly as a supplement to
the conventional forms in which geopolitics has been explored, queer studies has
incited a vast traveling archive of commentaries. *GLQ*, specifically, has over the
years opened itself up to special issues that have wrestled with questions of geopolitics and representation. As early as 1999, a special issue coedited by George
Chauncey and Elizabeth Povinelli addressed the conceptual knots and representa-

GLQ 22:2
DOI 10.1215/10642684-3428687
© 2016 by Duke University Press

tional flows through which spatialities were fashioned in queered genres. Focusing largely on contemporary predilections and repositories, the issue tuned in to the frisson between global traffic and local habits, urging readers to attend more vigilantly to the political economies underwriting such conversations (Chauncey and Povinelli 1999).

Yet even as such perverse implantations jostle settled notions of geopolitics, some pointed collusions emerge between the various publications. (1) With a few exceptions, the citational underpinnings that provide the theoretical conduit for such explorations were and continue to be resolutely contemporary and drawn primarily from the United States; that is, geopolitics provides the exemplars, but rarely the epistemologies. (2) By invoking non-Euro-American sources, settings, and epistemes as exemplars, queer theory mostly speaks to US mappings of queer, rather than transacting across questions from different sites, colluding and colliding along the way. Thus such concepts as loss, margin, normative, and nonnormative, to name a select few, animate many of these writings, without an attentiveness to them as productive and theoretical formations that concatenate US political projects. (3) One notes a studied avoidance of any engagement with area studies.[1] Most of the writings we read and researched around the queer-geopolitics nexus for this special issue do not name area studies as the form that they are working against, if that indeed is the case.[2] On the rare occasion that a collection, such as the excellent *Islamicate Sexualities*, does invoke the specter of area studies, it appears as a burdensome geopolitical category (incarnated, for example, in the term *Middle East*), to be jettisoned for a broader and more robust understanding of the cultures of Islam (Babayan and Najmabadi 2008).

Given such a strident refusal of area studies in the scholarly engagements with sexuality and geopolitics, why are we attempting to mine a formation so charged with obsolescence? Any quick review of the establishment of area studies in the United States would highlight its emergence as an intelligence-gathering force for consolidating US power, especially between World War II and the Cold War (Szanton 2004). The post-9/11 resurgence of a revised area studies further emphasized the linkages between state power and research on "sensitive" areas such as South and West Asia, the Levant, and North Africa, with money flows from foreign agencies and governments making the knowledge of such "areas" a new marketplace of speculation and profit (Miyoshi and Harootunian 2002).[3] Surely, returning to such a moribund and corporatized form would then seem futile, even dangerous, given the fraught legacies of its emergence. Yet how could we not? If area studies is a moribund form, it is outmoded in the same ways that empire is. At a moment when the celebration (or even complication) of concepts such as transnational and global in queer studies is accompanied by the torture and deaths of queer bodies marked by the legacies of area studies, we contend that there is little else to talk about. To give in to such disturbing scenes as mere exemplars of queer presence and absence, without scrupulous attentiveness to the convoluted densities of geopolitics, would paradoxically reinstate the queer as either exemplary or insular.

We are less interested in summoning up forgotten histories of geopolitics (through area studies) than in grappling with the reasons why certain vocabularies of the geopolitical achieve prominence and why others get relegated to the ash heap of (queer) history. In other words, does the elision of area studies within queer studies constitute a willed refusal to name the epistemological genres that US political initiatives have taken outside its territorial borders, a refusal to concede perhaps that these very commonplaces might hold the residue of post–Cold War settler colonial intimations? Vulgarly put, it is as though, if one did not speak through "area studies," the United States might be able to retain its hold as a homing device to which salutary queer epistemologies might be continually oriented, and the United States might hold its own as the home of intellectual reserve currency that underwrites the queer collaborations with "area" sans "area studies." Area studies, as we have pointed out, also suggests avenues into historical freightedness that might be usefully exploited in queer studies collections somewhat attentive to the questions of what the past might carry. After all, under the sign of capitalism, reigning ideas are hardly inimical to the forces of the market.

Our project here is not to provide a corrective or alternative, or to sanitize or otherwise pulverize such efforts to add queer to area. Indeed, any effort to chart or critique any intellectual current is, as we well know, ipso facto reductionist. There is no theoretical cataclysm on offer here. Neither is our invocation of area and area studies (especially as we hear the hesitant rumblings of discontent from within the ranks of our own contributors!) meant to summon up proper knowledge of the elsewhere, most notably the global south, which might circulate to restyle or commute the so-called provincialism of the north. Surely, area studies in its current form, like queer studies removed from the anthropological voyeurism of its early forays into sexuality, is no longer a simple effect of ventures, tourist or otherwise, into terrain whose purchase was in objects routed through ethnographic avidity or fervor or the bona fides of local habitations. In other words, we are unwilling to cull value from the hoary debates on the authenticity of such itineraries or tours to knowledge production. Rather, following Gayatri Spivak (2003), we wish "to approach the language of the other not only as a 'field language,'" or as "objects of cultural study by the sanctioned ignorance of the metropolitan migrant" (9), but as the "irreducible work of translation" (13).

Our epigram hints at one byway. A litany of names, neither of the global south nor quite Euro-American, balances tenuously on either side of "or" and "in a sea of stories," each a precarious impossible translation of another, each carrying or encapsulating or ferrying or freighted with the residues of the geopolitics of place, of lambent histories of capture, of traffic, of trade, of pleasures awaiting their possible or never-never time. "Kashmir, Kaschmir, Cashmere, Qashmir, Cashmir, Cashmire, Kashmere, Cachemire, Cushmeer, Cachmiere, Casmir . . . Kacmir, Kaschemir, Kasmere, Kachmire, Kasmir. Kerseymere?" (Ali 1997: 15). The names are spaced apart, their shapes and profiles obdurately mismatched so that they will not fold smoothly into one another, nor are they isomorphic: the *longue durée* of translation, area, naming, desire caught subtly by the lyric's contours. The question at the end leaves translation vulnerable, ajar, a choreography from which one might commence, rather than a conversion that occludes or wraps up its trajectories.

In sum, instead of staging area studies and queer studies as segregated field formations, we want to tell, in crude and *fabular* form, a different story of translation. As in the first volume of *The History of Sexuality* (1990), we have opted for the fabular because it can be thought of as the form through which one imagines a better or perhaps just a good enough analytic. Fables underscore peculiar commonalities and repetitions of belief and orient routinized habits of analysis while attending to the generation of value/capital that is implicit in both. Translation (especially in embodied elsewheres) could inadvertently slide into literalization, punctiliousness, or conversion, mislaying in the process the fecundity that the fabular can lug along. Rather, we want to relay something of the messy misalignments, the violating invocations that the epigraph offers, without revisiting salvific modes or completely capturing or captivating value. We want to read the politics of queer and area studies as coincident—if not quite isomorphic—activities, to read both as heuristic practices that see form (whether it be nation, gender, time, biology) as a placeholder that might partly express a promiscuous or incoherent desire or a desire whose content continues to be under erasure. That is, both fields (in theory) are immanent forms that effect a radically ambitious project of recontextualization, each bringing a world into being in such a way that each almost relinquishes or forgets the other. But each remains somewhat tethered to wanton legacies that do not quite overlap or map onto one another, as though each were a kite pulling away from hands or roofs; therein perhaps lie their seductions.

The biggest challenge to both fields has come through the renewed focus on geopolitics and on the thinking of racial difference across divergent temporalities and spatialities. In case our comments be read wearily as yet another cautionary tale of queer studies' shallow embrace of the geopolitical, its persistent flattening or myopic consumption of area studies (all of which is true), we want to suggest instead that such heuristic myopia works resolutely in area studies as well, in the form of highly reduced caricatures of complex queer formulations.[4] Each field formation (if we want to stage them as indeed separately complicit), though in divergent ways, works with the difference of geopolitics through a notion of "difference"; that is, they are not about simplistic expansion into sites of alterity to reach a whole but about a resistance to any form of totalizing knowledge. If, in queer studies, geopolitics forms the question that leads to new (altered) knowledges (problematic as they may be), in area studies, particularly in the global south, geopolitics has become an assertion that fixes knowledge in an anchored place and time. To explain: in queer studies, the geopolitical has posed a much-needed challenge to the spatial and temporal logics of the field (logics that had previously mired it in the United States), especially in the aftermath of the turn to transnationalism. Area studies has historically fashioned its domains outside US borders, but despite its range has remained somewhat tied to nationalist coagulations and formations. For area studies, the focus on diaspora, forced migration, and alternative trajectories of collaboration has equally unmoored the geopolitical from the stability of the nation-form. Renewed engagements with the geopolitical have thus shifted the angles through which the two field formations might begin to imagine collusions, collaborations, and conversations. Yet even as the embrace of the geopolitical (in all its avatars) has diversified queer studies' Euro-American holdings, some troubling analytic turns persist. Queer geographies have undoubtedly stretched to include hitherto untapped regions of the world (read: specifically spaces in the global south), albeit with the local/vernacular reappearing (once again) primarily through ethnographic salaciousness, if it is at all, as incident, exemplar, or evidence, as spatial fodder for the queer mill.[5] Area studies still continues to provide the kind of thick, linguistic, cultural detail that is needed, even if its limitations, which tie area in both its regional and disciplinary specificities, to US political or economic interests, have been signaled.

To continue the story, such geopolitical flattenings in queer studies are further extended through a second analytic form through which area has been displaced by a different ordering of empire: the neoliberal form. More recently, the origin story of neoliberalism (even under erasure) has centered the project of US Empire such that the local appears only in the guise of resurgent markets, emerging fiscal possibilities, risky terrains marked by the incursions of US capital.[6] Affect studies, too, does its best work here, resituating the United States as center yet again, even as it labors to unravel its effects and productions.[7] Of interest here is that it is precisely such a recursive centering of US Empire that has in the past, under the auspices of the Cold War model of area studies, led to a particular focus on area. These imaginings consume area as evidence and capital for US territorialism and expansionism. Instead of reproducing such maligned models of area studies, we are interested here in looking for ways in which to coagulate areas in the service of a queer geopolitics by focusing on the idea of area as a postcolonial form through which epistemologies of empire and market can be critiqued. If queer studies at its best attempts to grapple with its own ethical failures, an engagement with area studies draws attention to the temporal and epistemological asymmetries at work. The challenge here is to configure a queer form that attends to congealments, failures, and translations of knowledge through an understanding of area as both incommensurable and quotidian, recalcitrant and ordinary. The challenge here is to ask: what does area studies bring to queer studies, even in its providential failures?

Three possibilities come to mind. (1) We need to broaden our understanding of empire beyond the current renewed assertion of US Empire and US neoliberalism as the formative impetus for the politics of queer studies—one has only to look at the plethora of texts in affect studies, for example, that deftly uphold this traumatic origin story. Affect, in however generative a guise, turns into a transposable logic or schema traipsing along from the United States to elsewhere.[8] And just as neoliberalism as neologism does, affect pulls value back, in the ways that we have already highlighted, toward the places where the debates on this particular genre of global traffic are said to have begun and recapitalizes, perhaps even accidentally, the United States as that site; area continues unabated as the direction in which capital flows. To read empire(s) otherwise, subalternity needs to be translated not just as a conceptual turn but as a historical turn mired in the concatenations of enduring and multiple empires, British, Portuguese, French, et al.—something that, for example, even scholars working on South Asia equally deny, given their attachment to the singular story of British colonialism. In other words, how does one go back to write a history of orientalism in South Asia that is not the history of British colonial orientalism (an organizing move that would parallel those we have pointed out for the United States) but something that existed alongside or even before that? Let us emphasize here, these linkages are not just of the past but animate the everyday lives of queer subjects. (2) Of equal concern here is the pervasive understanding of race as understood primarily through the history of the transatlantic slave trade, such that this idea of race could be said to constitute the background against which all representations of racial formation take place. What would it mean to imagine an analytic of race that would take the transatlantic trade to the Indian Ocean and not produce African subjects in the same trajectory of slavery? Race has certainly enlivened the geopolitical turn in queer studies, but only to harden structures of representation that foreground the Atlantic model. How do we engage the complexities of racialization through a destination, even as bodies traverse multiple oceanic regionalities to produce extant political formations? (3) How do we create durable epistemologies through citational cultures that refuse certain kinds of overdeterminations? Despite the toxic ink spilt over mandating differences and elsewheres, queer scholars (and we are equally implicated in such a formulation) continue to bankroll our critical assets by returning to and retrenching particular hegemonic origin sites, homes, as it were, whether they reside in the United States or in British colonial trajectories. One au courant instance would be the petition before the Supreme Court of India to reinstate Section 377 of the Indian Penal Code (the sodomy statute, as it is more commonly known). Notwithstanding their best intentions, queer intellectuals and activists (here and there) banked on the singular history of British colonial legislation when, by recalling even Portuguese colonialisms, not to say French ones, they might have intimated other alliances and other avenues of intermediation or routes.

II. Couplings

Roaming/drifting/meandering from town to house, a vagabond misplaces
the road that gathers him home.
That which was once a possession
foresworn from memory
mine and yours no longer known.
Why question/pursue/hunt
how memory was forsaken.
Imagine it like this, its source no ethical lapse:
he simply forgot.
—Miraji, *Tin rang (Three tones)*[9]

I am writing to you from your far-off country. Far even from us who
live here. Where you no longer are. Everyone carries his address in
his pocket so that at least his body will reach home.
—Agha Shahid Ali, *The Country without a Post Office*

We have chosen to go with lyric, not only as our epigrammatic entrée to every section, but as the centerpiece, the very heart, of this introduction. Some readers might well wonder why. Two queer poets led us to these genres of the lyrical as epistemic possibilities that dodge, foil, or will not easily collude in the instrumentalist, intelligence-gathering, language competency–based early drivers of area studies programs.[10] Counterposed against these structural predilections of area studies, queer studies, on the other hand, has long trafficked in the literary, but not quite in the ways that we want to traverse here. Given these conditions, the two poetic snippets in our epigram point to alleys that might muddle some of the more routinized passages through queer studies and area studies: migration or diaspora, refuge or displacement. Where might epistemic homes be said to lie, especially those whose signposts have been waylaid, mislaid? What cartographic enigmas, riddles, or confabulations might be disinterred or exhumed when writing to you from your far-off country, where even you no longer are?

Miraji (1912–1949) and Agha Shahid Ali (1949–2001): our two lyricists are South Asian *musafirs*—vagabonds, itinerants—traversing cross-hatched lineages of geopolitics, gender, and aesthetics. Of Kashmiri roots, Miraji moved from Lahore (now in Pakistan) to the royal state of Baroda, from the colonial capital, Delhi, to the financial and film center, Bombay. Writing and scheming his way across the borders, languages, and patrons of colonial India, Miraji invites his readers to desire, to wander, and to forget. No origin stories, no routes home, no attachments to nostalgia can be summoned; after all, as he writes, we simply forget. In the excerpted form of the *ghazal* quoted above, Miraji plays with the form's penchant for transposition and recursivity, commanding us to come back, as it were, to a recitation of "home," only to have us forget and let go. The self-remonstration *bhul gaya* (I, you, one [or all] forget) creates a staged ambivalence around who stands for object and subject; rather, we have a poetics of translation (perhaps in a Benjaminian sense) where origins and destinations lose their way in relation to one another. Similarly, the name Miraji translates itself into another gendered poetic acronym (the feminine Hindu Meera, in sensual comportment with Krishna the divine lover, becomes the queer, unmarked Mira-ji) where another's name, another's voice forges the geopolitics of a radical queer aesthetic.

Miraji passed away in conditions of unknown displacement in 1949 (some say in Bombay, others say his remains were moved there only after his death), a mere two years after a genocidal partition that gave birth to modern-day India and Pakistan. Kashmir, the storied space of his birth, became the country without a post office, a region caught between the warring histories of a subcontinent unable to let go and forget its violent beginnings.[11] It is thus no coincidence that essays written on the life and work (*shaksiyat aur fann*) of poets such as Miraji return inevitably to such narratives of relocation where Kashmir inaugurates the itinerant form of the poet's corpus. Kashmir becomes an origin put into place after the fact, a putative home, even as such aspirations carry no ontological, genealogical, or historical freight in Miraji's writings. These staged lineages suture poet to place, form to geopolitics, eschewing Miraji's emphasis on the violence of origins and his call to forget and wander despite or because of such demands for geopolitical certitude.

For Agha Shahid Ali, born in Kashmir in 1949, the very year Miraji dies, the poetics of geopolitics speaks equally to the difference between a denizen and a citizen. Birthed in a landscape littered with the memories of bodies, lost and found, maimed and reconstructed through the vagaries of state and faith, Shahid writes to you, to us, to his beloved, to the unknown subject and object of a place with no sanctioned address. In Kashmir, the dead return through the poignancy of a voiced prose that proffers a nonliteral geopolitics, even as it marks the locational economies of labor and violence. We are always "far even from us who live here," writes Shahid, cautioning against the seductions of exile and nativism. One cannot, as it were, know, or even learn about Kashmir; rather, we are called to think through Kashmir without recourse to the fetishization of coverage or the placations of temporal linearities.[12] For Shahid, Miraji's poetic archive provided a much-needed aesthetics of location, an iteration of the necessary failures in comprehension that he desperately wanted to (but never could) translate. After all, what does it mean to wander (through readings of multilingual poetic and religious forms, from Japan to the United States, from Anna Akhmatova to Sappho, as did Miraji), only to forget the route home? What if exile, migrant, refugee, all figurations of geopolitical violence that conjure Kashmir, are deployed without the consolatory aspirations of return? What happens if the forgetting of home, self, lover, lineage holds no purchase, its value as loss dispersed?

Let us first say more about *bhul gaya* as the hermeneutic that allows us to speak to the nexus of area and sexuality that is our preoccupation here. *Bhul gaya* is literally a compound verb that brings together *bhulna* (to forget) with *jaana* (to go). The coupling, *bhul gaya*, as doubled verb, unmoors *bhulna* from settled meanings of loss and forgetting, and ferries it along the axis of space and time (*jaana*). As a compound verb, *bhul gaya* incites play between registers of memory and movement, between loss and return, drawing attention to the impossibility of both. We begin with this allegorical summoning of *bhul gaya* to draw attention to the languages of capitalization through which geopolitics enters the diversified holdings of queer studies. In other words, habits of analysis wander (travel the world, as it were) to precisely concatenate home ground, home territory within languages of ethical fortitude. *Bhul gaya* calls for a queer hermeneutics that refuses the seductions of homing devices, of theoretical pathways that suture geopolitics to forms (refused or otherwise) of region, area, nation. Instead, the forgetting that Miraji and Shahid proffer speaks of a recursive translation of spatialities that renders Kashmir, colony, metropole into a site of political contest rather than into nation.

Lest our prose be misread as a revitalization of the turn to geopolitics as ungraspable form, let us reiterate that it is not. Being caught up in the double bind of representation (as Spivak reminded us so early on) does not absolve us of an ethical attentiveness to the incursions of subalternity. Rather, our efforts here are directed at resisting the impulse (by now well-sedimented in queer studies) to overread geopolitical sites (particularly in the global south) as obdurately and enticingly unresponsive. Indeed, the seductions of such unresponsiveness (often cast in the languages of divergent spatialities and temporalities) accrue a certain political value where you cede to geopolitical difference precisely to lay aside the epistemic work such difference does. How often, we wonder, does the allure of site give way to citation?

Instead, *bhul gaya* gives way to a different economy of presence where the turn to incommensurability as the desired value-form is jettisoned, forgotten. In that vein, one might well ask, why we have opted to site our citations on Kashmir, given how fraught, beset, tense, and troubled the disputations on Kashmir have been? "Kashmir, Kaschmir, Cashmere, Qashmir, Cashmir, Cashmire, Kashmere, Cachemire, Cushmeer, Cachmiere, Casmir . . . Kacmir, Kaschemir, Kasmere, Kachmire, Kasmir. Kerseymere?" And "a vagabond misplaces the road that gathers him home." How do we hold to the ethics of attentiveness in delineating Kashmir without conceding to the formalized indexes and inventories of incommensurability, without returning homeward in some simple way as our poets evince? This is a question that ought to make anyone leery. It is not without its pitfalls, if one accounts for the displacements that are endemic to Kashmir's politics of place, or the impossible desire held so close by so many Kashmiris to come back to the home to which they feel they ought to belong.[13] Perhaps it is no accident, then, that two Kashmiri poets proffer routes to no return not as literal lodestones for the migrant, the refugee, the violently displaced.[14] Rather, they serve as tracks that relinquish epistemic domiciles and forgo holding places where politics stays the usual course. Perhaps it is the command to translation bequeathed us by these two poets that offers us a guide, if not a map, into how to enter its plangent and potent historicity, perhaps, or especially in fabular form.

"I write on that void . . . in a sea of stories." Kashmir elicits an entourage of tales, big and small, punctilious or playful, harrowing or lighthearted. Scribbled on the void (how can they not be?), the narratives swing between politics and aesthetics (Kaul 2015: 108–9). Kashmir's content and context is the effect of competing histories, and under such circumstances representation turns necessarily aporetic, cagey. Be that as it may, so many who have probed the current prevailing conditions anchor them in the history of the region that we cannot not also do so here; we thus open our foray there.

The contemporary configuration of the state of Kashmir resides in and is contested among India, Pakistan, and China. And by all accounts, Kashmir was nominalized as a territorial entity through the political jostling for power in the region in the mid- to late nineteenth century. Situated between Afghanistan, Russia, China, and British India, the region was parceled from hand to hand, beginning with the Mughals (1586), moving on to the Afghans in the mid-eighteenth century, and finally taken over by the Sikhs toward the early nineteenth century (Rai 2004; Schofield 2010). It became a token in British imperial machinations, a pawn in the great game between Russia, China, Afghanistan, and the British, arguably the precursor to and perhaps the model for postwar and post–Cold War geoterritorial imperatives (Brobst 2005; Hopkirk 2001; Schofield 2010).

The British colonial state crafted the princely Dogra state of Jammu and Kashmir in the mid-nineteenth century out of multilingual, variously ethnic constituencies. In doing so, it also set up many of the political exigencies for the socio-political-religious and internecine battles being waged on the ground to date (Kabir 2009; Kaul 2015; Rai 2004). But even as the British had set their sights on what was to become Kashmir, travelers, poets, and photographers reinvigorated Kashmir as an aesthetic object, sublating the jurisdictional, bureaucratic, legislative, and military precipitations of the great game in the opulent semiotics of the sublime.[15] That very same unutterably colonized aesthetic preoccupation continues as palimpsest into the postcolonial. For example, Kashmir emerges as the exquisite and elysian optic of pleasure in songs from 1960s Bollywood cinema bent on forging pastoral nationalisms, and as indispensable backdrop in militarized movies made from the 1990s onward that attempt to propel a virulently scopic patriotism, dropping by the wayside anything that might bring the people of the valley into view (Kabir 2009; Kaul 2015). In the face of such a history, where anachronisms from a long trajectory of areas perhaps impossible to still marshal so much sway, how can we not, along with Kabir and Kaul, turn to the aesthetic promise and peril of the lyrical *bhul gaya* as possible episteme? As Shahid, composing from afar in the face of the violence on the ground and the specific calls for Kashmiri autonomy in the 1990s, asks: "[Do] you now see why we give no interviews?" We turn in the next section to translations of that pressing question.

III. Translations

I hold your breath. Look, I slow my fingers.
Do you now see why we give no interviews?
When you leave, my hands will again be spiders.
—Agha Shahid Ali, *The Country without a Post Office*

The ambition (for better or worse) of this special issue is necessarily multiple, diffuse, even didactic, as are its subjects, a confabulation that holds close to the tenderest incarnation of the question: "Do you now see why we give no interviews?" Our aspiration (for better or for worse) remains one that transposes the myriad semiotic registers incited by calling for area without representation. Rather than inclusivity or coverage—the seductions that the interview form so often pulls into shape as it incites presence—the issue culled the provocations of dispersal / of the question.

What would it mean to hold someone else's breath, to slow one's fingers? To hold or grasp at some "thing" that by its very nature is ephemeral, can never be tangible, yet follows inexorably one after another? Can it be a "thing"? Our introduction cusps itself around Kashmir, the placeholder of provisional names with spaces between them, its territoriality fungible, wisped away constantly, however slow one's fingers become in futile gestures that venture to hold it still. Here lie the vulnerabilities of fabular intimations through translation, through which we oriented this introduction. Merely breath between the litany of names, Kashmir can never be marshalled fully as the site, as the thing that must speak its truth, even one that unravels its fulsome and torsioned history, for someone (you) standing before it asking for an interview from it. Rather, it facilitates the questions through which we weave our provocations and alignments. Even as one cannot not know it, Kashmir provisions the possibilities for epistemology without rendering itself as knowable, as the place constantly constituted as an object for geopolitical fracases, as the denouement in the games of geopolitics. What does this then entail for the contributors of this special issue who bring area to queer in however friable or fungible a fashion?

"Area Impossible" (the title serves as a lure and provocation) commences with a dossier, an array of meditations solicited as a roundtable with scholars, whose publications, though consistently seminal to our understanding of sexualities and geopolitics, are rarely positioned within area studies (given the insistent repudiations that dog any calls to return to it), alongside those who did not perhaps see themselves in regular conversations with queer studies. We requested our writers to ruminate on what they saw (or didn't see) at the joints between the field formations they inhabited and queer studies as a way of stirring critique, niggling at the very foundations of the joints. Neferti Tadiar's, Keguro Macharia's, Ronaldo Wilson's, Diana Taylor's, and Jasbir Puar and Maya Mikdashi's generously curious, pointedly indicative, capaciously aesthetic gestures generate openings that are picked up in the essays that follow. Scanning the pieces, readers will find that each broaches area, sexuality, desire in such a succinct and voluminous fashion that the very notion turns friable in their hands. Their interrogative reflections, "hands like spiders," splaying across the geopolitics of space and time, summon the willful semiotics of area and genre, and intimate routes to the questions with which we began the introduction.

In "Ground Zero" Tadiar tailors her intervention around the epistemological commonplaces that were thrown up as we surveyed queer imbrications with geopolitical. Tackling them head-on, she asks, "When we do the critique that we do so well, do we not employ the grammar of the police? . . . Do we communicate and traffic in the particular colonial, capitalist, real abstract codes of social and subjective being that make up an American grammar?" Tadiar pulls that particular uneasy call to commensurability away from the places where it perches so fervently or uncaringly or unheedingly in the guise of "transferable cultural logics" that constantly home in on or return back home to the United States, "these nearly Kantian categories," "'gender, race, sexuality'—the categories [that] roll off the tongue like dice"—which "inspire and organize practices of expropriation of value." Tadiar's mediation dumps value squarely into or at the heart of what it means to reside with our own volatile culpability in these forms that ferry sexuality, perhaps orienting it toward area, forms that we settle into so well, so succinctly. Setting the stage for all the essays that follow hers, Tadiar's grammar tunes into the porosity of the "diminishing plethora of verbs of action" immanent in the best lives people make for themselves, reaching for what they might yet obtain in areas conceived as "places of lives."

Macharia takes off from here to his place of life as an "Africa-based queer scholar." In other words, he reroutes queer to area in the beleaguered familiar formation of area studies. Here, if one can even describe where he is as a "here," Macharia's logics of transferability encounter an unwittingly obdurate blockage of fluency. Translation turns "dissonant" for him precisely where queer meets area, where the possibility of making sense of himself for another is no longer viable or legible in the phrases that he carried back with him from the United States. Neither queer nor (not) Africanist is portable; all they incite is puzzlement. Even race, however mutable into an Afro-Atlantic political genus, fails to conform; not even the "deracinating power" of "black queer" ferries any purchase. The question of value peters out not because Macharia is gesturing toward a utopian response to the lamination of place into sexuality but because translation goes awry. Macharia suggests picking up a word from the lexical world of his present. *Tala*, culled from the Kenyan scholar Neo Musangi, is a description, not quite sedimented into thing or identity, not quite even a fully fashioned form of identification. At stake here is a vocabulary that neither asks for nor fully refuses the nominalization "native." "What demands," Macharia asks, "would *tala* make on the concepts and histories in which queer studies is embedded?" What fluencies might queer studies have to abrogate? The pathways back to some notion of home dead-end with these questions, wending through the wayward stories with which he closes. As though invoking the Urdu poet Miraji whose itinerancy is the lyrical byway to misplacing home without an ethical lapse, Macharia closes his musings with waywardness as epistemic possibility: as a somewhat naive, somewhat nuanced "stubborn refusal to come to the point." What Macharia approaches through or ventures through waywardness is the indifferent native, one who often simply does not show up, sometimes simply wanders off, giving no interviews, unhitching himself from the provocations of area and queer, even as he subpoenas and beckons vocabulary that is of little interest to scholars from the United States, epistemologies that seem not to be able to accrue value there. "Because value," in Spivak's inimitable analysis when she was confronted with the question of Asia, "simple and contentless, is just a form in use when things are made commensurable" (Hairong 2007: 445). And when translation tarries or temporizes as it does here, commensurability falters as well.

Two of our contributors curve their ripostes around performances that also raise the specter of forestalled commensurability. Wilson jettisons the bared bones of the analytic for the spectacular striations of aesthetic that stages, voices, and visualizes analytic intersessions. In his prose-poetry-sketch-photo-performance "clicked on [to] play" through vistas that improvise each other in temporal scapes, area patterns into pretext, semblance, facade, phase. As Wilson traipses, struts, bolts, wends, welters his way through the sexual and racial geopolitics of encounters settled in the United States wearing literal and figurative masks, it is almost as though area mutes into breath, the between of the narrations, the scenes, the gap between mask and skin, the rent into which blackness, as racialized, might arrive torn. From bar to beach, dinner party to prize committee, Wilson inhabits a marketplace of circulation that moves through an are(n)a of encounters, spilling stories of space and time along the way.

Taylor promulgates the collusions between area and sexuality in yet another enunciatory mode. She recounts the lineaments of what ensues when the elsewhere is performed in Canada, a play by two Mexican artists that spawned a fraught series of politicized encounters when it faced an audience unwilling to breach the impossibilities of translation. Caught in an economy that poised two players against each other—the long legacy of gendered and sexualized colonial violence choreographed in contemporary valences through irony and parody against the so-called harms that the deployment of such representational spectacles might have induced in an audience unattuned to these registers—translation ground to a halt. It was as though the shop-soiled debates in anthropology about trucking the native back to institutions of knowledge production in the metropole were refurbished again in the currency of sexuality. The untranslatable provocateur here was perhaps the best of what can be gleaned if area studies conspires with sexuality, the studied droll absurdist handling and dramatization of anachronism (of what the past might carry) in the service of queer politics, an area impossible, one that in this case was unable to hail audiences fleeing to the shelter of their own epistemic homes. Is this the lesson to which we must attend?

What if the passages home were blockaded by provincializing queer theory, nominalizing it or reframing it as area studies? What alternative possibilities might be thrown up if area as "ground zero" was the temporalized biopolitical? Puar and Mikdashi's "cartography of critical theory" yields multiple registers of the biopolitical, but two stand out: the biopolitics of maiming and stunting as the quotidian condition of foreshortened everyday corporeality, and killing without mourning, the future congealed into the bodies of men marked by the regulatory impetuses that sediment heterosexuality. Can we claim such bodies, they ask, as queer, processing them through area? In response they route their germinal questions through the transnational Middle East to think through the work performed by "the temporality of the 'crisis.'"

Temporality, the promise and peril of area studies, then might provide an epistemic demeanor for the impossible nexus of area with sexuality. Each of the three long essays in this special issue is somewhat configured through time, in Wilson's words "capturing the patterns," a "poetics of asking what happens through improvisation, or in the gesture of writing about the scene, the area/arena where the story is experienced within time that folds through multiple modes of the event." The essays translate time through area, as it were, in possibly incommensurable directions. Mobilizing recombinant time as knots, as loops, Lucinda Ramberg dives into the curious promiscuity of the asynchronous temporal embodiments that flesh out the everyday household politics of Dalit communities. For Ramberg, theogamy as obsolescent anachronism splices across and cuts into the future-driven gendered proprieties that conversion into Buddhism as political deliverance brings in its wake. Aliyah Khan ferries in the historical legislative record alongside the labor of desire to translate shipboard intimacies between men and between women into kinship. The nominalizations *jahaji bhai and jahaji bahin* (ship brother and ship sister) provide her leverage into both the racialized landscape of the Anglophone Caribbean and the more contemporary lesbian fictional narrative with which she sites the "voyager who is not, however, a permanent exile." Home, then, through the crossed chronologies of desire, of sexuality, of traffic across water, loosens its vantage, dropping area in its wake. Ashley Currier and Thérèse Migraine-George turn away from the constantly renewed fiscally bounded bequests of Afro-pessimism, the metaphorics that toll the present of continental (albeit transnational) conditions, toward genres such as film and photography where the entangled timelines of queer and African studies might signal possible futures embodied in and gelled into Afro-optimism.

The translations of area that this issue conjures do not parse together easily in any settled vernacular of geopolitics. But perhaps it is exactly this refusal to easy legibility, even to the point of frugal dispersal or even exuberant disarray, that makes the coupling of area and queer as generative and confounding as it is. The historical and temporal markers that produce "area" as catalogs of representation are erased, in these pages, by singular and perhaps even peculiar reproductive historicities that envisage those markers as messy, vitalizing, and ultimately queer. The urgency here is to reinvent, from the are(n)as of the stories told, new queer idioms of the geopolitical. Attentive to itinerant provincialisms, such fabular figurations of area impossible remain vulnerable to wayward translations, forgoing settled orientations to home.

Notes

Our first words of thanks must go to our editors, Nayan Shah and Elizabeth Freeman. Nayan shepherded us through the early stages, while Beth made the whole issue possible with her caring and trenchant guidance. At many different moments, and in many different ways, Kath Weston and Lucy Mae San Pablo Burns have kept us sane through the myriad twists and turns of editing a special issue. We owe each of our anonymous reviewers a debt of gratitude for their tireless (and unpaid) labor. And last but not least, a big *shukriya* to our contributors who were painstaking, precise, and enthusiastic. This issue is dedicated to all the queer natives of area(s) impossible.

1.　We use the term *area studies* to demarcate an interdisciplinary approach to the study of "areas" of the globe. Even as area studies engages with questions of geopolitics, broadly speaking, its success (and failure) as a knowledge formation derives from a long history of state-sponsored programs. For example, in 1958, Title VI of the National Defense Education Act (renamed the Higher Education Act in 1965) provided funding for research and training in international and foreign-language studies. Title VI continues to be a significant source of funding for programs devoted to area studies that span fields in the humanities and the social sciences. For a short history of the emergence of area studies, see news.stanford.edu/news/multi/interaction/0507 /area.html.

2. A sampling of such efforts from the past ten years or so would include Al-Samman and El-Ariss 2013; Blackmore and Hutcheson 1999; Carpenter 2011; Downing and Gillet 2012; Hough 2013; Liu and Rofel 2010; Renne 2000; and Sahli 2008. There are, of course, too many such collections and special issues to list in their entirety.

3. See, for instance, Volkman 1999 and Szanton 2004. Collections such as Miyoshi and Harootunian 2002 speak to the failure of area studies, particularly in the context of a corporate university. For Masao Miyoshi and Harry Harootunian, knowledge formations such as gender studies and cultural studies must specifically intervene in reclaiming area studies from its entrenched Cold War narrative (1–19).

4. Influential collections such as *The Politics of Knowledge: Area Studies and the Disciplines* (Szanton 2004), for example, attend to questions of gender and sexuality by simply routing them through foundational categories such as woman, man, and occasionally homosexual. Even a collection such as *Learning Places: The Afterlives of Area Studies* (Miyoshi and Harootunian 2002), which acknowledges the importance of gender studies and cultural studies to the growth of a more robust area studies, does little to engage with histories of sexuality as histories of region or "area."

5. We are, of course, not the first ones to make such a claim. Scholars such as Elizabeth Povinelli have repeatedly called for "radical interpretations" of ethnographic studies of the non-West. Through her work on aboriginal communities in Australia, Povinelli pushes at the question of what is at stake in recuperating ethnographic details and what is entailed in how those details are collected and communicated. For Povinelli, it is crucial that we attend to the current demand for ethnographies of sexuality that resurrect "sex out of corporeal practices" and return us to the very knowledge technologies of colonial liberalism that we wish to abrogate. She calls for an engagement with the "breach and shadow" of the geopolitical forms that produce sexuality's difference in the first place. See Povinelli 2002: 73.

6. Texts that laid some of the groundwork for contemporary analyses of neoliberalism include *A Brief History of Neoliberalism*, by David Harvey (2005), and *Neoliberalism: A Critical Reader*, edited by Alfredo Saad-Filho and Deborah Johnston (2005). Whatever historical trajectory they offer for neoliberalism, all the books and articles written around this time imagine its directionality as from the west to the rest. Even Harvey's (2005) chapter "Neoliberalism with Chinese Characteristics," which might have pro-

vided an alterior course for neoliberalism, sets the west up as the stage that provides the conditions for the Chinese entrée as an emergent power in global marketing and finance (121). Though some recent books such as those by William Davies (2014) and Philip Mirowski (2014) challenge some of the premises that center the value accorded to neoliberalism, they still continue to hold on to that particular orientation. Another way to come at neoliberalism would be through the work of Kalyan Sanyal (2013), an Indian economist and historian. Sanyal tracks the historical nuances of the flow of development capital that does not begin in the West and suggests trajectories that ascribe a central place neither to neoliberalism nor to Euro-America.

7.   One pioneer in the US overtures into affect studies is the extraordinarily valuable collection *Compassion: The Culture and Politics of an Emotion* (Berlant 2004). Offering clusters of cases and genealogies, it has a curiously suggestive genealogical oversight that is pertinent to the concerns we are raising here: Buddhism. A religion and practice organized around compassion, or *karuna*, Buddhism has become workaday fare for the United States, routinized as religion, belief, or practice. Whether it is routed through yoga or Tibetan/Japanese/Indian meditation or through the more working-class movements such as Soka Gakkai, compassion in this key has become a part of the cultural politics of a quotidian Euro-American lexicon. These genres of lapses in attention to direction continue unabated in the introduction to the more recent 2010 collection *The Affect Theory Reader*, edited by Melissa Gregg and Gregory Seigworth. Though the editors are at great pains to show multiple descents for affect, all the lineages they offer stop short at Europe or stay within the purview of the United States, holding on to the United States as the most prolific site of the production of texts on affect. Gregg and Seigworth offer affect's blurred ancestries in the introduction, going as far back as the philosopher Baruch Spinoza. Given their attentiveness to some sort of historical genus, the exclusion of one of the earliest ventures into parsing, cataloging, and appreciating aesthetic and political affect is notable. We are speaking here of *rasa/dhvani* theory in Sanskrit where feeling assumes both "force and form" (5), is immanent and explicit. These are not lost histories of affect, especially as British and German Romanticism and invocations of sentiment were frequently deliberately curved around eighteenth-century translations, including those from Sanskrit by Indologists such as William Jones.

8.   Al-Samman and El-Ariss's 2013 introduction is a case in point. Transacting their invocations of affect through Heather Love's (2007) provocative and generative interrogation of the politics of feeling in *Feeling Backward*, they reinstitute the United States as the reserve currency holder for affect. Love, tracking some of her lines into feeling through British modernism, like so many before her, situates modernism firmly in the West. What would it mean to nuance that history through South Asian movements such as the Progressive Writer's Association, many of whose members were engaged in working discussions with British and American modernists (Patel 2002)?

In posing such interrogative interventions in how we might imagine the flows of literary capital embedded in affect, we are not attempting to regulate writing or take a hatchet to ventures that have an enormous amount of value. We are instead suggesting directions not taken that might have led to alterior pedigrees and sight lines.

9. For a manuscript version of the poem, see Miraji n.d.: ghazal 1.3; for an extended exegesis on this fragment, see Patel 2002.

10. See Cumings 1997 and Szanton 2004.

11. In its current incarnation Kashmir is uneasily balanced between India, Pakistan, and China.

12. In "Essay 3: The Witness of Poetry" Kaul (2015: 135–61) turns to the lyrical as the conduit for a possible futurity for Kashmir. Prior to Kaul's demands on the lyric, Kabir (2009: 138–41) deployed Shahid's lingual propensities to explore the lineaments of the poet as witness to the conflicts in the Kashmir valley. But lyric as the mouthpiece that speaks the truth to power, especially in cases of violence, had a spokesperson in Pandey 1992.

13. For meditations on the vagaries of the Kashmiri question, see Kaul 2015; Kak 2011; Rai 2004.

14. The lyric offers a salutary point of entrée for a beset region such as Kashmir, especially as marshalled by writers such as Kaul (2015) and Kabir (2009).

15. In fact, as Kabir (2009: 13–15, 93–97, 157) points out, the "great game" generated much of the thrill that underwrote aesthetic projects which may never have visualized or spoken them on their surfaces.

References

Ali, Agha Shahid. 1997. "The Blessed Word: A Prologue," "Dear Shahid," "The Correspondent." In *The Country without a Post Office*, 15, 43, 61. New York: Norton.

Al-Samman, Hanadi, and Tarek El-Ariss. 2013. "Queer Affects: Introduction." *International Journal of Middle East Studies* 45, no. 2: 205–9.

Babayan, Kathryn, and Afsaneh Najmabadi. 2008. Preface. In *Islamicate Sexualities: Translations across Temporal Geographies of Desire*, edited by Kathryn Babayan and Afsaneh Najmabadi, vii–xiv. Cambridge, MA: Harvard University Press.

Berlant, Lauren Gail, ed. 2004. *Compassion: The Culture and Politics of an Emotion (Essays from the English Institute)*. London: Routledge.

Blackmore, Josiah, and Gregory Hutcheson, eds. 1999. *Queer Iberia: Sexualities, Cultures, and Crossings from the Middle Ages to the Renaissance*. Durham, NC: Duke University Press.

Brobst, Peter John. 2005. *The Future of the Great Game: Sir Olaf Caroe, India's Independence, and the Defense of Asia*. Akron, OH: University of Akron Press.

Carpenter, Karen. 2011. "Introduction to the Special Issue on Sexuality in the Carib-
     bean." *Sexuality and Culture* 15, no. 4: 313–14.

Chauncey, George, and Elizabeth A. Povinelli. 1999. "Thinking Sexually and Trans-
     nationally: An Introduction." *GLQ* 5, no. 4: 439–49.

Cumings, Bruce. 1997. "Boundary Displacement: Area Studies and International Stud-
     ies during and after the Cold War." *Bulletin of Concerned Asian Scholars* 29, no. 1:
     6–26.

Davies, William. 2014. *The Limits of Neoliberalism: Authority, Sovereignty, and the Logic
     of Competition.* London: Sage.

Downing, Lisa, and Robert Gillet. 2012. "Introduction to Special Issue on European
     Culture/European Queer." *Sexualities* 15, no. 1: 11–15.

Foucault, Michel. [1978] 1990. *An Introduction.* Vol. 1 of *The History of Sexuality.* Trans-
     lated by Robert Hurley. New York: Vintage Books.

Gregg, Melissa, and Gregory J. Seigworth, eds. 2010. *The Affect Theory Reader.* Durham,
     NC: Duke University Press.

Hairong, Yan. 2007. "Position without Identity: An Interview with Gayatri Spivak." *posi-
     tions* 15, no. 2: 429–49.

Harvey, David. 2005. *A Brief History of Neoliberalism.* New York: Oxford University
     Press.

Hopkirk, Peter. 2001. *The Great Game: On Secret Service in High Asia.* Oxford: Oxford
     University Press.

Hough, Sigmund. 2013. "Special Issue on Sexuality across the Globe, Setting, Condition,
     and Age." *Sexuality and Disability* 31, no. 4: 299–300.

Kabir, Ananya Jahanara. 2009. *Territory of Desire: Representing the Valley of Kashmir.*
     Minneapolis: University of Minnesota Press.

Kak, Sanjay, ed. 2011. *Until My Freedom Has Come: The New Intifada in Kashmir.* New
     Delhi: Penguin.

Kaul, Suvir. 2015. *Of Gardens and Graves: Essays on Kashmir, Poems in Translation.*
     Gurgaon, India: Three Essays Collective.

Liu, Petrus, and Lisa Rofel. 2010. "Beyond the Strai(gh)ts: Transnationalism and Queer
     Chinese Politics." *positions* 18, no. 2: 281–89.

Love, Heather. 2007. *Feeling Backward: Loss and the Politics of Queer History.* Cam-
     bridge, MA: Harvard University Press.

Miraji. 1968. "Bhul gaya." In *Tin rang (Three tones),* 151–53. Pindi: Kitab Numa.

———. n.d. "Tin rang" ("Three tones"). Handwritten manuscript (unpublished). Posses-
     sion of Geeta Patel.

Mirowski, Philip. 2014. *Never Let a Serious Crisis Go to Waste: How Neoliberalism Sur-
     vived the Financial Meltdown.* London: Verso Books.

Miyoshi, Masao, and Harry Harootunian, eds. 2002. *Learning Places: The Afterlives of
     Area Studies.* Durham, NC: Duke University Press.

Pandey, Gyanendra. 1992. "In Defense of the Fragment: Writing about Hindu-Muslim Riots in India Today." *Representations*, no. 37: 27–55.

Patel, Geeta. 2002. *Lyrical Movements, Historical Hauntings: On Gender, Colonialism, and Desire in Miraji's Urdu Poetry.* Stanford, CA: Stanford University Press.

Povinelli, Elizabeth. 2002. *The Cunning of Recognition: Indigenous Alterities and the Making of Australian Multiculturalism.* Durham, NC: Duke University Press.

Rai, Mridu. 2004. *Hindu Rulers, Muslim Subjects: Islam, Rights, and the History of Kashmir.* Princeton: Princeton University Press.

Renne, Elisha P. 2000. "Introduction to Special Issue: Sexuality and Generational Identities in Sub-saharan Africa." *Africa Today* 47, nos. 3–4: vii–xii.

Saad-Filho, Alfredo, and Deborah Johnston, eds. 2005. *Neoliberalism: A Critical Reader.* London: Pluto.

Sahli, Zahia Smail. 2008. "Gender and Diversity in the Middle East and North Africa." *British Journal of Middle Eastern Studies* 35, no. 3: 295–304.

Sanyal, Kalyan. 2013. *Rethinking Capitalist Development: Primitive Accumulation, Governmentality, and Post-Colonial Capital.* New Delhi: Routledge India.

Schofield, Victoria. 2010. *Kashmir in Conflict: India, Pakistan, and the Unending War.* London: I. B. Tauris.

Spivak, Gayatri. 2003. *Death of a Discipline.* New York: Columbia University Press.

Szanton, David L., ed. 2004. *The Politics of Knowledge: Area Studies and the Disciplines.* Berkeley: University of California Press.

Volkman, Toby Alice. 1999. *Crossing Borders: Revitalizing Area Studies.* New York: Ford Foundation.

GROUND ZERO

Neferti X. M. Tadiar

$\mathcal{T}$he ground zero of gender and sexuality studies has not dramatically shifted, its "area" unsurmised. Or, it has at least not been sufficiently undermined, just relativized with the qualifying brackets of West, Anglo-European, US, or something of the like. And then the work that those concepts are set to do continues on its merry global ways. "Gender, race, sexuality"—the categories roll off the tongue like dice, and though we might yet feel the bitter fates that have made them fighting words, we also know how they have been pressed into imperial service, fashioned into a set of cognitive procedures for dealing with those other realities as so many reflections of, so many varying distances from, this center's own.

You think you already know that, but you do not. You tend to forget, if you really knew it at all. If you do not know it, it is because those other "areas" have these other brackets around them, which you call "context." It makes you feel cosmopolitan about your ignorance and comfortable with the provinciality of your nonconformist, subversive imagination. You know your theoretical acts are local, even as you are aware of the global, but still you cannot seem to retain the fact that this is the place where the brackets are made and placed, the areas conceived and implemented, the global defined (for those areas to demonstrate, resist, or elaborate), which sets the stage for all those other indeterminate "differences" not encapsulated by the ones you know so well to persist in some inchoate form that you are likely to call "cultural." Anthropology will surely take care of that. And everyone can keep their place.

Or, if you know all this and, more, you know (but do not readily "understand") at least one of these other "contexts" intimately, where smells as much as words call up associations that, loath to leave the premises, will enmesh you,

GLQ 22:2

DOI 10.1215/10642684-3428699

© 2016 by Duke University Press

maybe tear somewhat at the "subject position" you have worked hard to build and win for yourself (rather than giving rise to those generic thoughts so transportable into "theoretical" reflections), still you might forget when you are looking through these analytical lenses—these nearly Kantian categories—that you are seeing only as far as these imperial shores will allow: the familiar forms of life that an "American grammar" of power and marginality, visibility and invisibility, identity and difference, normativity and nonnormativity, being and becoming can help you make out.

Eurocentrism is one thing. This is something else besides. Sure, there is the epistemological problem, the problem of reading, making sense of gender, race, and sexuality "in a global context." In this endeavor, anti-Eurocentric, anticolonial critiques have not lost their pointed relevance, though now they too have brackets around them, like a third-string guest in a crowded party, nodded to in passing where there are more exciting conversations to be had with personages of field-making, field-troubling value (against which one would have to measure one's own assets). "Moving on," the academic shareholders say, as they make their way to the cutting edge with the highest profit margin.

Simply pointing this out might seem like you are going over to the other side of the culture wars, that side that wants to put an end to all this "identity" stuff, which has already rent the social fabric and its fundamental cultural values, a barbarism against which all manner of civilizational return is repeatedly proposed. They who, out of credence in Enlightenment humanist values or in post-Enlightenment, posthumanist theory, would underestimate the durable, even intensified salience of identity rationalities in the organization of contemporary statist practices do so in willful disregard of how this optic of abstract equivalence is a key function in today's dominant social operating system. Or it could well play into that conservative strain of so-called historical materialists who, in a hysterical defense of their own hallowed ground of critique, would relegate the matters of concern propelling feminist, antiracist, and queer critique as of secondary importance to the primary, ultimately determining structures and forces of capitalism. In one fell swoop, such a defense writes off entire radical traditions of critical theory that had in fact deepened the historical materialist understanding of actual material life as organized by and composed of these very "matters" of the body and bodily relations. But these qualms should not stop the point from being made: this business of academic thought production is part and parcel of the problem.

I will not dwell on this much—the fact that entrepreneurship is now required for thought to gain enough traction—since the observation sits well with no one (neither "winners" nor "losers"). Yet the financialization of everyday intellectual life cannot be gainsaid, nor should its effects on academic production be underestimated. No social stratum fully experiences the subjective condition of the falling rate of profit as do the middle and upper middle classes of the global north, of which the mid and higher tiers of the academic profession are solidly a part. The struggle to produce value from one's life/work to maintain economic buoyancy and mobility (one might say, a viable career) in an increasingly corporatized, intensely competitive industry can be relentless and insidious. It can make it such that our endeavors seem to heed the protocols of entrepreneurship more than anything else. I am no political puritan about these matters, despite the puritanical strains that shape all manner of politics in the United States (a puritanism that detections of "complicity" have the funny effect of intensifying), but I am beginning to wonder how much of what we "innovate" in our various fields in critical "studies" has become a form of cognitive app making (which gives new meaning to the notion of subscribing to an idea).

One could say, this is simply the latest development in a longer history of "difference" becoming incorporated, whereby the state and capital have found ways to mimic or adopt and politically evacuate insurgent practices through their institutionalization, such that we professionals may ourselves be doing our part in turning critical politics into policy. And is that not in fact the case when "gender" and "sexuality" figure so prominently in both governance and war? When feminist and gay and lesbian rights activism is embedded in the security and capitalist machinations of imperial projects? Many have already rightly called them out: imperial feminism, NGO feminist governmentality, homonationalism, feminist governance, pinkwashing, carceral feminism. What they all bring out in stark relief is the global expansion of normative society's modes of operation, even when supposedly working on behalf of the marginalized and excluded, that is, even in antinormative, antimarginalization critique. And while in certain places (I'm looking at you, Western Europe) one would wish that they had some of the more sophisticated versions of this critique where it seems to be sorely lacking (where tolerance and accommodation of diversity in the face of "multicultural" immigrant assault seems the best that can be mustered), still, there too it feels like it is the same family affair, despite the hopeful well-intentioned openness toward its odd new members.

It is not just that something like an identity politics can and has been placed on the side of states: we see political strategies of radical social struggle made over into *programs*, sets of procedures for the civil-service sector of global imperial democracy. *Are we not ourselves among these international civil servants, or their mentors?* When gender and sexuality become operative elements in the political campaigns of deadly, punitive, and genocidal states, the problem is not determining why and how these categories might (yet) make a critical difference. As Hortense Spillers (1997: 140) long ago put it: the question is "not so much why and how 'race' makes the difference—*the police will see to it*—but how it carries of its message onto an interior." Spillers was talking about how the poisonous idea of race insinuates itself into the psychic interior of the racialized. It is worth asking whether and how academic ideas of gender and sexuality are insinuating themselves into the ontic interior—the *codes* of being—of imperial expansion. Or whether and how they might have already been there, worming their way out.

Forget co-optation. Things are not so simple or easy. It might be comforting to think that critical forces are on one side and the forces of contemporary colonialism and capitalism are on the other, with the latter always appropriating, co-opting, the tools and methods of the former. Yet we know or should know better. We were forewarned about "the fascism in us all, in our heads and in our everyday behavior, the fascism that causes us to love power, to desire the very thing that dominates and exploits us" (Foucault, 1983: xiii). And we recalibrated our critical tools to work on ourselves, to critique our own critiques. That is the nature of struggle, one supposes: gender and sexuality studies' permanent cultural revolution.

But my sense is that it is not just, or primarily, that at all. When we do the critique that we do so well, do we not employ the grammar of the police? Of the slave trader and auctioneer? Of the entrepreneur and the investor? Do not we communicate and traffic in the particular colonial, capitalist, real abstract codes of social and subjective being that make up an American grammar?

As sociosymbolic, cultural logics, sex-gender systems extend beyond social identities/subjectivities and the ways these operate in liberal and neoliberal democracies in the north, with their particular fondness for juridical forms of political imagination. They are also sociosymbolic orders of allocation of power, labor, value, spirit, enjoyment, and moral ideals; they form the basis of protocols of personhood and sociality, of life and death, and the place of their before and after. Though sex-gender systems, systems integral to human life, may be many, it is the abstractable, transferable cultural logics that emerged out of the specific evolving sex-gender systems of an incipient Western European colonial capitalist bloc that dominantly inform and further develop out of the latest, global imperial projects. These are logics that inspire and organize practices of expropriation of value and expiation of violence not just in nations but across them *all the time* and not just in those exemplary, often fatal moments when sex-race-gender figures (numbers and names) loom large and spectacular, enough for us to force the brief consideration of the "structural" role of gender and sexuality alongside race in the making, and not just the interpretation, of the material world we inhabit.

Sexual economies are one way to highlight the organizing role of these cultural logics in the transnational regional and global conduct of economic trade and regulation and political-military alliance and cooperation among states. When some national economies are presumed and disciplined to service the needs and wants of others, sexuality is not a "mere" metaphor but the set of regulatory precepts of regional and global trade, of transnational production and governmentality. The cultural logics of gender and sexuality certainly operate in the ideological formation of key international state actors and policymakers from the age of world liberal development to the age of global neoliberal finance, Franklin D. Roosevelt and John Maynard Keynes, Margaret Thatcher and Milton Friedman. The old boys networks and the girls who are let in to the high-stakes clubs of the Fortune 500 and the G-8 as long as they play by the rules of the game are, after all, as socialized as anyone else in the ideological manners of the north. And undoubtedly the ships they "man" (the nation-states they lead, cut deals for, hock and sell) and the tanks they think-drive (military, financial, humanitarian) will translate their rosebud desires and the orders of gender and sexuality that such desires depend on, negotiate, rework, and transfigure into worldly, even worldwide, effects.

But the cultural logics almost do not have to pass through those privileged ideological actor-subjects to carry out the work of their meaning making. They are, after all, already at work in the domains of the "economy" and statecraft, domains that are themselves forms of perception and reading as well as orders of living, transmitting the codes of gender and sexuality they abide by. So that when the categories become critical lenses for reading the workings mainly of social subjectivities and identities and their "differences," there is a very good chance we will have lost sight of how these codes create the terrain on which these contestations take place, that is, the "area" that disappears into the ground zero of global gender and sexuality studies critique. And if so, there is an equally good chance that the latter, as a set of critical forms of perception and reading, will have lent themselves to a kind of cultural Keynesianism, a project of sociocultural reform that does not, perhaps cannot, unsettle that ground zero to the degree that it is now that ground's pioneering extension, its pseudopodia, as it were—the organs of its locomotion and prehension.

What is the evidence that this is so? Or at least what is to tip us off that it might be? Surely when such categories consistently spell exclusion from or failure to fulfill social norms, seeing through them expands the intelligibility of normativity as the operative regime of sociality and indeed extends the model of disciplinary society (and its model of "power") everywhere. The globalizing movements of critical humanism thus gain traction through gender and sexuality, which succeed less in establishing specific social identity norms (though they do that, too) than in shoring up the sex/gender order of capitalist relations—still so little understood—an order that imagines and institutes whole, integral bodies as the units, repositories, and subject agents of libidinal life and death drives, governed by economies of regulation and/or freeing, of privation and/or gain. Our bodies, ourselves—grounding "sex" (as discursive, constructed, constitutive bodily acts and practices) as the incontestable test site of power and protest, the territory and property qualification of political subjects and their claims. Are these not also elements of ground zero, maybe even its cornerstones?

How they will succeed in making us men and women: Like the strange newly made people in the H. G. Wells story "The Island of Doctor Moreau," we will all have to ask ourselves as we look no longer at our five fingers with the opposable thumb but now at the malleable, changeable, yet always bodily guaranteed subjectivity of our sex-gender life performances, "Are we not human?"

None of this is to say that the descriptors lie. Social formations and political formations are built out of the structures of identification, the exigencies and stakes of representation, the terms of legibility and viability, which have themselves become global forces of making human. Yes, of course, we are women and lesbians and trans and queer and black and of color and third world and more besides. And our bodies betray us as much as they allow us to survive, live, love, and find each other. These are lived formations. Yet everyone seems to endlessly repeat the political scripts and counterscripts of being and becoming for free individuals and collectivities as if in an ongoing dress rehearsal for a play that is always being performed "for real."

If we—and I mean we, not you—are not to make the ideas with which we struggle to undo this world simply into the place we already live, the territory to be expanded, then those ideas, like our selves, must remain alive to the permutations of other places, as forms of life. To be alive here means to be open (not "vulnerable") to transmissible forces, presences, and motions, to be mediums and mediators of what we are both a part of and apart from.

The problem is that we habitually mistake these ideas for the lived realities they critique and when you insist on them as the basis for social reform, you participate in making them the means of inhabitation for others. So libidinal forces are all too easily tailored to the social dresses of subjects and objects, where they might instead come across as modes of action, behavior, communication, and relation—modes of "happening"—that would be constrained to fit the familiar characters and props of "real" everyday life. The dynamism of nomadic morphing performed as a form of survival—a living—by so many of us who are by definition of history ill-fitted for that freedom, which is the axiomatic state of an achieved humanity; the convertibility of one's personhood in and out of, to and from things, pertinent existences, organic and inorganic beings; our habit and ability to make ourselves into the *verbs* of others—these are also what animate the world.

And yet even those who feel keenly the need to claim that the places of their being are not simply elsewheres to the here of ground zero but somewhere in their own right ignore these vital forms that are in abundance in those other places, part of the leftover and condition of life after colonialism. They too reproduce the terms of their apprehension—we too participate in our own theoretical arrest. How could we not? Fight back and affirm what is denied, defend what is denigrated, uphold what is decried, make ourselves subjects in our own right. "We" (*dakami*) they and I say in contradistinction to you. But what about when I say "we" (*datayu*) to mean you (they) too? What about when any "I" is only a part-subject, and what if even together "we" do not add up to a whole subject or at least one that has any staying power as a political subject? When people habitually make themselves the instruments or vehicles for a "happening" or a "making" (*pangyayari*) without necessarily being the cause or the author or the object of the action; when some one of us—some lesser member—might serve as appendage or organ of an amorphous extended self of which she is a part, from which she is apart; when one might be as porous as a sentient medium for transmissions of certain and uncertain origin and remain as active as an intransitive verb without a subject or the agent of a noncausative action? These are, I believe, ordinary facts of social grammar for many. And what if that is not a problem but the historical form of our enabling and our caring, our creative living and enjoyment? And freedom is neither the condition nor the issue of well-being?

You may already know that this is the case, except the bodies pile up and always amount to a known quantity/quality, a collective or political identity/idea maybe, if not a community. Every day we are enjoined to keep accounts, measure and be measured, devalue in order to value, determine the I and the not-I, the body and member (*bagi, kabagi*) and the not-body, nonkin, nonmember, nonbody politic. These are pleasures as much as duties of our most mundane everyday struggles as well as of our most noble revolutionary efforts. It is what we get to have and do and what is exacted from us when we keep playing these scenarios of valuable life for real.

The enjoyment of devastation and carnage; the thrill of unimpeded muscular will either on behalf of or against the soft flesh, the pure seed, the redemptive soul; the gratifications of frigid control or inebriated sovereignty; the *jouissance* of self-dissolution or dissolute indulgence in warm waters as the counterpoint of erect, moral standing; the contentment of the violently protected. Are there other libidinal modes and forces, other "kinaesthetic" orders of potential, besides these and more that are still making ground zero and its domestic and overseas possessions? What can other "areas" offer to a gender and sexuality studies struggling to decode these dominant forms of unconscious attachment, which hold things together while they are falling apart, while the rot is flying off the handle?

Language, organism, and race can be areas, too, if by area we mean places of life that are willfully, "structurally" (though humans are indeed always involved) denied the creative dynamism and honor of autopoetic being by master codes, which alone can confer their integral sense. If one were to carefully attend to these fully social areas that transgress existing geopolitical territorial boundaries—be alive to what they might say and be open to their effects and suggestions—one might oneself experience or remember, maybe get caught up in, and not simply recognize, maybe even become a component of, the way things occur and are made to occur when people are not simply playing "for real" but also for possibility, for realizability. What is realizable, both cognitively and practically, is suggested in people's ways of communicating and organizing experience, which are sedimented and codified in the "live" archives of language, and in the ways of inhabiting and using physical and virtual being (not just "the body"), which are themselves transmitted "live" through intimacy, association, affiliation, and accompaniment. In this way, the realizable pleasures and powers of sentience and sensuality—and the "politics" they enact and imply—cannot be removed from how one moves and dwells in the material world, with and among others, including those who are dead but have not ceased to exist, who make their presence known and felt, and those who may not speak or breathe but compel consideration and response nonetheless.

Outside freedom, or within the conditions of nonfreedom, is a diminishing plethora of verbs of action, of happening and making happen, beside which the vocabulary of acts and practices, processes, events and structures, being and becoming is so purposefully impoverished, enamored as everyone is to conceptions of power and erotics that are the shared foundation of our material world. Learning and communicating in the semantic-kinaesthetic networks—plural, linguistic as well as nonlinguistic, languages and mixed tissue of shared existence—that are intrinsic to and immanent in the ways people not only make their lives in the best way they can in the material worlds they build and accommodate but also reach for the possibility of other lives in the ones they have or in the ones they might yet obtain, we might glean the invented and inventive forms of people's personal and social thriving and enjoyment, forms of life set up in quiet and noisy defiance of the debasement, obsolescence, and elimination mandated by compulsory orders of kin or kind. To be alive to these other "areas" in this way might then, maybe, maybe, serve as a path for us to finally get somewhere, else.

References

Foucault, Michel. "Preface," in Gilles Deleuze and Félix Guattari, *Anti-Oedipus: Capitalism and Schizophrenia*. Minneapolis: University of Minnesota Press, 1983.

Spillers, Hortense J. "All The Things You Could Be by Now, If Sigmund Freud's Wife Was Your Mother," in Elizabeth Abel et al., ed. *Female Subjects in Black and White: Race, Psychoanalysis, Feminism*. Berkeley: University of California Press, 1997.

ON BEING AREA-STUDIED

A Litany of Complaint

Keguro Macharia

I am an Africa-based queer scholar. I am an Africa-based scholar who has accepted an invitation to participate in a conversation that will live behind a paywall and, thus, will be inaccessible to many in Africa. I am an Africa-based scholar trained in the United States, struggling to unlearn the fluencies that so readily grant me access to conversations in mainstream queer studies. I am an Africa-based scholar who has chosen to publish most of my thinking on queerness and especially queer Africa on a publicly available blog as an ethical and political act that refuses academic gatekeeping as the price one must pay to be legitimized as a scholar. My blog is called "Gukira," a Kikuyu word that, depending on how one reads it, translates as to keep silent, to cross (as in cross a road), more than, and, if one really stretches it, to awaken. *Gukira* is a wandering word, a wayward invitation to linger in and on spaces of fugitivity.[1]

I am an Africa-based queer scholar trying to find the right way to enter a conversation whose premises seem much less clear after more than a year spent away from the US academy. From here, my protestation, "I am not an Africanist," meets with puzzled looks. Stella Nyanzi, a Uganda-based medical anthropologist, asked me, "What is an Africanist?" suggesting that this geodisciplinary designation does not travel well, if at all.

Other terms are troubling.

I am a queer scholar. By which I mean to say, I am trained in and identify with a field that does not exist in my present geography. A sense of deracination overwhelms me. But I say this with trepidation, because deracination has so often been fetishized, if not celebrated, in queer studies. Consider John D'Emilio's urban-based queers; Judith Butler's abject; Lee Edelman's early proclamation, "Queer theory is no one's safe harbor for the holidays; it should offer no image of home," now morphed into the "antisocial" thesis; Sara Ahmed's "affect alien";

GLQ 22:2

DOI 10.1215/10642684-3428711

© 2016 by Duke University Press

Elizabeth Povinelli's autological subject; and Michael Cobb's "single."[2] Faced with so many demands to un-be and un-belong, one understands Robert Reid-Pharr's (2001: 103) comment, "You say black gay. I hear nigger fag." This dissonance between the said and the heard registers Reid-Pharr's unease with queer articulations of race: "I still have to resist the impulse to flinch when someone refers to me as a queer and to positively run for cover when someone refers to me as a black queer" (ibid.: 102–3). From Nairobi, even the deracinating power of "black queer" seems inaccessible, and I must face other illegibilities. Perhaps we might call this the geohistories of location. Or, following Katherine McKittrick (2006), the peculiar ungeographies generated by particular bodies. Here's one point of entry by the Kenyan queer scholar Neo Musangi (2014: 54):

> The Akamba people of Eastern Kenya are my people. And sometimes they are not. The thing that I am they call *tala*. They do not call me *tala*; it is the thing that I always was. A thing that I became; a thing that I am becoming. *Tala* is the thing that I am. But *tala* is not even a name. It is a description. To call myself "a thing" is to choose to exist outside of myself. . . . To think of *tala* is to imagine a state of being and not being. Neither this nor that. This and that but not. I live as a description.

What if one were to refuse the instinctive recoil that says "native informant," the queer assimilation that gathers yet another term to prove that "we have always been everywhere," or the anti-identitarianism that fetishizes "description" over identity? What demands would *tala* make on the concepts and histories in which queer studies is embedded? What would queer studies have to unlearn about its geohistories to encounter *tala* on shared ground? What fluencies would queer studies have to give up to enter into conversation with *tala*? What geographies and geohistories would have to be generated and contested? Who could occupy them and how?

More.

I am an Africa-based scholar who trained in and taught about the black diaspora. For hiring committees dedicated to what Kandice Chuh (2014) critiques as "about-ness," black diaspora translates into an accumulation of racialized geographies. In some imaginations, it means I can teach the United States, the Caribbean, black Britain, and Africa. For me, the black diaspora is a s/place from which to contemplate the relationship between deracination and encounter, to focus on how black individuals from across the world interact with each other: how we imagine worlds, inhabit ungeographies, and produce fugitive temporalities, not simply "other" or "alternative" or even "counter" modernities but different configurations of time altogether, located in the afterlife of slavery, occupying what Christina Sharpe (2014) might term "wake time."[3] What did it mean, for instance, when Afro-Caribbeans encountered Africans in Paris and London in the 1930s and 1940s and, subsequently, in Ghana and Senegal in postcolonial Africa? How did these encounters generate forms of being together unimagined and unimaginable within white supremacist frames that grant significance to black life only as it becomes visible to a white gaze? What forms of geography are generated by these encounters? What kinds of impossibilities? How does deracination become not only the condition under which such encounters might take place but an ongoing outcome of these encounters?

I note, for instance, that the work now circulating as queer African studies in the United States is indifferent to many of the conceptual frames in African studies. Reading through this emerging body of work, it is difficult to imagine that African philosophers, including John Mbiti, Kwasi Wiredu, and Nkiru Nzegwu, have ever written anything that conceptualizes personhood, individuality, or community. African intellectual contexts disregarded, queer African studies becomes simply another trick in the queer backroom.[4] In fact, the work of thinking through queer Africa will be mostly illegible to US and European ears trained by and embedded in LGBTI studies. Or, as is happening too often, queer African voices and experiences will be absorbed as "data" or "evidence," not as modes of theory or as challenges to the conceptual assumptions that drive queer studies.[5] Even now, an army of well-meaning European and US researchers descend on Africa with notebooks and digital recorders to capture the belated entry of Africans into queer modernity.

In a gesture of profound rudeness, I now ignore e-mails and requests for meetings from US and European researchers who travel to Africa to search for queers.

In recent years, I have returned to Barbara Christian's "Race for Theory" (1987). There, Christian critiques the whiteness and aesthetics of theory, the languages and bodies assumed to be capable of theorizing, the racialization (and tokenism) of theory. She insists that "people of color have always theorized—but in forms quite different from the Western forms of abstract logic" (Christian 1987: 52). "Form" lies at the heart of race-making distinction, for the being envisioned and theorized in much Western thinking, the being Sylvia Wynter (2003) terms "Man," emerges from and occupies a genealogy of thinking and practice of living that is simply unavailable to black people. Hortense Spillers (1987) teaches me that the genealogy of blackness in modernity—a genealogy that creates and sustains slavery and colonialism—produces a different relationship to those philosophical figures supposed to describe one's being in the world: the individual, the subject, the person, the human. The thing-making labor of colonial modernity demands rubrics other than those of inclusion/exclusion, inside/out, subject/abject, majority/minority.

And nothing is quite as futile as trying to occupy or reclaim a negating space.

My thinking emerges from and tries to inhabit the s/place between an ungeography called Africa and a deracination called the black diaspora. From this s/place, archives become tricky. I could pursue and reproduce my negation by attempting to use the archives of colonial modernity. But I am tired of describing all the ways racism unmade black people. Too, I am radically uninterested in the colonial-era archives now brandished with much excitement by those who insist that colonialism brought homophobia, not homosexuality, to Africa. Instead, I am interested in how different black people across multiple geohistories have co-imagined each other and attempted to create a shareable world. This means the sites and scenes and objects I examine—the disparate pieces that make up my archives—are often uninteresting to mainstream queer studies. When I examine, say, how wearing trousers was an important moment in Gikuyu colonial modernity when gender and sexuality shifted in radical ways, or how shifting practices of labor and punishment in pre- and postemancipation Jamaica remade notions of gender and sexuality, I see the yawns lining up in mainstream queer studies. Where are "the queers"? Sometimes, the question is, "where are the white people we can care about?" and at other times, "where are the Europeans and US inhabitants we can care about?" Or, where are the US thinkers we can care about?

I am interested in tracking the dissonant intimacies that emerge as black figures encounter each other: the uses of what Audre Lorde (1986: 61) terms "heterocetera" to create shared ground, the frictions created by geohistorical origin, the uses and failures of blackness to create shared ground, the uses of what Tavia Nyong'o (2014: 76) terms "critical fabulation" to imagine conversations that might occur. Location matters.

When I was still institutional in the United States, before I resigned, it mattered more that my thinking demonstrate I knew how to speak, to conversate, if you will, with mainstream queer studies. Now, I am much more interested in thinking with people for whom blackness is not an afterthought. It means that much of my thinking will remain illegible and uninteresting to mainstream queer studies, as I insist on populating it with names like Neo Musangi, Stella Nyanzi, Zethu Matebeni, Nkiru Nzegwu, Kwasi Wiredu, and Wambui Mwangi. As I stage conversations that skirt the United States, learning from Kamala Kempadoo and Rinaldo Walcott, refusing, in the process, the notion of an "area studies" model that centers the United States as the place to which information flows.

I recognize the irony of making such a claim for a conversation in *GLQ*. Perhaps my task here is to be a complaining native.

Since returning to Nairobi, I ask how being here can be made more possible. It is a here that extends across borders, a here that tugs between ungeography and deracination, an insistent here too often full of displacement. So I form my sentences carefully, learning, from Barbara Christian, how to find the forms I need to survive.

As I return to this writing, Nairobi is in the grip of what used to be called the long rains, which run from March to May. Or, at least, they used to. Now, as February turned into March, and March approached April, phone calls would start with the same question: "Is it raining there?" It has become difficult to know when to plant and what to plant. Food prices have become erratic. Tomatoes are smaller. As are onions. When it rains, electricity becomes erratic. Traffic gets worse. Flying termites fill the air—birds and geckos eat well. The tap water, supplied by the city, shifts in color from clear to mud brown. And when it clears again, it is still difficult to use.

Perhaps it is the rains. As I kept trying to respond to wonderful comments about how to imagine and reimagine area studies, about what a decolonizing university or academic practice might look like, about the kinds of knowledge practices and archives that might remove queer studies from its imperial perch, I kept getting stuck on the story of the scorpion and the frog. You know how it goes: a scorpion begs a frog for a ride across a body of water. Though at first reluctant, the frog eventually agrees. At some point during the trip, the scorpion stings the frog. That is its nature. We know the conversation the frog and scorpion have before they enter the water, and we know the conversation the two have as the frog is dying, but what do they say to each other as the frog begins its journey across the water?

The opening lines of Audre Lorde's "There Are No Honest Poems about Dead Women" have been nagging:

> What do we want from each other
> after we have told our stories

I think the scorpion always has an answer to this question. I think the scorpion always knows what it wants. To cross the body of water, to meet another frog, to cross the body of water again, and to meet yet another frog. Perhaps the frog always knows it is going to die. And, to the extent that it can, it chooses where it will die. In the water. As it is swimming. Perhaps the story of the frog and the scorpion is less about the scorpion's nature and more about how the frog chooses to die. What does the frog want? More precisely, how should the frog choose how to die?

Increasingly, I admire a certain African genius for waywardness. As practiced by Stella Nyanzi, waywardness accumulates odd stories, little moments, folksy wisdom, and seemingly disconnected anecdotes. Some stories feel juvenile— and those looking for profound insights in them will be disappointed by their simplicity. And also revel in their sophistication. Others will nod sagely and with well-practiced condescension praise the simplicity of African philosophy found in odd stories. Waywardness revels not in the secrets found as it strays here and there—it is not a scavenger hunt. Nor is waywardness necessarily interested in forging new paths that others can follow. Often, it is a stubborn refusal to come to the point. And I find myself asking what kind of refusal the frog might stage.

I am not really sure I have anything to say about area studies—about the maps of the world it created, about the maps of the world it still uses, about how it assembles knowledge, about the academy's complicity in it, about the role of native informants, about the possibilities of antinomian practices, about decolonization (a term whose current use in online communities makes little sense to me), about earnest US-based scholars who promise not to replicate imperial strategies as they travel around the world to discover, if they dare, that they hold US passports, and this means something they cannot escape. I could think about what that means for those who travel with good intentions, but I do not really see the point.

How will the frog choose to die?

A final wayward moment: primary school history taught me how to think about Africans. There were two kinds of Africans: those who collaborated and those who resisted. Later, I would encounter the native informant, a role that I could not not perform, and Gayatri Spivak offered me the language of complicity. Others entered the frame: the sly native, the trickster native, the desiring native, the sage native, the agential native, the undeveloped native, the homosexual native, the queer native, the deracinated native. Increasingly, I have been interested in the indifferent native. This native haunts colonial archives and, if you check, recent NGO reports. This native fails to speak in the correct way. Chooses not to answer questions. Rarely shows up. Shows up when not expected. Offers banal observations— perhaps about flying termites. Perhaps the indifferent native understands that the scorpion does not really care about conversation. Perhaps the indifferent native never has to say no. Perhaps the indifferent native simply wanders off.

Notes

1. Thanks to Cervenak 2014, "wandering" has become a newly available term to think with.
2. Many of these works are now vernaculars and need not be cited. I would draw attention to Edelman 1995.
3. I learn "s/place" from Philip 1994.
4. I address some of this in Macharia 2015.
5. I owe this formulation of how nonwhite figures appear as "evidence" or "footnote" to Soto 2005.

References

Cervenak, Sarah Jane. 2014. *Wandering: Philosophical Performances of Racial and Sexual Freedom.* Durham, NC: Duke University Press.

Christian, Barbara. 1987. "The Race for Theory." *Cultural Critique* 6: 51–63.

Chuh, Kandice. 2014. "It's Not about Anything." *Social Text*, no. 121: 125–34.

Edelman, Lee. 1995. "Queer Theory: Unstating Desire." *GLQ* 2: 343–46.

Lorde, Audre. 1986. "There Are No Honest Poems about Dead Women." In *Our Dead behind Us*, 61. New York: Norton.

Macharia, Keguro. 2015. "Archive and Method in Queer African Studies," *Agenda* 29, no. 1: 140–46.

McKittrick, Katherine. 2006. *Demonic Grounds: Black Women and the Cartographies of Struggle.* Minneapolis: University of Minnesota Press.

Musangi, Neo S. 2014. "In Time and Space." *Reclaiming Afrikan: Queer Perspectives on Sexual and Gender Identities*, curated by Zethu Matebeni, 53–58. Athlone, South Africa: Modiaji.

Nyong'o, Tavia. 2014. "Unburdening Representation." *Black Scholar* 44, no. 2: 70–80.

Philip, Marlene NourbeSe. 1994. "Dis Place—the Space Between." In *Feminist Measures*, edited by Lynn Keller and Cristanne Miller, 287–316. Ann Arbor: University of Michigan Press.

Reid-Pharr, Robert. 2001. *Black Gay Man.* New York: New York University Press.

Sharpe, Christina. 2014. "Black Studies in the Wake." *Black Scholar* 44, no. 2: 56–69.

Soto, Sandra K. 2005. "Cherríe Moraga Going Brown: 'Reading like a Queer.'" *GLQ* 11, no. 2: 347–63.

Spillers, Hortense. 1987. "Mama's Baby, Papa's Maybe: An American Grammar Book." *Diacritics* 17, no. 2: 64–81.

Wynter, Sylvia. 2003. "Unsettling the Coloniality of Being/Power/Truth/Freedom: Towards the Human, after Man, Its Overrepresentation—an Argument." *CR: The Centennial Review* 3, no. 3: 257–337.

THE ARE(N)A OF THE STORY

Ronaldo V. Wilson

Ronaldo, I want to apologize again for the situation you experienced . . .

What I am attempting to do here is to tell a story by unveiling this situation, but more importantly, through examining the experiences that move around it. This is a narrative that is fractured, something insofar as the story might inherently get split, broken apart by time, by others, by any attempt at its telling, or perhaps it is in the telling that there is some failure of reclamation, as in the fact that I can't quite render any particular start of the situation, or recognizable order, let alone gauge its impact through what I hope to share in this telling. In this sense, the story constantly travels from the source of its origin, part quickened, part protracted, all veering back into its source, a beginning that neither it nor I can escape.

. . . last night and remind you of the $30 credit I placed on your guest room account . . .

The story is not, in a sense, difficult to unveil, not because it is simple to narrativize, but mostly because it has remained with me since it *happened*, though I realize that before it did, it was bound to happen, or had happened, in some ways, many times before, or was linked to other sorts of accounts of assaults, almost or deadly.

(Say, the chair in the Chelsea Dallas BBQ that hit the white head, say the head that got chaired was taking mad shit, say that the head that got hit was hit by the force of an anger more complicated than any straight hate crime. Say a mother's spine severed at the base by her two enraged daughters, say an avatar of a black body in a TV commercial, towering as threat-check to the viewer.)

GLQ 22:2
DOI 10.1215/10642684-3428723
© 2016 by Duke University Press

And even then, with these projections, the story moves like a track—clicked on play—in Garage Band, tucked away via an illuminated bar, leading away from the start in a beat, or low hum. This is a reminder, a conduit of expectation, production, metronome turned off, but still, there remains the continuous, cycling experience.

But what of its measure?

In fact, it is not sound that holds the story in place at all. Or the facts. Or any record of event. It is a photograph that I am thinking about. In it, I am wearing a blond mullet wig on my head and a Venetian full black mask over my face. The mask has a slight shovel-vent for a nose, and some of what I recall is revealed from my memory, of being told by one of my two "dates" that night, that despite the sweat between the inside of the mask's face and my own, I couldn't take it off: *You're committed. Just think of the cast of* Cats! *All night they went!*

I am at the Association of Writers and Writing Programs main conference bar in Minneapolis with one of my dates, a familiar-looking white man on my arm. You may have seen him anywhere: thin or fat, bald or not, blond or not, grey. Brown tweed jacket or elbow patches, slate. Square or round. Hard-hitting, lanky, or soft-jawed.

We walk into the bar's lobby, which is, again, not the beginning of the story but something I recall, perhaps, as in respite. Or the start could be a white woman in front of me, one I do not know, nor do I recall her look, and then another, her homegirl, both of whom figure, they sorta-know-me.

One charges: "Why are you hiding?"

"Why are *you* hiding?" is what I say back. Or I say, bass in the voice: *You're the one who's hiding*, headswerve,

wig-whip.

I am tired.

But too, I am inspired: by recalling the line, so long ago, in Sacramento, in front of *FACES (Gay Night Life Built for You!)*, an older white, Greek looking, or Latino, and a woman on his arm, she passing (idonotrecallherracebutshelookbrown-tome) enough to tell me and us, *I got him.* Woman enough to remind me of what was possible in desire, in the space of getting in, of being visible in that line as who she was, and is, even now, in my memory as return.

Later, the known and familiar white man, my date, who kicks it with one of the two white girls, tells me she feels bad for saying what she said. Or maybe she was scared. But I was over it in that stupid, long hotel lobby maybe; or maybe, I was scary in my mask, wig, and heels on an imagined catwalk?

I do recall when she rolled her eyes. I'm starting, again, not with this image, nor with the reproduction of my performance as an attempt to be seen, or even represented, *for her eyes only*, or *for her eyes at all*, but as a performance in the very space of representation itself (forme,foranimaginedviewer,forus,forit,forits shifting) that could be akin to Stefano Harney and Fred Moten's (2013: 20) call to "renew by unsettling, to open the enclosure whose immeasurable venality is inversely proportionate to its actual area."

That my attempt was not to provide a spectacle to be seen but to disrupt the very sight of being seen in order to expand the site of my own inquiry is a way to move, to mark the impossibility of the marked subject, something captured by Harney and Moten where they acutely report: "We cannot represent ourselves. We can't be represented" (ibid.).

Here, I offer another picture, perhaps of what *cannot* be represented, a picture of not what I was wearing; instead, I pursue another image altogether, the line (a shadow) that leads from my stilettos below my boxed-in, curved torso to the wig, an orange-red and black wave on a cement ledge, just below the worker, hunched (and gazing into the blue) in a neon-green vest.

Figure 1. *Blue.* Directed and performed by Ronaldo V. Wilson. Center for Art and Thought (CA+T), 2014. Film (still)

What moves the story comes *from* within this image, and remains *in* it. The imagination suspended, projected. Caught. Or a still, revealed. Not the subject, but a scene. For your eyes only, and, also, for all. Or to be more cautious: what moves around this narrative is what was me then, in relief, or what is me now in the red-brown suede stilettos TEAR-E-AVATAR wore in their videos "Pink," and "Red," and "Blue" (Ronaldo V. Wilson, 2014).

At Seabright beach in Santa Cruz and in Port Jefferson Station in New York,

On opposite sides of a country, near the harbor, near the Long Island Sound,

under a lighthouse, or near a Ferry, or Carousel, near the Puget Sound—

what kept me, then, above the critique?

> *From, in.*

> It was NOT me in the cab, stil
> ettos on for the night.
> I wouldn't have walked.
> I couldn't leave them on. As
> Lucille Clifton says:
> *the way a poor man*
> *learns to carry everything.*
> Yet still, my Wireless Bose
> speaker prevents my pumps'
> invisibility. Camouflage, I'm
> caught in my BLK pebbled Coach.

In "Radical Nature of Experience," from *The Public World / Syntactically Impermanence*, Leslie Scalapino (1999: 3) writes that "in language, horizontal and vertical time can occur at the same moment." Through several other poets, Lyn Hejinian and Philip Whalen in particular, Scalapino presents a case to consider the idea of a "non-hierarchal structure in which all times exist at once. And occur as activity without excluding each another" (ibid.).

I am taken by this collapse between horizontal and vertical time, between her exploration of these authors, whether through courting the unexpected, as in one writing one line, and letting a long time pass between that one and the next, "making the line unfamiliar to herself," or in Whalen's writing lines over an extended duration, so as not to "collage" them, but to capture patterns through "comparisons of different moments or periods of time and his own mind at those times" (ibid.: 4).

For Scalapino, time, and perhaps the subject within time, moves along multiple axes. One might say that this could allow one to return to the event, say the escape, say the bashing, say the stabbing, say the slight, say the erasure, say the split of it all, because the area of the narrative remains far from occupying the story itself.

Especially as in, *Hey victim, you are both the agent of the story, and the consequence of your own victimhood—but most importantly, consider what you might make out of these transpirations?*

What Scalapino understands in time as "activity," I follow, here, into a poetics of asking what happens through improvisation, or in the gesture of writing about the scene, the area/arena where the story is experienced within time that folds through multiple modes of the event or in what Scalapino (1999: 9) notes as "the disjunctive present, which is: 'then' is 'now,' and the future is the same 'now' (they occur at once, but not hindering each other, being entirely those times, separate from each other—in a 'present' as being disjunct)."

Boxing

The gloves are hidden next to the wall
in a corner, near weights and speakers,
in the room marked: *PERSONAL TRAINING.*
They are red, and for speed, so too,
is the bag, which shakes at my jabs,
& straight punch. My hips turn in impact,
and the struck bag wobbles at the base
of its pendulumn: spins, stops, tagged.

At the moment when RPH took this picture, I was dueling with another black, who was reclining in almost a vestibule, with Dreds that featured yellow tips at their ends, and he was glaring at me, while he was lovingly (at least it seemed so) surrounded by a crowd of whites, each of whom resembled fan girls, or in the least, they was his crew. Stroking him? Angels?
Yet at me, he was clearly, throwing shade—
Sulfur in the night—
I began to vogue in front of him, or at least to pose, some controlled movements,

Figure 2. Photograph courtesy of Roxi Power, 2015

lines of power from the thighs, wavering, as if unbalanced.

Two could play at this game, of indignation,

or survival, of whatever.

It was a kind of fight.

One might say that this is where the story gains its traction

in the realm of desire that fuels one to take the risk,

in leaving a bar,

half in heels, half in drag, in a cab, all alone—

Or one is never alone. In the conference bar, at a shared table, I tried to seduce an old white man with an almost equivalent dinner jacket as mine, though not as modern, or as well sought, mine, Patrick James: *West Coast Classic.*

He told me about his girlfriend who'd died only days before AWP. *She was strung out on crack*, and died of the same. *I miss my little crack baby.* This is also what he said, when we (I thought) had a window to pursue the possibility of what would never happen.

My short-term goal: to get my stiletto to touch his leg. I told the lady cock-blocker next to us—we were all talking—that this was going to happen. And we watched, together, my success at connecting the tip of my heel with the curve of his

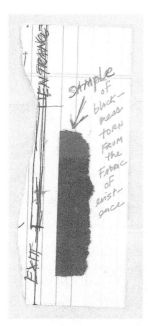

pant calf. I touched him, or at least something did. Despite his sending the blocker (her) the message to meet him in his room (shewould,ithink,rejecthisazz), despite their similar lives, the family pics, immediate reminders—in the very shadow of my mask—they could barely see each other.

Against this image from William Pope.L— taken from his notes on *The Black Factory*—I do not remember how either of them looked. He more than her, but only the small shape of his head. I am thinking of the space between my heel and his leg, the area between my mask and face that night, the inner arena between who I was, what I wanted, and how I played. What was against, or up in my face? A black shadow contained for whom?

Figure 3. POPE.L. Black Factory Object 2004. Courtesy of the artist and Mitchell-Innes of Nash, NY. © Pope.L

Perhaps this rendering (asexploration,device, grid)—I've been thinking about it since I first saw it—is part of the reason I wore my mask into the bar that night, the belief in fun, trouble, the faith in collaborators, unexpected, the reason I walked around the nearly empty lobby of another hotel with a plain, thin white man on my arm. We were together. We passed the other writer-blacks near the fireplace, then. Now, I borrow Pope.L's materializing the production of an extant racialized possibility through a shard, a fragment of race as the idea to illustrate blackness as fluid, yet flattened, *torn* from one area of existence into—or to make—another:

> Sample
> of
> black-
> ness
> torn
> from
> the
> Fabric
> of
> exist-
> ence

In my photograph, I notice the droop in the V-neck of my cheap (H&M) long-sleeve black cotton crew, my forehead, my eye sockets, the brown skin that matched Dreds's own. Or perhaps he could see the way that I could not care less about how whack was my Rite Aid blond wig, all the way from Palm Springs, the part of the costume I was unable to use in "Hummingbird," a video in progress in which I am wearing only shades (Oliver Peoples), a midnight and cobalt blue polyester shirt (printedhummingbirds&florainthefabric) with a broad matching tie—a blended set of faux-silken life to augment my ticking in front of the desert rock and mountain terrain. Maybe it is in that dance, these movements where the story waves into fact.

This is what happened.

I pulled up in a cab, driven by a Somali driver, one of many in Minne-apolis, having been just driven from around the corner by another. Earlier that night, I performed as TEAR-E-AVATAR. On the stage, with my mask, and without glasses, I could not read what I prepared, so I had to improvise a song to the beat of a band that blasted generic hard rock in the adjacent room.

I sang a song about a major poetry prize committee I was on with some very well-established white American poets, a prize in which the two women of color poets I presented—the only WOCs offered by any of us—multiple books and extensive careers—who have won no similar prizes, nor are in any rich belly of prize-winning whites, but have been qualified for this prize—and all these prizes—like forever, but who are not from here, who do not work in a familiar and worn language, who come from deep in a belly of knowing how to capture erasure and loss—well, they were, by and large before this moment and after—ignored.

Here are some takeaways: Their names were not once repeated by my fellow jurors, until I pointed out this fact. And then all the candidates' names were repeated. Even so, there was no discussion, really. There was no debate. Chairs became involved. A director. And as it turns out, the first name named—a usual suspect by a usual suspect—would secure the prize from the very start. I wrote a response. It went unanswered. I was asked for my blessing. I sang a song about this in a bar. I sang a song against a beat from within an adjoining room, where a band played something. I improvised. I found joy. Or, at least, I tried.

There was no consequence, yet there was every consequence in that the person who won is the same person who always wins, and so it went, and so I did not fight. I was afraid. To say too much. I sang into where there is no answer, at least for me, no answer quite yet, and the correspondence still lingers. Here, from my inbox, is some of what I wrote to the rest of the jury:

Figure 4. Photograph courtesy of Roxi Power, 2015

This is the work of poetry that is so often overlooked, particularly by women of color poets whose work is deserving of mainstream attention and reward. Please note, I am not saying that _____ work is not deserving, or that, _____ too, does not mine loss, and seeks to make visible the inequities of our world, but I say, this work has been generously prized, and alternately recognized, and I feel that this might be an opportunity to present other figures with similar treatment.

Did I carry this loss (mineforthe-team,or,myowninabilitytowar,or,myneedtokeepitmoving) into the night? Whatever the case, a feeling did tell me to refrain from walking the several blocks that late to the next spot; and what made it simple was the pain in my feet from my Dollhouse heels or the ease of my cash, my exhaustion, the weight of the speaker in my bag—the copy of Amiri Baraka's collected *S.O.S. 1961–2013* on the lobby table left with a card, propped up against it reading "Free," was not among—

    Too much weight, in fact, a weight as heavy as the story that came up after on my Facebook feed, about another black in the AWP Convention Center hallway, *SMH*, shitting himself in a diabetic fit, or the words *I can't*, was one response of another in the feed, the many people walking over his body, because it was explained to them by the guards that he, in all likelihood—a black man lying prone on the convention floor—*Well, him, he's high, on heroin*, or some other thing, such a common, common.

    I suppose I am working at thinking of being in time, or in the world with this endless beat, this relentless hum, the falling, the lament, the cycling song as essay, as the poem in formation, freestyle performance, gesture, document. Perhaps this vantage point comes from what Wanda Coleman reminds us in her quest to mark the body in time with violence as systematically tied together, however fraught, however wandering. Seeing is popping! Coleman (2005: 57) points out that

> on the part of White Folk there is no longer pity for the plight of Black Folk. The amused contempt resonates. The troubled State of the Race has become the product of a deeper, more calculated condition. . . . And so I have grown another eye, a primal orb density that provides me with constant double view. With it I observe with such intense focus that I become emotionally cockeyed, my vision so skewed I can't witness any racial incident without relating it to my personal circumstances.

So maybe I wanted to keep my stilettos on (and on the move) for the night!

    In the cab ride, I remember double-checking. Was my wallet there? Was my speaker? Was my room key, my shoes? And my mask? It was not on my face. It was over. That is, at least, the performance was over. I was going home and I was not the crack baby. Not to be missed. There are two white men. I know they are larger than I am. And they are wobbling, but it is not the men who tug at the cab door, which is locked. It isn't them, actually, that I notice first. It's the white woman (isshetall,orthin,orisherbagperfect?thewayitsettleslateronthecounter) who is tugging with so much force, as if, she too, is convulsing, her hand the only one on the car door. We are barely stopped, and I am watching the locked door from inside. I have all my things. I am not enraged when somehow, it opens:

"I'm not finished," or, I think I say, "Rude . . ."

This is a trigger. This is a feat. This sets the white fight, and us, into motion. They are ready to bash.

WP (WhitePerson/WhiteProle/WhiteProblem): "You're gonna mouth off!" "You gonna give us mouth?"

T-E-A: (TEAR-E-AVATAR): "You need to wait." I think I drop my voice, or I say, "I'm not done."

Who knows what I called them—*Proles, Trash, Primates, Animals*—names to divide us, to create a shield, a closed door where there was no door.

WP: "Look at his shoes. Look at his shoes. You faggot. He's a fag. He's a black cocksucker! You want it up the ass! He needs a dick up his ass!"

The Somali cab driver wants me to exit the cab, but I tell him that I will not. "That won't happen," and I tell him, "What you need to do is to pull forward. I'm not getting bashed, *uh . . . no.*"

Wander

I would run when the cars slowed in the meatpacking district,
the tricks in the TrannyNight, heat cooled by a Gin&Tonic.
In the bar across from the ManHole, and on the walk
from Bank to 11th Avenue / Hot eyeballs and baseball bats.
Fat ice cubes in a huge tumbler.
>   & this summer still grabs back the braids,
>   the gun pulled on the little
>   black girl in a bikini, and the big Texas cop
>   goes, shut your mouth you now know sit down stay down
>   sounds not dissimilar,
>   but familiar:

Shut your mouth. Fix your mouth.

. . . if I may be of any further assistance, please don't hesitate to reach
out . . .

I look for my phone. Will I call 911? Somehow the door gets closed. Maybe she
closes it. Maybe I close it. Maybe this was so I could recall, on YouTube, when
the dad of the family on a safari in Africa, who exits the jeep to get a close-up, is
jacked by a pride of lions and ripped apart, bloody clothes and pieces tucked into
a body bag, and driven from the kill site. So, too, his kids are safely whisked away.
    Maybe this is why I closed it, or she closed it, that door, and I am looking
out of the cab's back window. My muscles did not feel threatened, nor did my back,
nor did my skull. In fact, I don't know where I felt under threat after the door slid
shut.

I am, though, aware of a fist. But I am not on the end of that fist.

(WP's start to punch each other in the street!)

"I had your back bro!"
    Or some other tongue,
        crossjabs to the face, and someone's in the street,
            vanishing into a pile.
                We drive a few feet to another entrance, and I make
    it in:

Bitching. I want to recount the space in which the attack and nonattack
elongate. What was the area between us that allowed me to not get snatched out
of the car to move, instead, more deeply into the seat, to demand being pulled forward to a safer exit? To watch my would-be assailants turn on one another? How
did I understand, to a certain extent, my safety to be my right, as in, *How dare they
touch my precious, rich body, my priceless self?*
    Does the story of our interaction begin with the song I sang in the bar?
Does it begin with the refusal of the poets I presented, as valid, clearly worthy of
every prize? Does it begin when I am told I am hiding, simply for being present
in the modes of performance in which I choose to operate? Does it begin with the
weight of my body on the tip of a single stiletto digging into the lobby floor, or its
shadow cast on a cement ledge?

Let me start again, by saying I was invited to tell this story at a dinner party, as if this could serve as penetrating entertainment, or even still, as if I could actually retell the story without feeling similiarly elated, or sick, ejecting, dejecting, inspired to figure out how to actually reveal it, enough to speak, laugh, or carry on. Pass the Blend. And the story becomes coupled with a dream, or a snippet of one at least, a dream in which I am, in fact, not arrested but queried by a white cop—but it is I who flashed him with my brights, driving behind him, to get his attention.

Not a dream. Above us, a great ceiling dome, painted in burnt reds and dark browns, and lit enough to cast a light over one of the men—maybe it is the winner of the fight—who made it inside. He is being held, surrounded somehow, by people, and revealed by what appears a soft, crimson light. In it, I remember the shape of his mouth, a bashful curve, and the resignation in his drunken song:

WP: "C'mon he's a Ho, a Black Ho. He needs a dick up his ass. He's a Homo." "You know I'm tellin' the truth." "You know I'm tellin' the truth."

The counter is another story. I make myself small behind it. I don't think I'll get shot, or stabbed, or kicked, there. To me, this isn't a game, but I am playing one where I am crouched next to a small trough of rocks, also lit by a similar, though brighter, crimson light.

Lora, who met me halfway, just beyond the counter, in the lobby, will escort me into the elevator, and later walk me to my room. Lora, who asked if I was with them, when I stomped in—as if I could be with them—who, me, a part of the flow of punching bodies drifting in unison from the street fight into the W?

In where I hide, though, Lora realizes I am not. Lora gets it. She does not budge. Lora is on my side. She protects me, me near the rocks, out of reach, in my own world, my eyes scanning up, where I fake not hearing, all the yelling, yelling.

WGDT (White Girl Door Tugger): "You called him trash! He is not trash! Tell them, you called him trash! Tell them!"

Soliloquy

What comes out of his drunken mouth,
more than he knows, is perhaps true.
Maybe I did need a dick up my ass!
This morning, I see a pile of bi-couples,

leftover on my screen, some cuckold

ramping up on a bed into a mouth.

And one whispers: *You like that white daddy dick,*

Nigger? So sweetly—or the name of the porn

could be *Pink*. How I said, *Look*

at your shoes! I rev him up, get him to crack.

I am playing, I think to live, yet somehow,

bringing us together by way of pursuit.

I did not want to escape,

which is not the same as running

to attack his shoes, a chunky loafer,

a bold square toe, so hideous, the raised seams.

His cuff's mouth is frayed, wide boot cut,

so only the scuffed head peaks out.

How to bring this together with what I'm thinking:

That those white teens killed those black teens,

then they surfed their corpses: *a zombie noise—*

a final gasping sound, a song of evacuating bowels.

They were all friends. Then the living whites fucked

the dead black boys, who went to school where

my father went, in Joliet, Illinois. Poor.

I'm not, and unafraid in the rocks. *They wanted to keep*

their teeth as trophies. Untouched, I chill behind

the counter, and the next day, I fortify.

I drop pounds with a "Bro" in the lobby, a witness:

That was so fucked up, and maybe, too, he says *sorry.*

How did I throw my weight into it, when I boxed

the bag the next morning? Elliptical: Yellowstone

Grand Loop, Moraine Lake, I hiked the Virtual

Australian Bush Quiet, to attack

the fear of being jumped in the elevator?

At the Breakfast Buffet? Ifitwereawhitewoman

inthatcar,andyou,withanotherblack,pulledatthecardoor,

you'dbedead! The mayonaise is yellow on the knife

& the bread, hardening, is white. The turkey is cold,

the bacon too. This is far from the best sandwich in America

I ate with DLM, fried fish on a warm bun, and then

later, after a nap, I awake to Minneapolis, view at dusk—

. . . warmest wishes, Lora and the W Team . . .

There's a rainstorm coming, and lightning breaks
over the grey city. Thunder, too.
And the bear bar I see online is far,
so far from here.

References

Coleman, Wanda. 2005. *The Riot inside Me: More Trials and Tremors.* Boston: Black
    Sparrow Books.
Harney, Stefano, and Fred Moten. 2013. *The Undercommons: Fugitive Planning and
    Black Study.* Wivenhoe, UK: Minor Compositions.
Hejinian, Lyn. 2001. *A Border Comedy.* New York: Granary Books.
Pope.L, William. 2002. *William Pope.L: The Friendliest Black Artist in America.* Edited
    by Mark H. C. Bessire. Cambridge, MA: MIT Press.
Scalapino, Leslie. 1999. *The Public World / Syntactically Impermanence.* Hanover, NH:
    Wesleyan University Press.
Wilson, Ronaldo V. 2014. Dir. and perf, "Blue," "Pink," and "Red." Online: The Center
    for Art and Thought.

WE HAVE ALWAYS BEEN QUEER

Diana Taylor

To María Elena Martínez, the *primogenita* of the research on Juana la Larga, who did not live to see this essay published.

$\mathcal{I}$n June 2014, during the Hemispheric Institute's Encuentro (an eight-day conference/performance event) in Montreal, a very queer dispute erupted in the assembly of some one thousand participants. A "queer" dispute, I call it, because everyone on all sides of the clash self-identified as queer and because it questioned the meaning, scope, and politics of the term as well.

Jesusa Rodríguez and her wife, Liliana Felipe, two of Mexico's most radical performance artists and activists, had presented a play, *Juana la Larga* (*Long Juana*), developed from archival documents unearthed by the queer Mexican historian María Elena Martínez of the University of Southern California. Juana Aguilar, an eighteenth-century intersex person from Central America, was accused by the Inquisition of committing "abominable sins" with women.[1] Aguilar is depicted onstage as an anatomical model. Esparragosa, the physician played by Rodríguez, examined her genitals and declares that Juana has no sex at all ("se es nada"), and is therefore a nothing, and cannot be prosecuted and executed by the Inquisition.

Here, in fact, Rodríguez and Felipe took liberties with Esparragosa's findings that categorized Aguilar as gender "'neutral,' like some bees" (as opposed to "nothing") (Martinez 2014: 159). For Esparragosa, gender identification relied on visually distinctive genital markers and functionalities. His findings, based on his observations that Aguilar could not physically have committed the acts attributed to her, may have released her from the grip of the Inquisition. The eighteenth-century debacle was all about anatomical definition and difference, defined by hegemonic authorities, as the basis for "the administrative technologies," as Martínez (2014: 164) writes. The assumptions, she notes, were "that a man or woman is defined fundamentally by the capacity to reproduce" (ibid.: 165). Aguilar is merely

GLQ 22:2
DOI 10.1215/10642684-3428735
© 2016 by Duke University Press

an object to be dissected. I could go into detail here, as Martínez does in her essay, about the violence of Western medical classification systems and taxonomies, the brutal and dehumanizing ways that medicine has produced, labeled, and treated nonconforming subjects, not to mention the merciless scrutinizing powers of the Inquisition.

Rodríguez's "nothing" stems from a different genealogy—Mexico's *ningu-neo* (making someone a nobody, a nothing). Octavio Paz (2008: 188) notes that the "operation that consists of making Somebody a Nobody. Nothingness becomes individualized, it becomes body and eyes, it becomes Nobody" (Una operación que consiste en hacer de Alguien, Ninguno. La nada de pronto se individualiza, se hace cuerpo y ojos, se hace Ninguno) (my translation). As easy as it might seem to align Aguilar's sexual "deficit" with a Freudian notion of the phallus or a Laca-nian theory of lack, *ningunear* is not a psychoanalytic paradigm but a radically misogynist and racist act of ontological dispossession. Paz continues: "I remem-ber one afternoon I heard a noise in the room next door and I called out 'Who is there?' The voice of the domestic servant who had newly arrived from her village responded: It's nobody, Sir, just me" (ibid.). The genealogy of producing "absence" also dates far back—at least back to the conquest. Domingo Sarmiento, an Argen-tine schoolteacher, intellectual, writer, and political activist who became presi-dent of Argentina, 1868–74, tellingly described Argentina in *Facundo*, his mas-terpiece, as empty, desolate, completely without human habitation, nobody there but some Indians, "salvajes" (savages).[2] Juana Aguilar, according to Rodríguez and Felipe, is a nobody, one more in the long line of people who do not fit into the identity-granting values and categories and, thus, are forcefully or discursively disappeared. Fittingly, the documentation about Aguilar's fate has vanished from the archive.

While Esparragosa's designation might have saved Aguilar's life, the rea-son for the shift in the performance, I believe, is far more existential and political, suggesting that women have been treated as nonhumans in Mexico for a long time. The play was humorous as almost all of Rodríguez's work is, at times pushing (some would say exceeding) the boundaries of acceptable taste. As the pompous, deliciously self-admiring Esparragosa, she struts about the stage in the french-ified velvet long coat, white stockings, and fine slippers so popular in the period. His first name, Narciso, fits him perfectly. She, as he, caresses the words in his mouth. "Seminal pollution" sounds like a delicate and fine wine. She makes fun of herself as she forgets her lines and has to peek at the subtitles projected on the examination table downstage center to catch up. She even asks the person running the translation slides to back up a little. She makes fun of Spaniards, Argentines,

Barbie from the United States, the Canadian immigration service, and everyone else. She does a particularly offensive rendition of yellow face to depict the Japanese doctor who studied female sexuality.[3] The history of conquest, slavery, and continued exploitation is told through various characters and accents. "Coño!" (a common expletive meaning "cunt") Felipe repeatedly exclaims as a macho Argentinean character.

Using caricature, vaudevillian gags, oversimplifications, double entendres, and other forms of wordplay, they make their point, but the point is sharp. The two artists call out the continued and escalating violence and nullification of women. *Feminicide*, a term coined in Mexico to describe the gendered nature of the viciousness, continues to escalate. Two thousand seven hundred and sixty-four women were murdered in 2012 alone. Every three hours, they tell us, a woman is brutally murdered in Mexico. The "brutally" refers to the frequent practice of stoning women to death, flaying them, desecrating them, cutting their nipples off; their murderers wear the nipples as necklaces because they can. The police do not bother to investigate the crimes. The government takes no action. The women are "nothing" to them. A United Nations representative reports: "Violence against women isn't an epidemic, it's a pandemic in Mexico" (Diaz and Rama 2014). Throughout the play the tension oscillates between the desire to destabilize gender and sexual categories and point out the violence of medical and archival categorization that historically cemented current notions of "difference" and, at the same time, make an urgent point: that "women," products of that systematic and violent differentiation, are being targeted and killed for being women. The "women" include lesbians and trans women. The play attempts to resolve this tension between "women" and unsettling gender in the last line with a celebration of "women of all sexes."

The next morning, via Facebook, the one thousand or so participants of the Encuentro learned that a transsexual member of the audience felt humiliated and laughed at both by the artists and by the audience members during the performance. He said that it had brought him to the point of tears and that he had resisted the temptation to walk out. A number of queer friends agreed and reposted the text widely. Those who had not seen the post heard about it at breakfast. The buzz circulated in Spanish, French, Portuguese, and English via the morning chatter and the did-you-hears.

The next hours were full of discussions, accusations, and demands for clarification. In a brief impromptu town hall meeting that I called that same day in the midst of a packed performance schedule, Rodríguez explained that her intention had never been to make fun of trans people—on the contrary. Her artistic and performance work has always pushed for gender rights, sexual rights, and other forms of human rights. She did mean to offend machos, she added, who define themselves by annihilating femininity in all its manifestations. A tall, strong, trans woman in a red dress, pearls, and high heels came up to the three of us on the raised platform and thrust her hand within inches of my face. "It's not their fault," she shouted at me. "It's your fault." I let the gesture pass, even as I felt physically attacked. For all the talk in the audience of the need to create "safe" spaces, I did not feel safe. Again, Rodríguez reiterated that the violence against women, including trans women, in Mexico is so virulent that she and Felipe had wanted to bring it to the foreground. She apologized if they had inadvertently hurt people in the audience.

A contingent of the Encuentro's participants wanted more time to talk about the issues that had been raised. Stephen Lawson, the queer Canadian performance artist (of 2boys.tv) and curator of the Encuentro, asked us all to postpone the discussion until the next day so that artists who had come from throughout the Americas to share their work might be able to continue with the programming. The majority of those in the room agreed, and the performance artist Lois Weaver organized a Long Table for the following afternoon at the Library of Performing Rights that she created for the Encuentro. Long Tables, developed by Weaver in 2003, offer an alternative form of discussion to traditional roundtables and town hall meetings. Based on the notion of a dinner table conversation, she developed an "etiquette" that allows anyone to speak as long as they are seated at the table that normally accommodates twelve people at a time. If all the seats are taken, the person who wants to speak taps someone at the table on the shoulder and requests the chair. While allowing for full participation, the Long Table also requires that we look at people as we speak to them. The face-to-face offers a different form of engagement than a disembodied Facebook communication. Language, affect, self-presentation—everything, in short—becomes part of the transmission. Rodríguez sat at the table, and Felipe chose not to. The trans man who posted on Facebook sat next to Rodríguez but did not speak. The trans woman who confronted me did not participate and said that she would not talk to any of us. She did not attend the Long Table. Others at the table, nontrans queer activists and theorists, made some points: the trans community bears the burden of always having to explain itself—we should not contribute to that burden; the trans movement is a central one that needs to be heard and understood; there were language issues and points of untranslatability. What (and who) was the audience laughing at? Was the audience laughing at what the artists said or at the translation that kicked in a minute or so later? Some pointed out the dangers of censorship; others reiterated that

Rodríguez should have explicitly referenced the trans population as she played with genitals; others felt uneasy with artists being called on to apologize for their work. Larry La Fountain, a queer theorist from Puerto Rico who is a professor at the University of Michigan, pointed out the dangers of mistranslation and misrecognition around terms and concepts combined with the challenges of engaging historical documents. The play after all, he stressed, dealt with the eighteenth-century Spanish Inquisition! "I understood it was a parody and that Jesusa was opening a space for conversation," he said. But he added that "it sounds to me like the white people from the North are once again telling the women of color from the South how to do their work." The Jamaican artist-scholar Honor Ford-Smith agreed that the discussion reflected a north-south divide: "the huge gap between what Jesusa was trying to get at" and the attitude that "those backward Third World people need to be taught things." The queer performance artist Peggy Shaw expressed her position succinctly: "If you have a problem with a show, go make your own fucking show." She added that women have never been safe and women have had to explain themselves for centuries and have become used to seeing themselves ridiculed onstage and off. For the first time, a self-identified trans person spoke, saying "the only person I can speak for is myself" and told Rodríguez, "I want to be in solidarity with you."

And so it went.

Rodríguez repeatedly asked for someone to explain the specific thing or image that had offended them.

At the end of the hour and a half Long Table, the trans man who posted leaned over to Rodríguez and asked her quietly if he could have time to speak with her.

The discussion did not end there.

The queer theorist Jack Halberstam, who was present at the exchange, referred to the incident in "You Are Triggering Me! The Neo-Liberal Rhetoric of Harm, Danger, and Trauma" (2014), "a play that foregrounded the mutilation of the female body in the 17th century was cast as transphobic and became the occasion for multiple public meetings to discuss the damage it wreaked upon trans people present at the performance." Halberstam notes that "recent controversies within queer communities around language, slang, satirical or ironic representation and perceptions of harm or offensive have created much controversy with very little humor recently, leading to demands for bans, censorship and name changes" (ibid.).

Rodríguez's answer to Halberstam's essay sidestepped the "harm" issue (which has not yet become a "topic" in Latin America) and noted instead the cultural differences around humor. She also pointed to different understandings, or perhaps assumptions, around queerness:

> I've dedicated my time to studying ancient Mexican culture, our heritage. Its worldview is based on a dual conception. This dual principle is male and female at the same time . . . (Ometecuhtli and Omecíhuatl). This dual principle encompasses everything in our culture. From the very origins, opposite forces are conceived as complementary and not simply as opposites (which is the case in Christianity). This duality, simultaneously male and female, shapes everything and includes everything. So the hermaphrodite dual concept is integrated into all that exists, it is a basic concept that imprints Mexican culture with a special seal, including, of course, sexuality. This doesn't mean that we don't follow the controversies taking place in the West, or that we're unaware of the predicaments of so-called "modernity," but no matter what, we see them through this lens because it's in our roots and our origins, and is therefore reflected in our language.[4]

In other words, riffing off José Esteban Muñoz, in Mexico we have always been queer. According to Muñoz (himself a gay US Latino) (2009: 1), "We have never been queer, yet queerness exists for us as an ideality that can be distilled from the past and used to imagine a future." Queerness, for Muñoz, "is essentially about the rejection of the here and now and an insistence on potentiality or concrete possibility for another world" (ibid.: 1). For Rodríguez, among many others, queerness has always been with us, has always been us, although the same inquisitional forces that tried to execute Juana la Large have attacked and literally demonized it (as "cosas del diablo") for over five hundred years. The encompassing conception of queerness, for Rodríguez and Felipe, I believe, is a given. At stake, rather, is communicating the brutality of the *ninguneo*—reducing the someone to a no one.

As Rodríguez and Felipe make clear in the performance, many concepts were brought in with the conquest and colonialism—linear temporality (and thus the belief in anachronism) among them. For indigenous populations in Mexico and other parts of the Americas, as with many communities of Afro-descendants, time does not function as past, present, future. Where native languages and cultural beliefs and practices survive as living forces, the future is indistinguishable from the past. We move forward into the past; our present simply enacts the second of alignment between the past that is never over and the future that is always here. Guillermo Bonafil Batalla (1996: xvi–xvii) analyzes the "living presence of Mesoamerican civilization" and calls this Mexico "Mexico Profundo" and the Western imposition of civilization "the imaginary Mexico." When at the end of the perfor-mance Rodríguez and Felipe circle back to the conquest using a wooden puppet of a conquistador (and speaking with an outlandish Castilian accent) and place it next to the tiny doll figures of the Zapatistas, it is not to underline the five hundred years since the conquest but the continuation of conquest by other means. The struggle against imperialism continues. Yet the move also underlines the ongoing force of indigenous people and worldviews. Close to 15 percent of Mexico's popula-tion is indigenous, although a greater percentage actively engages in indigenous cultural and belief systems. One of the system's underlying principles is that iden-tities exist in a state of constant change. While this holds true everywhere, changes occur differently in various contexts. Rodríguez embraces the power of constant transmutation. She writes elsewhere of her desire to transcend categorizations in her work and "leave behind its gender prejudices—what's important is that specta-tors confront their own capacity for transformation, male, female, bird, witch, shoe, or whatever" (Taylor 2016: 7).

The understanding that such terms as *gender* and *sexuality* and *queer* and *trans* are not understood the same way throughout the Americas, and—more importantly—cannot be reduced to one more north-south tension, was again underlined at the Encuentro by the keynote delivered by Thompson Highway, a Cree queer writer from northern Canada:

> Aboriginal languages divide the universe into that which is animate and that which is inanimate, that which has a soul and that which has not. In this conception, gender has no place whatever. Whether male or female biologically, we are all he/shes emotionally, psychologically, and spiritu-ally, as is God. And the resulting superstructure is thus not the straight line of monotheism but the circle of pantheism, a system wherein god is biology is nature is the land. A yonic—that is, womb-like—superstructure as opposed to phallic is what we speak of here, a design where there is room for many genders.[5]

In this very queer cosmology, he laments the loss of spaces and geographies that allow for his language and culture to survive.

The Long Table, then, became one more site for the difficult practice of self-naming and self-localization—in addition to other negotiations that we perhaps failed to recognize, let alone name and locate. As Anjali Arondekar (pers. comm., March 30, 2015) notes, one becomes "non-trans through seizing political affect . . . non-US through seizing political affect."[6] The process of self-constitution, she writes, entails designating whomever one deems "improper as anachronistic" (ibid.). Instead of focusing on violence, risk, and harm, the conversation became about where people came from, whom they spoke for, on what authority, and how they labeled themselves. Highway's keynote, in fact, had explicitly connected location, naming, and risk—he knew that in the capitalist, expansionist economy, he was deemed an anachronism, an improper outlier, a Cree, queer subject who understood himself as part of a yonic system of constitution in a phallic world and thus doomed to disappear. The death sentence had been passed—it was simply a question of time. He had resolved to die laughing. Humor, for him as for Rodríguez, was a political affect highlighting the very concrete danger: in this economy of subjectification, certain populations are disposable.

Highway's keynote, in fact, anticipates several of the issues raised by the Long Table—the impossibility of communication, the perceived anachronism of "other" ways of being and doing, the nontransferability of humor. The participants at the Long Table did not all understand one another across languages and cultures. The "anachronism" explicitly addressed at the table was not Highway's understanding of himself as a doomed subject in a system he could not control, a throwback to other times and spaces marked for disappearance, incompatible with neoliberalist, masculinist expansion. Rather, the discussion pointed to what Martínez (2014: 174) warned against as "trying to make [Aguilar] a part of 'gay and lesbian history.'" "Succumbing to a classificatory impulse," she adds, is "not unlike that which is present on Esparragosa's investigation" (ibid.: Introduction). This might have been a warning for those who insist on labels, but it is a warning too about the very power of labeling, a sovereign power of determining or delimiting rights and legitimacy. Ultimately, of course, the two understandings of anachronism are related; the differences lie in perspective and positionality (who classifies? who gets classified as "nothingness?"). Translating humor, of course, posed yet other problems. Some at the Encuentro felt that Highway was making fun of them. "I love white people, don't you?" he asked, laughing himself silly as he stopped to "readjust his girdle," as he put it. Many, however, followed the laughter to where he was asking us to go. All these challenges severely complicate even the most well-meaning cross-cultural discussions.

My feeling at the table, however, was that the disconnect was less about understanding the important trans movements and more about the ways that identity struggles can blind us to related forms of violence. We were all talking about violence—the violence that trans communities face every day, the violence against women, the violence of dispossession of indigenous peoples, lands, and worldviews. Moreover, these forms of destruction are connected—sharing roots to patriarchal, imperialist pasts that have become our neoliberal presents. But turning the violence into a personal grievance put it beyond discussion: "I felt Highway was laughing at us" or "your representation was hurtful to me." Conversation stops: I cannot argue with your feelings. But talking about violence as relational allows us to develop strategies of co-resistance. Women have always been explaining themselves; feminists have always been explaining themselves; people of color have always been explaining themselves; queer, transgender, and transsexual groups have always been explaining themselves; indigenous peoples have always been explaining themselves. And, clearly related, they are all at risk. Surely, as the one trans person who spoke at the table noted, there are grounds for solidarity. As Peggy Shaw reminded us, if we are going to cast everything as a war, we need to remember who our enemy is.

What does "at risk" mean here? Communities and groups of peoples referred to in this discussion—women, gays, lesbians, and trans people, communities of color, and indigenous groups—are at risk of physical violence, de-subjectification, discrimination, and economic marginalization at the hands of the very same forces. These are not sequential forms of oppressions—old ones resolve, giving place to new. The violence is lived as past and very present. Rather than separate past and present, I turn to anachronism as a viable politics to call attention to the seemingly constant state of againstness of dispossession. In 2014 the Long Table performed the failure of the "dramatics of discourse," Michel Foucault's scene of enunciation (2011: 68). "Injury" seemed to be the main subject of debate, and people spoke past one another. At risk, however, was the possibility of envisioning modes of co-resistance. But something tells me this particular conversation has only just begun.

Notes

1. For selections from the archival accounts of the case, see Martínez 2014.
2. See Sarmiento 1921.
3. When I asked Jesusa Rodríguez why she did this, she said that the facial expression was one she used to represent the late Mexican president Luis Díaz Ordáz, who was noted for his pronounced overbite (pers. comm., June 24, 2014). She liked it, she said, and thought nothing of it. The term *yellow face* is unknown in Mexico and critiques of racial impersonation almost nonexistent. While Rodríguez is not sensitive to the topic, I have tried to explain to her, on more than one occasion, why people might find racial impersonation offensive.
4. Translation by Marlène Ramírez Cancio.

5.   For a video of Thompson Highway's keynote, see Bautista 2014.
6.   Thanks to Anjali Arondekar and Geeta Patel for their editorial comments.

References

Batalla, Guillermo Bonafil. 1996. *México Profundo: Reclaiming a Civilization*. Translated by Philip A. Dennis, xvi–xvii. Austin: University of Texas Press.

Bautista, Victor, ed. 2014. *The Place of the Indigenous Voice in the Twenty-First Century*. Montreal: Concordia University.

Diaz, Lizbeth, and Anahi Rama. 2014. "Violence against Women 'Pandemic' in Mexico." *Reuters*, March 7. www.reuters.com/article/2014/03/07/us-mexico-violence-women -idUSBREA2608F20140307.

Foucault, Michel. 2011. *The Government of Self and Others: Lectures at the College de France, 1982–83*. New York: Picador.

Halberstam, Jack. 2014. "You Are Triggering Me! The Neo-Liberal Rhetoric of Harm, Danger, and Trauma." bullybloggers.wordpress.com/2014/07/05/you-are-triggering -me-the-neo-liberal-rhetoric-of-harm-danger-and-trauma/.

Martínez, María Elena. 2014. "Archives, Bodies, and Imagination: The Case of Juana Aguilar and Queer Approaches to History, Sexuality, and Politics." *Radical History* 210: 159–82.

Paz, Octavio, ed. 2008. *El laberinto de la soledad*. Madrid: Cathedra.

Sarmiento, Domingo. 1921. "Aspecto físico de la República Argentina y caracteres, hábitos e ideas que engendra." In *Facundo: Or, Civilization and Barbarism*. www .gutenberg.org/files/33267/33267-h/33267-h.htm.

Taylor, Diana. 2016. *Performance*. Durham, NC: Duke University Press.

QUEER THEORY AND PERMANENT WAR

Maya Mikdashi and Jasbir K. Puar

*C*an queer theory be recognizable as such when it emerges from elsewhere? This is the central question that guides our thinking on the intersections between queer theory and area studies, in our case the study of the Middle East as transnational. We come to this question in thinking through disciplinary and archival locations of knowledge production, and the political, economic, and social cartographies that animate both queer theory and the study of the Middle East. Finally, we outline some of the recent theoretical contributions of work that thinks across the boundedness of "queer theory" and "Middle Eastern studies," and revisit the question of what queer theory may look like when it is not routed through Euro-American histories, sexualities, locations, or bodies.

The United States remains foundational to queer theory and method, regardless of the location, area, archive, or geopolitical history. (This is still largely the case even in Europe, Australia, Canada, and New Zealand.) US archives and methods appear to make legible and illegible all other geohistories. We note that this is not a new problematic.

Much of the early work of queer theory in the 1990s sought to trace the flows of "queer" as a hegemonic traveling formation that followed the circuits of US Empire. In attempting to mark the complex negotiations and resistances to such purported external impositions, the "local" in the global south was unwittingly reified as raw data, often through the purview of "sexuality studies," in relation to an ever-entrenching "global."

And yet, several decades later, despite many trenchant interventions, such epistemic issues remain. Commodifications of area, and of the local, result in a twofold movement. It is not just that queer theory is unconsciously enacting an area studies parochialization: queer theory as American studies. More trenchantly,

GLQ 22:2

DOI 10.1215/10642684-3428747

© 2016 by Duke University Press

other areas become visible and refracted only through this parochialization. Thus the formulation of this roundtable is notable. "Queer Theory and Area Studies" suggests that queer theory itself remains unmarked and unencumbered by location. (We could, in fact, rename this roundtable "American Studies and Area Studies," or "Queer Theory as Area Studies.") This may well be a problem hardly specific to queer theory and more generalizable in terms of the US academy as a hegemonic and traveling formation. After all, both authors of the present article were educated at the graduate level and now research and teach in the American academy—one is trained in or teaches area studies and anthropology, while the other is an "Americanist," an invisibilized area studies formation from which all other area studies are derived and defined. Another example of this is the number of US women's, gender, and sexuality studies departments that have now set up franchises in not only western European countries but also eastern and southern European as well as global south locations. This geopolitically uninflected variety of queer theorization, which does not recognize itself as redoubling homonationalist tendencies, also tends to be resistant to knowledge produced under the purview of an "area studies formation." This is perhaps due partly to the fear of the area studies disciplinary mandate to situate, locate, and circumscribe, a mandate that might seem antithetical to the antifoundationalist impulses of queerness. Furthermore, rarely is the scholarship of queer theorists hailed as epitomizing the best potential of area studies formations. At the outset, the work of queer theorists in area studies (rarely read by queer theory as "Queer Theory" and often relegated to "sexuality studies") is understood as a "case study" of specifics rather than an interruption of the canonical treatments of the area studies field at large.

While we are thoroughly convinced of the critique of area studies that transnational feminist theorizing instantiated more than three decades ago, and while we are critical of the (changing) conservative nature of the field (the *Journal of Middle East Women's Studies* and the *International Journal of Middle East Studies* have been key to this change), we remain observant of certain aporias. The transnational frame, popular in contemporary queer theory and sexuality studies, is often routed through the west, resulting either in west to the rest or in theoretical and comparatively based triangles with the United States or western Europe at the apex. Rarely are the locations of area studies themselves understood as transnational; the Middle East, for example, is a historically, politically, and economically deeply transnational region unto itself.

Is there any way to negotiate or avoid altogether this call-and-response circuit that continually repositions the United States as arbiter and funnel for the legibility of theory elsewhere, and the arbiter of what is to come, to be learned or apprehended? We would call for a politics in queer theory that works to displace the United States as the prehensive force for everyone else's future—the arrival point on a transnational journey of progress. That is to ask, why is the critique of the production of US nationalism within queer theory itself not not central, rather than incidental, to queer theorizing, given that the privileged site of the United States so thoroughly shapes what queer is, what it can do, and how it forms a field of knowledge that can affect the rendering of queer bodies elsewhere? Is queer theory in the United States indeed homonationalist, indebted to an uninterrogated nationalism in order to further its capacitation, its (imperial) reach? Further, as Joanne Barker (2011) and Scott Morgensen (2011) and others point out, queer theory enacts a settler subjectivity in its invocation of futurity and its narrative of progress. We must complicate or reject the prehensive force of histories and presents of the United States precisely in order to study the relations between settler colonialism, colonialism and imperialism on the one hand and queer theory on the other. Other imperial histories, including Ottoman, British, German, Italian, and French, are crucial. These imperial networks, much like the imperial network of US hegemony today, were global and transregional and, crucially, often in competition over different parts of the Middle East. Techniques of rule, representation, sexual regulation, and morality, in addition to colonial bureaucrats themselves, traveled within this imperial network—from Bombay to London to Cairo to Calcutta and from Paris to Sudan to Algeria to Syria and back to Paris. The theoretical archive that forms the background picture of queer theory is itself deeply invested in, and in part produced out of, these imperial, colonial, and settler colonial contexts and conversations. Queer scholarship in Middle East studies is diverse and full of debate. One framework suggests understanding the rubrics of sexuality and gender as multiple and translated across geopolitical locations and homo/hetero, queer/hetero binaries (e.g., Najmabadi 2005, 2013). Yet another argues for the need to posit sexuality as a form of colonial governmentality that legislated an affective and structural relational of modernity through its cohesion in legislative but not necessarily populist arenas (e.g., Massad 2008, 2015).

We are interested in recent work in the field that reads the registers of sexuality and queerness as infinitely imbricated in biopolitical forms of control. Jasbir's work on Palestine demonstrates how pinkwashing and the activist response to it displace the intense regulation of racial reproductive technologies of the Israeli state. Her current work on Gaza looks at practices of bodily and infrastructural debilitation that challenges biopolitical distinctions between living and dying through the production of radically altered corporeal forms (Puar 2015). Maya's work attends to the ways that mainstream sexuality rights discourse is conversant with the masculinist, capitalist, racial, and sectarian nature of the Lebanese state and with discourses on Islam, homophobia, and secularism in the War on Terror (Mikdashi 2013, 2014a). She places heterosexual women and the regulation of heterosexual relations at the center of her queer analysis. Another project of hers attempts to think through the gendering of heteronormative men as available for killing (without mourning) in contemporary Palestine, using both settler colonial and War on Terror frames of analysis and thinking through the work that the temporality of the "crisis" does, for example, in Gaza (Mikdashi 2014b). Other examples include Paul Amar's work, which reads against the presumption of an insistent imposition of East/West binaries, revealing a whole human security-state system that reformulates the stakes in the regulation of sexuality. In his analysis of the Queen Boat incident as about disenfranchising women's bohemian economic circuits of ownership, he suggests that Joseph Massad's response to Cairo 52 is quite homonationalist (Amar 2013). Sima Shaksari's (2013, 2014) work on the sanctions regime and trans migrations and asylum politics in a War on Terror era in Iran teaches us that the biopolitical and the necropolitical technologies of war and state regulation place particular injuries above others through technologies of neoliberal recognition and international law.

The aim of this body of literature is to ask what different locations, archives, and histories generate in terms of new conversations, connections, and directions in queer and feminist theory—in many ways we aim to provincialize the United States. The larger project is to shake the cartography of critical theory itself, as Edward Said (1978, 1993) and Gayatri Spivak (1988, 1999) both argue—where "regions" are largely studied through epistemological and theoretical frameworks generated from the archives of the global north—archives that cannot be divorced from imperial histories and archives of colonialism, that cannot be read away from strategies of domination and extraction.

The transnational Middle East is a region beset with strife. There is the ongoing US occupation of Afghanistan and Iraq and the preceding two Gulf Wars. The Israeli settler colonial regime in Palestine is financially enabled by the United States and has resulted in the dispersal of Palestinian refugees across several states, including Lebanon, Syria, and Jordan. A cold war between Saudi Arabia and Iran is being fought via proxy throughout the region. The current wars in Syria are being waged by over eight foreign states in addition to the Syrian army itself and multiple transnational Islamist movements. Kurdish national aspirations continue to be colonially dominated by Turkey, Iraq, and Iran. The Western Sahara continues to be colonized and settled. ISIS repeatedly bombs civilians, captures cities, and kills and makes life hell for apostates and religious and sexual minorities in addition to the women in the regions they control. There is regional widespread poverty and underdevelopment partly as a result of neoliberal economic restructuring and, in the case of Iraq and Iran, internationally imposed sanctions regimes. People are living in the aftermath of the Arab uprisings and revolutionary and counterrevolutionary zeal and upheaval in Egypt and Tunis. There are also many other regional and international conflicts and forms of permanent and semipermanent war and warfare.

In such a context, what kinds of queer organizing, archives, theory, practices, visibilities, institutions, knowledge production projects emerge? The precarity of queer life is not exceptional in these sociopolitical spaces: it is additional precisely because war, genocide, occupation, oppression, dictatorship, terrorism, and killings are part of the everyday fabric of life for many people who live in the region. What kind of queer emerges in the face of revolutionary overthrow of the Mubarak regime, for example, or in the context of Lebanon, where one out of every three residents in 2015 was a refugee fleeing war in a different part of the Middle East? What animates the impulse to search for something to call or to theorize as queer? What must the queer body do, or be, to be recognized as such, and by whom? Do we want this recognition, and if so, how and for what purposes? How can we generate theory out of these locations, and if doing so, are these bodies of theory routed through area studies rather than recognized as queer theory?

For example, perhaps the term most used to describe injury against same-sex relations is *homophobia*. As a term, *homophobia* is an apt descriptor for discrimination against queers in several urban areas of the contemporary Middle East—and we have written about its circulations between the United States and the contemporary Middle East (Puar and Mikdashi 2012). However, homophobia is also a homogenizing and flattening discourse. In Beirut, the naming "homophobia" aggregates aggressions that might also be understood as gendered or racial or economic. For example, the sign "homophobia" is the marker most used to describe incidents where working-class or racialized migrant laborers engaging in male-male sexual behaviors are attacked or brutalized. Perhaps this is not surprising given the everydayness of violence (sexual, physical, psychological) directed against migrant labor (including "domestic labor") or refugees. With the description of homophobia, the ordinariness of these assemblages of racial and classed violence are marked and are routed through LGBTQ rights groups and organizations and discourses that circulate transnationally. These organizations and discourses operate by universalizing particular injuries. Transnational LGBTQ rights discourse, meanwhile, is not only anchored in US-based queer histories and movements. It is also anchored in, and anchors, white, cisgendered, masculinist, and middle-class queer histories that are elevated through the elision of race, sex, and class domination in the United States. Once emptied of located and ongoing histories of domination, the "global LGBTQ movement" can emerge as such.

We are turning from the now obvious preoccupation with queer organizations, activism, and the naming of queer bodies, optics that are largely mobilized in queer theory as American studies as evidence of queer vitalism or "sexuality studies." We note, rather, that an urgent issue for those who work in and from the perspective of transnational Middle East studies (those of us whose archives are located there) is: How can queer theory emerge and converse with the mass corporeal losses and debilities of war? Does queer theory (still) require a sexual or gendered body or a sexual or gendered injury—particularly if part of the project of homonationalism is to produce and stabilize transnational, imperial, and settler colonial forms of sexual and gendered injury? Perhaps, thinking from a location where war and colonization are quotidian contexts of life, we should rethink what sexual injury is, and the economic, political, and military work that designations of "sexual" or "gendered" injury and violence does in the first place. How do these designations affect which deaths or injuries are internationally nameable and mournable and which deaths are merely "collateral damage" in the contemporary Middle East? What gendered and racial archives are being invoked with every deployment of those now ubiquitous words, *collateral damage*?

In Palestine, for example, the kinds of quotidian practices that are restricted through intensely militarized securitization and border surveillance produce a severely restrained economy of corporeality. There are and have been organizations such as Aswat, Al-qaws, and Palestinian Queers for Boycott Divestment Sanctions that name queer resistance as primarily about resisting the occupation. But other forms of bodily experience, such as stunting, the medical diagnosis for the slowing down of childhood development which prohibits "normal" maturation into adulthood, occur through Israeli practices of calorie counting, shooting to maim, exposure to weapon toxicities, and the erosion of water, health, and electric infrastructures. These practices create populations of altered and experimental corporeal humans, the transfiguration of human forms sustained through the decimation of health infrastructure that could transform the crippled into the disabled. They do so structurally, as medically impossible rehabilitations that might redeem the cripple as the disabled. Do we want to claim cripples as queer bodies, especially when those bodies neither present a challenge to the normative nor signal a transgressive nonnormativity but undo this very binary opposition through their endemic presence?

The proliferation of corporeal difference is multiple and diffuse. Depleted

uranium in Iraq from both Gulf Wars has led to an astonishing increase in con-
genital birth defects and cancer rates (Dewachi 2013). Afghanistan has the largest
population of people living with prosthetic appendages, from legs to arms to eyes
to penises. Do we want to call these bodies—partly the result of US imperial occupation and domination—queer bodies? (This claiming of disability as queerness
has been proffered in the US context by disability studies but is rarely taken up
in queer theory. On the rare occasions that disability is central to queer analyses,
it is deployed as an intersectional figuration—disability as queerness/the queer
disabled—rather than seen as a biopolitical vector that might alter the terms of
queerness and its legible corporealities altogether.) Should we remain wedded to
queer theory's general obsession and commitment to the sexualized human form to
recognizable "queer sexualities," given that the war on terror has thus far killed
at least 1.3 million people (a conservative estimate) in Iraq, Afghanistan, and
Pakistan alone? These casualty numbers do not reflect killing in Syria, Yemen,
or Somalia, arenas that have also been declared by the United States as part of
the Global War on Terror—nor do the numbers reflect US allies' own self-termed
wars of and on terror in the region, such as Saudi Arabia's war on its own people and on Yemen or Israel's folding of its colonization of Palestine and its wars
on Lebanon into the United States led War on Terror framework. The 1.3 million
dead statistic also leaves out the vast number of injured and permanently disabled
and debilitated that conveniently drop out of the calculation of collateral damage.
The men, women, and children in these countries and regions have been made
available for killing, brutalization, and debilitation partly through sexualized, gendered, classed, and racialized transnational discourses about Islam, Arabs, and
the Middle East. Importantly, these discourses were not created in 2001 with the
launch of the War on Terror, but the War on Terror does represent the contemporary pinnacle of the circulation and weaponization of these sexed, gendered, and
raced discourses.

Different contexts have the potential to push conversations in queer theory
in surprising directions precisely because they disturb the "taken for granted"
background picture of queer theory as American studies. The relationship of area
studies to queer theory is multiple, invigorating, and potentially groundbreaking—
but only to the extent that both fields allow their archives, theoretical presumptions, key terms, and areas of inquiry to suffuse, confuse, and destabilize each
other.

References

Amar, Paul. 2013. *The Security Archipelago: Human-Security States, Sexuality Politics, and the End of Neoliberalism*. Durham, NC: Duke University Press.

Barker, Joanne. 2011. *Native Acts: Law, Recognition, and Cultural Authenticity*. Durham, NC: Duke University Press.

Dewachi, Omar. 2013. "The Toxicity of Everyday Survival in Iraq." *Jadaliyya*. www .jadaliyya.com/pages/index/13537/the-toxicity-of-everyday-survival-in-iraq.

Massad, Joseph A. 2008. *Desiring Arabs*. Chicago: University of Chicago Press.

———. 2015. *Islam in Liberalism*. Chicago: University of Chicago Press.

Mikdashi, Maya. 2013. "Queering Citizenship, Queering Middle East Studies." *International Journal of Middle East Studies* 45, no. 2: 350–52.

———. 2014a. "Sex and Sectarianism: The Legal Architecture of Lebanese Citizenship." *Comparative Studies of South Asia, Africa and the Middle East* 34, no. 2: 279–93.

———. 2014b. "Can Palestinian Men Be Victims? Gendering Israel's War on Gaza." *Jadaliyya* July 23.

Morgensen, Scott Lauria. 2011. *Spaces between Us: Queer Settler Colonialism and Indigenous Decolonization*. Minneapolis: University of Minnesota Press.

Najmabadi, Afsaneh. 2005. *Women with Mustaches and Men without Beards: Gender and Sexual Anxieties of Iranian Modernity*. Berkeley: University of California Press.

———. 2013. *Professing Selves: Transsexuality and Same-Sex Desire in Contemporary Iran*. Durham, NC: Duke University Press.

Puar, Jasbir. 2007. *Terrorist Assemblages: Homonationalism in Queer Times*. Durham, NC: Duke University Press.

———. 2015. "The 'Right' to Maim: Inhumanist Biopolitics in Palestine." *Borderlands* journal 14, no. 1.

Puar, Jasbir, and Maya Mikdashi. 2012. "Pinkwatching and Pinkwashing: Interpenetration and Its Discontents." *Jadaliyya* August 9.

Said, Edward W. 1978. *Orientalism*. New York: Vintage.

———. 1993. *Culture and imperialism*. New York: Vintage.

Spivak, Gayatri Chakravorty. 1988. "Can the Subaltern Speak?" In *Marxism and the Interpretation of Culture*, ed. Cary Nelson and Lawrence Grossberg. Basingstoke, UK: Macmillan Education.

———. 1999. *A Critique of Postcolonial Reason*. Cambridge: Harvard University Press.

Essays

BACKWARD FUTURES AND PASTS FORWARD

Queer Time, Sexual Politics, and Dalit Religiosity in South India

Lucinda Ramberg

*W*hat are the possibilities of being out of sync with the linear time of histori-cal progress? What are the consequences? To be queer is to be out of step with the reproductive rhythm of sexual maturation, conjugal matrimony, and patri-lineal descent. To be Dalit, or a member of a community formerly designated as "untouchable," is to be backward, not yet modern. The question I am interested in here is twofold: How is asynchronicity inhabited by those deemed backward?[1] How might the answer to this question speak to the geopolitics of queer theory and the sexual politics of Dalit studies?

I come to these questions through ongoing ethnographic research on sexu-ality and religiosity among communities formerly designated untouchable in Kar-nataka, south India. In particular I have focused on two contemporary practices: theogamy and conversion. Through both practices, those deemed backward unset-tle the time that has been set for them. By marrying a goddess and converting to Buddhism, Dalits occupy and dislocate their marginality to historical progress, sexual convention, and capital accumulation, making futures out of different kinds of sex and distinct ways of relating to the gods. In learning how to think about these practices and their effects, I have long drawn on both queer theory and Dalit stud-ies. As fields of study rooted in emancipatory political projects, they have much in common. They share a secular modern conception of human subjectivity; privilege

GLQ 22:2

DOI 10.1215/10642684-3428759

© 2016 by Duke University Press

epistemologies of the margin; and denaturalize and resignify embodied stigma to mobilize forms of political and social transformation. Yet they also bypass each other, and in drawing on both fields, I have often come upon a conundrum. Dalit studies brings a thoroughgoing critique to the social and economic hierarchies produced through caste distinction and the stigmatizing attribution of "untouchability" to Dalit bodies. However, in Dalit studies the theogamous and sexually illicit female and male women (*devadasis* or *jogatis* and *jogappas*) with whom I have worked are typically understood to stand in need of reform, if not rescue, for their own good and for the good of the community.[2] This need for reform is presented as self-evident. That the need for reform is self-evident is itself an indication that desirability of sexual respectability has been naturalized: or so a queer reading of this inclination in Dalit studies would suggest. By contrast, sexual respectability is put to shame in queer theory. Queer bodies that are more than just sexually different—also marked as female or feminine, trans, brown, black, or native—are all too often subsumed within the temporality of white North American masculinity. Muscular, youthful, endowed with disposable income and unencumbered by family, the normative subject of queer studies remains white, masculine, and middle class. To put it somewhat differently, projects of sexual rehabilitation are frequently housed in the territory of caste critique, and modes of geopolitical imperialism travel all too easily under the sign of queer rights and recognition. I am echoing here a point others have made: the woman question and the question of geopolitics are often made to displace each other even as they are mutually configured. This displacement is observable in the politics of queer liberalism and caste radicalism as well as the configuration of fields such as queer or Dalit studies.[3]

In the context of her work on debates between Indian elites and British officials in the nineteenth century over sati, or widow immolation, Lata Mani (1998: 79) offers a useful formulation: "Women are neither the subjects nor the objects, but the ground of the discourse on sati." As she argues, what was at stake in these debates was the future of India. The status of women in the practice of sati functioned as the occasion for a struggle over the moral right to rule. Here geopolitics occludes sexual subjectivity, that of the widow who would burn or be burned upon the death of her husband. Struggles for sexual liberation can also occlude the difference that geopolitical location makes, such as when tolerance of gay men and lesbians becomes a litmus test for the moral right to national sovereignty, a phenomenon Jasbir Puar (2007) calls "homonationalism." My premise here is that one condition for the possibility of this occlusion is a particular temporality, in which the past, and those places and people consigned to it, is made to secure the present of those seen to be the bearers of the future. The question becomes how to unsettle this temporality, how to queer the relationship between the past, present, and future that it enacts.

Before I begin to expand on time, I discuss the two Dalit communities my research has focused on: Yellamma women and converts to Buddhism. Yellamma is a popular South Indian goddess to whom both girls (mostly) and boys (sometimes) are dedicated as children by their families. Those dedicated are called *devadasis* (servant/slave of the deity) or *jogatis* and *jogappas*. This dedication is conducted as a rite of marriage or theogamy. They do not marry anyone else, but may take patrons or clients. These female and male women embody the goddess whom they call mother and husband and conduct her rites of fertility in their communities across northern Karnataka and southern Maharashtra. Marginal but powerful, *devadasis* are widely framed as prostitutes, and their theogamous relation with the *Devi* (goddess) is not valued or recognized as a matter of legitimate religion or valid kinship under the law. Indeed, in the most recent wave of over one hundred years of reform, the practice of dedication—as well as all the rites it authorizes *devadasis* to perform—has been criminalized. *Devadasis* are enjoined to sever their ties to Yellamma and forgo the forms of ecstatic embodiment she provokes and enables, or to face fines and imprisonment.

Conversion to Buddhism in the same region follows the call of Dr. B. R. Ambedkar, an anticaste activist and philosopher who took *diksha* (became initiated) in Nagpur in 1956 at the end of his life. His initiation into or conversion to Buddhism has been widely emulated by Dalits since, especially in Uttar Pradesh and Maharashtra, such that Buddhism has become the fifth-largest religion in India according to the 2011 census. Conversion to Buddhism has been widely understood as a mode of political dissent and a way to move out from under the forms of social subjugation and stigmatization attached to "untouchability." Indeed, this is how Ambedkar (1956) conceived it, as a way to exit what he called "the hell of Hinduism." Women bring up the rear guard of this movement; they are widely perceived to be less able than men to leave the gods and embrace Ambedkar's project of secular modernity and rational Buddhism.

At first glance, the temporalities entailed—the backwardness of *devadasi* dedication and the forwardness of conversion to Buddhism—might seem obvious. Yellamma women are widely seen to embody a degraded past that undermines the possibilities of the present time and that cannot be admitted into the future of the community or nation. Dalit converts to Buddhism embrace education, equalitarianism and rights discourses, work and time discipline, and scientific rationality. However, what I show here through ethnographic attention to everyday practice is that both *devadasis* and Dalit converts are out of joint with the straight time of domesticated gender, capital accumulation, and national coherence. Moreover, they are working on time—cutting, splicing, looping, and knotting time—making what I am calling recombinant time.

Temporizing

What is the temporality of emancipatory histories, whether sexual or national? To draw on Anjali Arondekar's (2010: 113) terms, what politics of time has emerged in relation to our will to knowledge and stance toward otherness? Present-day Hindu nationalism anchors itself in the provenance of the Vedas and proscriptions of the Manusmirti, the texts taken to found the religion that we have come in the modern era to call Hinduism. According to this narration of time, the ancient Hindu past of Hindustan (India) authorizes Hindu rule in the present and should guide the future character, composition, and sexual comportment of the nation.[4] Geeta Patel (2000: 49) characterizes this way of telling time as "a future thrown forward from a past, a past produced in and through the present, which excises other possible pasts, other possible histories," and therefore, I would add, other possible futures.

This way of telling time is exemplified in two contemporary controversies in India. One is drawn from the annals of politicized religion, the other from the territory of sexual citizenship. In an ongoing campaign called Ghar Wapsi (homecoming), the Hindu political organizations Vishva Hindu Parishad (VHP) and the Rashtriya Swayamsevak Sangh (RSS) have been calling on Muslims and Christians to "return" to Hinduism. The call itself asserts Hinduism as the original religion of the inhabitants of the Indian subcontinent and portrays converts as prodigal sons who will be welcomed back home. The long and distinctly Indian histories of both Christianity and Islam are elided in this Hindu nationalist framing of Hinduism as every Indian's proper home.[5] Histories of caste are also elided from this way of telling the past and future of Indian religion; most converts to Islam, Christianity, and Buddhism were historically members of so-called untouchable communities. Proponents of Ghar Wapsi do not even mention Buddhism, which has already been subsumed under Hinduism in their minds. As one Ambedkerite Buddhist put it to me, laughing, "They think Buddha is an avatar of [the Hindu god] Vishnu. So according to them we never left. But we know the truth, we were never Hindu, we were always Buddhist."

This way of telling time is also evident in one argument made by legal activists for overturning Section 377 of the Indian Penal Code, a law introduced by the British in 1860 criminalizing "carnal intercourse against the order of nature." The petition filed by the Delhi-based Naz Foundation in 2001 sought to establish an indigenous history of same-sex relations in the subcontinent as a way to counter the argument that such relations constitute Western aberrations.[6] But, as Arondekar (2009) argues, such history telling elides the unknowability and complexity of sexualities' pasts and risks reproducing the very temporality it is trying to exceed, one that fixes the past through the political imperatives that drive conceptualizations of the present, whether those are instantiated in sodomy as unnatural vice or homosex as a universal and transhistorical practice. This historian's call for an antifoundationalist relation to the archive is akin to the anthropologist Kath Weston's (1993) warning about "ethnocartography" in sexuality studies, an epistemological operation in which the sexual cultures of others are mined for evidence that might secure the universality of the field's categories and serve as evidence of the global queer.

The question becomes how, in our efforts to secure the present for sexual dissidence and caste rebellion, do we enact a different temporality? How do we eschew the epistemic violence, the imperial gesture of this temporality that "excises other pasts" in its effort to secure its own? To temporize is "to let time pass . . . to procrastinate; to delay or wait for a more favorable moment. To act, negotiate, parley, treat, deal (*with* a person, etc.), so as to gain time."[7] The provocation here is, as we tell the time of sex and otherness, to learn to dwell in time in such a way as to linger over its multiplicity and its movements and to delay its fixing in the teleologies that have come to be so self-evident. Here I am working through ethnography as a way to temporize everyday practice, allowing it to rub against the deployment of history and its emplotments of gender, caste, and sexuality, the ways it fixes time and us in it.

Beginning with Backwardness

In most accounts of *devadasi* dedication, its persistence marks the ignorance and backwardness of the families with Yellamma in them. I have written against such narratives of spoiled virtue and peasant unreason, taking "ignorance" and "backwardness" as explanations for persistent nonmodern practices to be symptomatic of the "denial of coevalness" (Fabian 2014), a mode of representation and appraisal that fixes so-called moderns in the present and others in the past, eliding the productive effects of their practices of self making and world making in the present time and place (Ramberg 2014). I have been interested in situating *jogatis* and *jogappas* as capable of illuminating possibilities in lifeworlds beyond their own.

The region where I have conducted most of my fieldwork is commonly referred to as a backward area. The area's "backwardness" is evident, people have taught me, not only in the presence of "archaic" practices such as dedicating children to deities but also in the way people live, talk, have sex, and comport themselves. It is also legible as a lack of infrastructure, or absence of "development." That is, it is invoked both as a characterological trait that marks civilizational lack and as a socioeconomic condition of state neglect and marginality to capital. In 2002 when I was living and working in a village in this region, one of my queer friends in the city once said to me, laughing, "I don't get it—why you want to go there, it's so backward." Backwardness is also a sexual condition and remains a feature of queer existence. My friend's inability to imagine wanting to go to the rural places where I was working is one example of how this condition functions.[8] She herself had fled the (sexually backward) feudal hinterland for the (gayly forward) cosmopolitan center. Her comment held a lesson for me: my rural peregrinations as a white-skinned queer American doing research encountered different possibilities of recognition than her metropolitan queer Indian of Punjabi descent would in the hinterlands of India. However backward a place and people I preoccupied myself with and retrograde my sexuality seemed (I was self-evidently unmarried and childless and unaccountably uninterested in seeking a husband and having children), I was always already forward, modern, and rational— characteristics evident in advanced formal education, white skin, and Americanness. The meaning and consequences of being untimely are unevenly distributed across geopolitical terrains of difference. They are also embodied. To draw on what the differences between *devadasi* futures and Buddhist futures have taught me: if a future is what you want, it is better to be forward in a backward place than backward in a backward place. *Devadasis*, as *devadasis*, have no future. Buddhists do.

Yet backwardness has its possibilities. "Backwardness" in India is not only a trait ascribed to nonmodern others but a bureaucratic and legal category delimiting a condition of social and economic lack and therefore entitlement to state-sponsored forms of redress such as access to food rations and reserved seats in universities and government jobs. For this reason, backwardness in India is also an aspirational state, as communities strive to accomplish the designation "backward caste" to gain access to state-sponsored benefits. The designation of backwardness thus performs a double function; it marks a degraded condition that fixes you in the past even as it constitutes the means for your forward mobility by providing a positive basis for claims before the state. To lay claim to those benefits is to mark yourself as backward and therefore to dwell in an oscillation between backwardness and forwardness. A genealogy of *backwardness* in the Indian context indicates the ways the term is heir to the colonial designation and census category of "depressed classes" applied to those deemed not yet capable of self-government.

The present-day bureaucratic category of "backward castes" is a category of citizenship that speaks to one's relationship to the state. Members of backward castes are, in Andrew McDowell's (2012: 352) words, "subdivided by distance from a forward, participating liberal citizen [governed by market principles and logics]." In other words, backwardness marks those communities that have not yet entered the time of market capital. Caste is the prime indicator of backwardness in the contemporary bureaucratic calculus of the Indian state.[9] The renunciation of Hindu deities, especially of the practice of dedicating children to their service, is one way that those designated "outcaste" have sought to move themselves forward once and for all, into the time of capital accumulation, political modernity, and sexual respectability. Conversion to Buddhism is another.

But what might be foregone in the movement forward, away from backwardness? Writing about what he calls the "pre-history" of Dalit emancipation in India, Milind Wakankar asks us to consider what is lost in the movement from subalternity into what Partha Chatterjee calls political society. On the one hand, a willed forgetting of the past is necessary to the project of "empowerment"; on the other hand, "what is irrevocably lost nonetheless leaves its trace in the mourning subject" (Wakankar 2010: 85).[10] José Muñoz's (2009: 1) invocation of queer time as a not now but past forward—"queerness exists for us as an ideality that can be distilled from the past and used to imagine a future"—resonates with Wakankar's description of the position of the Dalit convert as temporally suspended: "forever in between" (2010: 51). Wakankar calls for attention to this Derridean trace, the absent presence of the past in the present understood as "a contemporaneity in which we look to the future but also seek to be 'haunted' by the past." I am interested here in this trace as it marks *jogatis* beckoned into reform as well as Dalits becoming Buddhist. The questions as I would put them are: How do those caught "forever in between" make of this position an unsettled and unsettling harbinger of temporal possibility? How do they pass time, making futures out of backwardness?

Cutting Time

Upon hearing that I had come to her village to learn about the *Devi* Yellamma and the women who are married to her, Shantawwa declared: "No one believes in Yellamma in this village anymore, only in Ambedkar. In my brother's house, we are not allowed to perform puja for any of the gods." In the village I call Nandipur in northern Karnataka where this conversation took place in 2002, twin offprint posters of Ambedkar and Buddha adorn many a household wall. Shantawwa's account marks shifts in both the time and the place of the gods: they have been left behind—"no one believes anymore"—and they have been exiled from the house.

Converts to Buddhism interviewed in 2014 echoed this narrative of transformation to me in interviews. In the words of an elegant, thoughtful painter who took diksha from (became converted by) Ambedkar at the age of seven along with all the members of his family and half a million other members of communities designated untouchable: "I came home, thought about what Ambedkar said and took all the gods from the house and threw them in the well." Smiling in his studio almost sixty years later, he made an illustrative gesture with his hands. Out with the gods, away from casteism and into the secular time of reason and political recognition—this is the call of conversion, its promise of progress.

At the same time that the gods are being consigned to the past and cast out of Dalit households in Nandipur, Shakta rites of fertility and prosperity continue to be performed by the women with a goddess for a husband. These rites continue even as they are condemned by Ambedkarite Buddhists such as Shantawwa's brother and banned by the government in an effort to eradicate a practice widely understood to constitute the sexual exploitation of Dalit women under the cover of "false religion." For those who had converted to Buddhism, the practice of dedicating daughters was but another example of the exploitation of Dalits, noxiously mixed with Brahmanical predatory desire. As one political organizer, Rajeev Kamble, described it to me: "They want our beautiful daughters so they spread this superstition among the people." Rajeev drew on Ambedkar's work to place the practice of dedication within an ongoing and centuries-old struggle between hierarchical Brahmanism and egalitarian Buddhism. When I asked him where non-Brahmin goddesses like Yellamma might fit into this schema, he reiterated the fundamental opposition Ambedkar posed in his later writings between religion/Brahmanism/casteism and rationalism/Buddhism/democracy. Rajeev outlined it in tones of practiced and quiet deliberation as we sat facing each other in my rented house in one of the Dalit lanes of Nandipur: the solution for Dalits lies in escape from feudal land relations, conversion to Buddhism, proper marriage, access to education, salaried jobs through the reservation system, and political mobilization as a voting bloc. He framed conversion as caste critique and Dalit future. The horizon of social and political equality he looked toward is predicated on the respectability of Dalit women and the straight time of endogamous heterosexual reproduction. *Devadasi* dedication, in this framework, is just one more impediment to the progress of the Dalit community. I have found a general consensus on this point in the community in Nandipur.

For the *jogatis*, the horizon brought other possible futures into view. They are no less critical than neo-Buddhists of caste and land relations, but in their narratives Yellamma is present as an agent in the world and she acts on their behalf.

"Yellamma was hungry," Durgabai began one afternoon over steel tumblers of tea, resting her back against the cool stone wall. Wrapping the end of her sari over her head, she eased her way into the devotional tale, displaying the rhetorical grace and skill I had come to expect from her storytelling.

> Yellamma was hungry. She was walking through a farmer's fields and she was hungry. Her stomach was empty and the fields were full. She was walking in the fields and she plucked some green onions and eggplant to eat, to fill her stomach. The landlord saw her eating from his fields and became angry. He ran into the fields swinging his scythe and shouting. Shouting and shouting, swinging his arms and that scythe. Yellamma ran and ran to escape him. She ran into the Dalit quarter. She was running and running to get away from the landlord. Even into the [Dalit quarter] she ran to escape him. Yellamma ran into Matangi's house, and Matangi said, "Here hide under these skins," and Yellamma concealed herself in the tanning pits under an elephant hide. The landlord followed Yellamma into Matangi's house. Rushing into Matangi's house, he demanded, "Where is she? Tell me where she is or I will cut you," he said, holding up his scythe. But Matangi did not say. She did not reveal Yellamma. "Who are you, what are you looking for?" she asked calmly. In anger, he cut off her nose and left. Yellamma came up out of the tanning pits. Seeing what he had done, she restored Matangi's nose, saying, "Because of what you have done, you will always be my sister."

Durgabai's account of the origin of Yellamma's relationship to Matangi is not contained entirely within the ambit of historical time, the march of nations and generations. Instead, it reaches into the time and realm of the gods, a space/time that runs alongside the modern institutions of private property and landlordism. Who takes care of the goddess when she is hungry? Yellamma's kinship with Matangi is between women, unmediated by brothers, husbands, or fathers—indeed, forged against male aggression. It is lateral rather than lineal and out of caste rather than within. This perverse kinship is born through a cut that marks both a history of violation and its possible healing.

In some versions of this devotional tale, the landlord cuts off Matangi's breast. The sense of sexual violation is more explicit in this version, but it is evident even in the other. Wearing a nose ring—along with toe rings, bangles, and marriage necklace, or *mangalasutra*—marks the marital status, active sexuality, and auspiciousness of women. To cut off Matangi's nose is to violate the integrity of her fertile body, to make her a widow. But Yellamma has the power to heal this cut, to restore Matangi to her auspicious state.

How are we to think about this cut in relation to time? In the context of a documentary film about Indian practices that exceed nationalist scripts of purity and respectability, the filmmaker Kirtana Kumar had the following conversation with an audacious *jogati* who spoke on camera sitting among a group of dedicated women in rural northern Karnataka. In her account sexual backwardness has its gendered possibilities.

> Because a man ties a tali [marriage necklace] on a girl's neck . . . even if he kills her he thinks this is his right. This is the arrogance of men.
>
> Q: Won't this happen in a *devadasi* relationship?
>
> Why? I am a woman who has been dedicated. Did you tie a tali for me? You didn't. If you want to come to me, come. If not, that's OK. I have my children, land. I'll struggle and live. All these "wives," as soon as their man dies they are called "randi"—widow. But for a *devadasi*, even if her man dies, she is not "randi." No one will ever call her a "randi-mundi" (shaven-headed widow). She is a *devadasi*, you have to treat her like the *Devi*. If a *devadasi* does "arathi" [worships her with a flame] for the God-dess, it is very auspicious. Do these wives do arathi for the *Devi* when their man dies? They cannot. But the *devadasi* is pure till the day she dies. The nose ring is given to us when we are small by our mothers and our sisters. . . . Why should we take it off when our man dies? A *devadasi* will not [remove her nose ring] whether her man is a landlord or a pauper. Dedi-cated girls will not take their nose ring for anyone. She is the woman and she is always auspicious.
>
> What do you say to that? (Kumar 2000)

Once married, a woman is auspicious, but this status is tethered to the timeline of her husband's life. If he dies, she becomes inauspicious, and her hair is cut off. Once given or married to the *Devi*, this *jogati* explains, dedicated women cannot be cut away from auspiciousness; they are tethered to the *Devi*, who does not die. A man may come or go, but he cannot claim any right over her life, nor does the time of his life subsume hers. He may provide or not provide; in any case, she has the means to survive. Her sexual capacity is not delimited to the lineal future a wife might be able to give to a husband in the form of a "legitimate" heir. And her mobility is not delimited by his proscriptions, a fact that one *jogati*, contrasting her position to that of conventionally married women, put to me like this: "They have to get permission from their father, husband, even their son just to put one toe outside the house, but I go wherever I please. I don't need permission from anyone."

Jogatis may claim that they are *nityasumagali* (always married, thus ever auspicious) and many do, but they too have often been subjected to a cutting: that of the matted locks of hair said to mark the presence of the *devi* in the body of the one with such hair (Ramberg 2009). In the words of one reformer, "We used to go and convince women with jade [matted locks] to cut their jade. Some would voluntarily come forward to cut their jade. Others would say, 'we will not cut our jade,' but we would not let go of them, we would drag them, cut their jade and wash their hair with shampoo."

Jogatis are also enjoined to sever the knotted string of distinctive red and white beads tied at the time of dedication to Yellamma. These cuts are not the "arrogant" violations of husbands and landlords; they come from the benevolent hand of the state, working to better the lives of dedicated women by separating them from archaic practices. However, the ever auspiciousness of *jogatis*, a generalized fertility that extends beyond mere biological reproductive capacity, cannot be cut. Or, this auspiciousness may be cut, but dedicated women will not remain arrested in time, dismembered. This is the lesson both Durgabai and the *jogati* speaking to Kumar offer. Put in the terms of queer theory, theirs is neither the straight time of reproductive futurism nor the queer refusal of such future but the past forward of a cut in time that ties a past (violation) to a future (possibility). This is what I am calling recombinant time.

This cut and recombinant time is also present in the origin story *jogatis* tell about their *devi*, Yellamma. She was married to a sage. She was so pure that she was able to collect water from the river for his morning *puja* (ritual, worship) without a pot, carrying it on her head using a cobra as a pot rest. One day, however, she was distracted, tempted by desire at the sight of erotic play among bathers in the river. She lost her concentration, the water spilled, the cobra slunk away, and she returned empty-handed to a husband who immediately saw that she had lost her chastity and ordered their sons to cut off her head. The eldest two, whom *jogappas* claim as their ancestors, refused, but the youngest did his father's bidding and chopped off his mother's head. In what the *devadasi* interviewed by Kumar might call the arrogance of his swing, he inadvertently also severed the head of an outcaste woman who happened to be walking by. Pleased with his son's obedience, his father offered him a boon, and the son asked for his mother to be restored. The heads of the two women were mixed up, and so Renuka Yellamma became a *devi* with an outcaste head and a Brahmin body who embodies a reversal of the Varna caste order. Landlords, husbands, and sons might be arrogant and violent, but outraged women can become goddesses whose capacities to recombine would seem to exceed the futures spelled for women by patrilineality and patriarchy—wifehood or social death.

Still, cutting constitutes a violation; it exacts a cost. A *jogappa* taught me this in describing his own choice not to cut—that is, not to self-castrate as *nirvan*, or "true," *hijras* are expected to. *Jogappas* identify Yellamma's eldest sons as their ancestors. These are the sons who risked and earned their father's curse of impotence by remaining loyal to their mother and refusing to cut off her head. Most of them identify themselves with their ritual work, as people dedicated to the service of Yellamma, and they distinguish themselves from those seeking worldly pleasures. In the words of Kallappa: "Why run behind all these things? I want to keep my body as it is. Being a *jogappa* is better than becoming a *hijra*. They have taken off their organ [*anga*]." I asked: "*Jogappas* don't cut [self-castrate]?" He continued:

> Sometimes, but their lives are not very good if they cut. They are kept outside the village; nobody will come forward to give their daughters for their brothers; no one will speak with them. They will have to pay a penalty if they want to come into the community; they have to pay money and feed all the people. *Hijras* have their own guru; if a *hijra* dies, only *hijras* go to their funeral. If no *hijra* comes, their body will rot. No one will go to cremate them. If a *jogappa* dies, all the *jogappas* will come; they will be cremated by the village people. . . . I want to keep my body as it is, I won't marry, I won't keep anyone [take a patron].

In Kallappa's account, to self-castrate, as true *hijras* are expected to, is to exile oneself from community and kin, to lose life, and to risk being refused death rites and left to rot in the open, to lose death. *Hijras* frequently leave, or are abandoned by, their natal families. They join communities of their own that are linked to lineages or houses whose membership extends across the subcontinent. They are widely understood to wield a kind of sexual power—the ability to confer or withdraw fertility sometimes said to be drawn from goddesses—and are often present at celebrations of marriage or birth singing bawdy songs and asking for money (Cohen 1995b; Reddy 2010). Their embodied potency is the result of the cut they have made; they threaten to lift their saris and expose their lack, thus communicating the curse of infertility.[11]

What is a cut in time? On the body? How might these two be related? Castration and penectomy is a cut in reproductive time that opens possibilities, as well as exacts its price. Kallappa wants "to keep his body as it is"; he is willing to follow Yellamma, but not to sever himself from his natal family and his community. A cut is an opening, a break, a wound. It might mark an end, an irremediable death, loss, or injury. It might also open into the possibility of new direction, a graft, a suturing onto another, transformation, transubstantiation, or the beginning of a different trajectory, a break with the progressive time of bodily integrity and maturation. Cutting produces possibilities of recombination and renewal, here not through new forms of science spelling progress but through timeworn tales of backward folk and their archaic practices. Renuka's head was cut off. "Her husband was cruel," as one *jogati* put it to me, "but now she is ruling the world." Readings that celebrate the reversal of symbolic and social hierarchies of gender and caste that these cuts enable—outraged and beheaded women who become powerful goddesses capable of bringing men to their knees and compelling them to wear a sari (as Yellamma is often described), or castrated and penectomized persons who can confer and withdraw fertility—risk eliding the bloody basis and deep costs of these reversals, as Kallappa reminded me and Lawrence Cohen (1995b) argues in his work on the anthropological consumption of *hijras* as India's "third gender."

What concerns me here is how these literal and figurative cuts on the body enact a particular temporality. Neither simply a subaltern reckoning of time nor a refusal of or drag on progress, this temporality is a way of acting in time on time to recombine its elements, producing pasts forward and backward futures. For instance, Yellamma is always already cut. Her fall from chaste wife to beheaded is represented in clay dioramas all along the road leading to her main temple and in poster arts sold in the markets across the region where she is felt to be especially powerful. Her past (and origin) are made present across the landscape where the possibilities of the future rest in the maintenance of good relations with her. She is also always already a *devi* with an untouchable head and a Brahmanical body whose incorporated reversal of Varna caste renders untouchability untimely. Devotees touch the feet of the *jogatis* and *jogappas* when they are acting as *pujaris* (priests). Many of the same devotees avoid touching *jogatis*, *jogappas*, and members of their families in other moments.

What about the time of capital? How might the teleology of capital accumulation be unsettled here? Consider that in addition to being a celebration of the power of Yellamma, the story accounting for the sisterhood between Yellamma and Matangi offers a critique of that property relation in which the labor of landless outcastes is extracted to produce the surplus wealth of the landholding farmers. In a context of a highly stratified rural agronomy in which subsistence living among Dalits is not uncommon, this is no abstract matter. Hungry men, women, and children from the communities designated outcaste are surrounded by fields of grain, vegetables, and sugarcane in which they might labor but whose yield they have no right to, except, possibly, as payment for their labor. Traveling the range of the village, *jogatis* claim this right for themselves, plucking fresh vegetables as they go roaming with the *Devi* and making the rounds at harvest time to ask for grain, bringing it home to their families, the households that they typically head. This story, and others like it, does not alter the conditions of Dalit struggles for survival in the rural Central Deccan, conditions that have only been exacerbated by national and international policies of economic liberalization. It does, however, articulate a critique of Brahmanical reckonings of power and purity and of private property rights. It also asserts an ethic of redistributive justice. We might consider Yellamma rites as a territory in which caste critique and public forms of Dalit female authority find expression.

This was not how the sons of *jogatis* saw their mothers' storytelling on the thresholds of the landholding farmers' homes. "Why must you go on such rounds 'begging' at the doors of the Vokkaligar (a landholding upper caste), bringing shame on us?" they asked their mothers. This perspective, evident in the careful historical and structural analysis Rajeev brings to his thinking about caste relations, is rooted in the idea that the way out of the violence and indignity of caste society and into the time of capital is through Dalit self-sufficiency. Forms of caste interdependence can only perpetuate caste-based inequities, and the ritual mendicancy and exogamous extended sexuality of *jogatis* can only bring shame on their families. Dalit futures are predicated on breaking away from such relations. A different calculus of relations is at work for the *jogatis*. They work to maintain a flow of exchange in which their dependence on landholding farmers for grain is counterbalanced by farmers' dependence on them for access to the favor of Yellamma. This interdependence exists in tension with the objective conditions of labor relations and property rights, as the story of Matangi's violation suggests. The recombinant time and backward future that *jogatis* enact in these ritual and economic relations of caste hierarchy and interdependence are not a future anyone can want. This, again, is an aspect of what it means to be backward in a backward place.

Time Knots

Writing about Hindu nationalist invocations of the *kisaan*, or farmer as a figure situated in the present but also able to embody the rural past of "real India" and redemptive future of capitalism, Geeta Patel (2000: 51) writes, "The kisaan was a point at which different kinds of temporality were *knotted together*" (my emphasis). Her point is not just that historical time and the time of the folk, their gods and spirits, interweave in the present (Chakrabarty 2009) but that temporalities are tied up together in embodied subjects. This point has implications for the possibilities of recognition, especially in relation to the question of history making, as well as for how temporalities make bodies.

Converts to Buddhism and Yellamma women occupy time and caste differently. Those tied to Yellamma enact a backward future, a present that persists in its attachment to a caste-specific nonmodern and nonsecular organization of sexuality: theogamy. Ambedkerite Buddhists bring the past forward, calling for a future without caste that throws itself forward from an equalitarian religion. As an ideology, Ambedkerite Buddhism stakes its future on the elision of *devadasi* pasts as anything other than degraded existence. In practice, Dalit futures are more knotted in time.

Yellamma women claim rights in the fruits of the land as persons who embody the *Devi* and transact in the fertility she is understood to bestow. The future, as they see it, is up to the *Devi* and contingent on the character of her relations with devotees, which they mediate. If she is pleased, things will go well in the household, the village, the world. If she is neglected, she will afflict those who have displeased her—the fall of politicians, failing crops, and infertility of neighbors are all regularly attributed to her displeasure. Such misfortunes, however, can be turned around through the intermediation of Yellamma women and, through them, the restoration of your relations with the *Devi*. However, the forms of efficacy and capacity that they embody as Yellamma women do not translate into the idioms of modernity, secularity, and positive state recognition. They cannot be thrown forward.

This is at least partly a consequence of how religion has come to be configured under modernity as a matter of propositional belief as well as how "Western concepts and practices of religion [have come to define] history making" (Asad 2009: 93). "Superstition" is that mode of religiosity and unreason consigned to the past, which cannot be brought into the future, cannot be made modern. Unlike the Buddhism that Ambedkar retrieved from the past as a basis for a more equalitarian future for Dalits, the form of Dalit religiosity enacted by Yellamma women cannot be made into a matter of belief that might be defended (Viswanathan 1998). In this sense, Shantawwa was right; no one believes in Yellamma, and indeed they never did. They may transact with and through her, but this, as we have been taught, although it may offer forms of caste critique, cannot be religion: it cannot be rendered a basis for a Dalit future or politics anyone wants. On this point, Yellamma women agree: they say, we will not dedicate our daughters; this will end with us. In other words, we will leave this practice and the relations it produces behind in the past; we will not carry them forward into the future through our children. Our children will have a different future, one predicated on the renunciation of this way of life. This past will not come forward in our communities; our future will not be backward.

The consignment of these relations between women and a *devi*, their possibilities and powers to the past, is partly an effect of the modern configuration of religion. It is also a question of sexual politics. In a variation of the devotional tale recounted by Durgabai, it is not the farmer who chases Yellamma but Parashurama, her warrior son, who cuts off her head at his father's bidding. In this version, as told by Dalit women pujaris, Parashurama pursues but does not kill Yellamma, who escapes into Matangi's home. Parashurama is upset because he does not know who or where his father is. Running after Yellamma with his axe, he demands, "Who is my father? Why do people call you randi [widow/whore]?" Here sisterhood between Yellamma and Matangi emerges in the face of a son's brutal demand for his patrinymy, and the *jogatis* who tell this story articulate a critique of the violent regulation of female sexual respectability through a call that the father be produced.

Jogatis have no father's name to give their children. Indeed, reformers seize on this lack as a prime indicator of the tragic condition of children of *devadasis*. In street plays sponsored by a government reform project, young Dalit men dramatize the stigma that children who can claim only god as a father are made to feel. In one performance that I observed in Saundatti at Yellamma's main temple during the high pilgrimage season in 2003, the daughter of a *jogati* was singled out in a classroom of children as the one child unable to provide a patronym.[12] The child's quiet response, "My mother is a *devadasi*," was drowned out by the teacher's demand, "Who is your father? Who is your father?" To be sure, the stigma of being fatherless is difficult to bear, a fact that many of the sons of *devadasis* I knew made clear to me.[13] But the images of the schoolteacher shouting at a student, demanding her father's name, and Parasharama chasing after his mother bring another stigma into view: the one attached to the randi, whose uncontained sexuality is felt to stain family honor. Her reproductivity is out of joint with the straight time of family and community. It cannot be made part of the forward past of Dalit progress.

Dalit respectability founds itself on the bodies of women. The standards of comportment signifying sexual restraint have been reformulated in the context of anticaste politics, and Dalit women have long been exhorted to conform to them. In a meeting with women from the *devadasi* and *jogini* communities in 1936 in Bombay, Ambedkar challenged them to "give up this degrading life" if they wanted to join the movement. A changing room was set up to teach them how to properly

wrap their saris (Rao 2009: 66, 310n139). The gendered character of respectability is evident today in Dalit political discourse in which women figure rarely
as revolutionaries or visionaries, which they surely are, but often as figures of degradation (*devadasis* being the paradigmatic such figure). This degradation, we are
told over and over again, is a matter of caste. Such rhetoric installs the family
as naturally heterosexual, monogamous, reproductive, and patrilineal. However,
as historians such as Indrani Chatterijee (2004), Tanika Sarkar (1992), Mytheli
Sreenivas (2008), and Patricia Uberoi (1994) have well documented, this form of
the family is far from the only configuration of domestic, reproductive, or sexual
relations to obtain across the historical or cultural record in India. A long history
of legal and social consolidation underwrites this form of the family, and in this
sense, Dalit aspirations are consistent with the postcolonial consolidation of the
family around monogamy and patrilineality. Critical histories of the family lead to
some questions for Dalit historiography: what might the histories of the Dalit family look like if the labor histories, exogamous and transactional sexual relations,
and reproductive lives of dedicated women were not erased from them? What if
jogatis and *jogappas* were situated in such histories as something more than the
spoilers of their sisters' sexual respectability, their brothers' manly self-respect?
What if Yellamma, that *devi* called husband and mother, was included in the history of the families that have married themselves to her? After all, within living
memory the children of *devadasis* were called *devaramakalu* (god's child).

The desire to be sexually acceptable—evident in both the gay pursuit
of same-sex marriage and the *jogati* embrace of a new identity, that of the ex-
devadasi and the conventional marriage she can enter—can be understood as the
desire to be free from violence and humiliation. At the same time, to the extent
that we lack a critical language for the gendered character of community respectability, we continue to fold the value of women into the status of the community
without accounting for such value, and we naturalize a sexual economy in which
men have rights in women that women do not have in themselves, and same-sex
relations are taboo (Rubin 1975).[14] *Jogatis* and *jogappas*, I am suggesting, offer
such critical language, but they offer it in terms that fail the norms and forms of
secular political modernity and which therefore cannot be thrown forward.

By contrast, Dalit converts to Buddhism call for a future that throws itself
forward from the ancient history of Buddhism, that conceives of that history
through a present-day collapse of caste into politics and politics into religion, a
past that "excises other possible pasts, other possible histories" (Patel 2000: 49).
The past forward of Dalit conversion might be characterized as looping; it reaches
back into ancient time to bring forward into the present the as-yet-unsubjugated

Buddhist for Dalit future emancipation. This recuperated time effectively rewrites the history of untouchability in the subcontinent as the mark of those practicing a minority religion, rather than of those associated with "polluted" forms of labor in Brahmanical reckoning.[15] This might be called a past forward in which a recuperated history of Dalits not only spells a different future, one that bears no past stigma, but also writes a new history of India as never the land of caste and its hierarchies and always the place of contested religion. This is a counternationalism, a history from below that rewrites the history of untouchability as a Brahmanical imposition on those early Buddhists who refused to become Hindu when Buddhism went into decline. But there are other elisions; the history of dissident Dalit sexualities can only come forward as stigma and degradation into the future opened up by Ambedkar's Buddhism.

At the same time, the temporality of Dalit conversion is more out of joint than my account might first seem to suggest. The path of conversion laid out by Ambedkar prescribes a complete departure from the past. The twenty-two vows he took and gave to followers include "I shall have no faith in Gauri, Ganapati and other gods and goddesses of Hindus nor shall I worship them" as well as "I shall not perform Shraddha nor shall I give pind" (forms of ancestor propitiation). Conceptions of conversion as a radical break from the past and time as a forward march aptly characterize Ambedkar's vision of Dalit emancipation as well as contemporary ideological accounts of community uplift and social mobility through the embrace of Buddhism. But attention to everyday practice suggests that time is not so easily straightened.

On the one hand, modern antinomies between the past and the future, true and false, transcendental and material are upheld by the pedagogical and popular model of conversion as break; on the other hand, these same antinomies are confounded in the everyday practices of Dalit men and women. As the officers of an "Ambedkar Cooperative Society" explained to me when I expressed surprise upon seeing the installation they had put up for Lakshmi during Divali in front of the cooperative building: "But whatever wealth we have is due to her, how can we fail to recognize her?" This statement by a Dalit convert to Buddhism signals what Milind Wakankar (2010: 51) calls the "in-between" subject position of the convert, "one who cannot assume a given religious, social or economic identity, and must remain temporally forever 'in-between' all ascription of place, location and identity."

Buddhists have narrated this in-between position to me over and over. It is evident in the gendered division of religious labor in households in which, in the words of one young married woman, "the men worship Buddha outside, and we worship the gods inside." This statement describes a gendered division of religious labor that is producing new forms of gendered difference and sexual conduct in which men inhabit a politically emancipated rational Buddhism and women confine themselves to the interiority of the household as that space of sexual honor and life renewal where food is cooked and ancestral and fertility rites are kept. Rather than being thrown out, the gods are privatized and familiarized; no longer will they roam the village with and as *jogatis* and *jogappas*. My interviews with Dalit intellectuals in Bangalore and Delhi suggest that this division of religious labor is widely recognized and discussed among Ambedkarite Buddhists across India as a problem for the community. As one Delhite put it to me: "We know we must give up such backward practices, but it is difficult for our women to give up their gods." What are the implications of such a formulation for Dalit futures in relation to gendered subjectivity? The Delhite's statement is embedded with a number of assumptions about change and time. He conceptualized conversion as a radical break with the past, a break that women are somehow less able to make. Time is progressive. A convert should move forward, away from past practices and toward a present and future emancipation. To fail to leave the gods behind is to remain "backward," caught in the past. In the religious division of labor I have observed in Ambedkarite Buddhist households, women are "bad subjects" of rational modernity. Over and over, they are described and describe themselves as unable to leave the gods, unable to make the break that signifies "true" conversion. At the same time, their keeping of the ancestral and familial gods is widely understood to be a way to secure the future—the fertility and prosperity of the family and its lineage. In this gendered division of religious labor, might men and women be said to be securing different kinds of futures for the household?

What kind of a time knot is tied in a mangalasutra? In the context of my first project (Ramberg 2014), I began thinking about state efforts to reform *devadasis* as a kind of conversion project itself. This "conversion" from false religion ("superstition") to true religion (nationalized Hinduism) and prostitute to wife is achieved by the annulment of theogamous unions between *devadasis* and the goddess to whom they were dedicated and the arrangement of conventional marriage for women who come to call themselves ex-*devadasis*. This thinking led me to consider marriage as a site of conversion, not only because it makes "fallen women" into "good women" but also because many Dalit women in the central Deccan rural communities I work in become Buddhist at the time of marriage in response to their husband-to-be's desire for the marriage to be conducted "in the Buddhist way." Conversion and marriage ceremonies are typically conducted at once such that, for women, becoming a Buddhist and becoming a wife are of a piece, and sexual respectability and neo-Buddhism are sutured in time.

In November 2014 I interviewed a Buddhist social activist in Kalaburagi, who described to me the essential elements of a properly Buddhist marriage, which he often officiates. "But sometimes they bring other things." "Other things?" I asked. "When the time comes to exchange garlands I ask for the mangalasutra, which should go over the bride's neck along with the garland. But quietly they say, 'carry on, it's already been done' and that is how I learn that the mangalasutra has already been tied in front of the manedevaru (household shrine). Sometimes they even go to the temple!" "How do you feel?" I wondered. "I feel angry, because they have called me to do a Buddhist wedding, but they don't want a Buddhist wedding. But also I feel some sympathy. If I insist the bride take off the mangalasutra so it can go with the garland, she starts to cry and all the women begin to crowd around saying, let it be, let it be." The Buddhist activist is frustrated to find Hindu practice brought into his Buddhist ceremony. These converts have failed to make the break away from Hinduism. But he is also moved by the press of women and their gentle but insistent claim that the bride be allowed to have both—her mangalasutra, tied in the Hindu manner, and her Buddhist rite of marriage.

In 2015 I attended a double Buddhist wedding, where two sons in the same family were getting married. As the two brides faced their future husbands, waiting for the exchange of garlands, I saw that one already wore her mangalasutra. This did not appear to distress either of the two monks leading the ritual. Confused, I turned to the women behind me, members of the groom's family, to ask. "Yes," one explained, "today marks the auspicious time for only one of the couples. That mangalasutra was tied at the auspicious time for that couple." "Where?" I asked. "In front of the gods," she said with the air of one stating the obvious. "Is Buddha in that household shrine?" "Yes, of course, we are Buddhists," she said. In the mangalasutra a knot is tied between the backward future of superstitious attachment to astrological tellings of time and the forward past of rational and equalitarian Buddhism.

The keeping of multiple kinds of time in Dalit Buddhist households problematizes the linear progressive time of secular modernity, the recuperative singularity of Hindu nationalism, and the Christian teleology and epistemology of true conversion as against false belief. In Dalit everyday life practices we find recombinant time, the backward future of the ancestral gods and the forward past of a recuperated Buddhism held together in a household, unsettling the domestic time kept by obedient wives, the Christian secular time of true converts, and the Hindu time of national hegemony and coherence. The promiscuous sexuality and theogamous marriages of *jogatis* would seem to more readily lend themselves to a queer reading than the heterosexuality and monogamous marriages Ambedkerite Buddhists pursue. But these marriages are polytheistic. They queer time by multiplying enacting it, recombining the cut time of conversion with the auspicious time of life renewal. Tying these two temporalities together in a knot, they pervert the reproductive time of Hindu nationalism and multiply the possibilities of the Dalit present through forward pasts and backward futures.

Along with ethnic studies, critical race studies, and Native American studies, area studies may be able to corrupt the universalisms that queer thinking that does not locate itself in time or space continues to perform. Especially in the form of ethnography, however, it risks merely generating parochialisms and performing the colonial operation of fixing others in past times and remote places. As an antidote, I am suggesting that we dwell with the question: who are we fixing in the past in how we narrate and enact queer futurity? What the *devadasis* and Ambedkarite Buddhists I have worked closely with have taught me about temporality, and what I hope to have communicated here, is not just that we all inhabit multiple temporalities or that we all, in one way or another, fail the norms and forms of sexual modernity, but that if we hope not to be caught suspended in the time others have set for us, we must find ways to temporize, gathering stories of dissidence like so many threads, cutting time, making knots that recombine the promise of the past with the legacies of the future in the present time and place.

Notes

Earlier versions of this essay were given as talks at the Association for Asian Studies 2014 annual meeting, at Brandeis University, and at Harvard University. I want to thank Jon Anjaria, Ulka Anjaria, Anupama Rao, Ram Rawat, Ajanta Subramaniam, and Mrinilini Sinha for their comments on those occasions. I am grateful to Anjali Arondekar, Geeta Patel, Lawrence Cohen, Jonathan Boyarin, and two anonymous readers whose generous provocations helped me work out my thinking here.

1. I am inspired to ask this question partly by Carolyn Dinshaw's question: "How does it feel to be an anachronism? . . . one way of making the concept of temporal heterogeneity analytically salient, and insisting on the present's irreducible multiplicity, is to inquire into the felt experience of asynchrony" (Dinshaw et al. 2007: 190).

2. Anticaste radical B. R. Ambedkar himself was quite clear that nonconjugal forms of sexuality were incompatible with Dalit progress. The following quotation from a history of the Dalit movement documents Ambedkar's views on the subject as well as the historian's perspective, one that is widely shared among scholars and activists to this day: "On 13 June, 1936 a meeting of the Devadasis and Jogalins was called at Domodar Hall, Bombay. It was addressed by Dr. Babasaheb Ambedkar. He advised them to abandon their contemptuous way of life and lead an honorable life" (Kshīrasāgara

1994: 118). While some feminist treatments of dedicated women have situated them as paradigmatic figures of the double victimization of caste and gender (see, for instance, Rege 1995: 23–38), others have attended closely to the politics of caste masculinity in the reformulation of dedication as a stain on the community (see, in particular, Pak 2014 and Rao 2009); for community self-redefinition and transformation without erasure, see Arondekar 2012.

3.   See Arondekar 2010: 113; and Boellstorff 2005.

4.   This way of telling national time has been deconstructed by many critics and observers of Hindutva. Consider, in particular, the secular and Christian temporalities of Hindu nationalism as analyzed in Bacchetta 1994.

5.   As one reviewer pointed out to me, the taken-for-granted singularity and purity of ritual performance assumed in Ghar Wapsi discourse is historically absent in Christian, Hindu, Buddhist, Jain, Sikh, and local Sufi Muslim communities in the subcontinent. Further, the idea of conversion as "break" has been provincialized in Middle Eastern–South Asian historiographies as beholden to a Christian epistemology of religiosity that has not been born out in the South Asian contexts of religious transformation. At the same time, Ambedkar himself explicitly called for a break from Hinduism and used the language of "conversion," leading some scholars to frame Ambedkerite Buddhism as "protestant." To this day the English-language term *conversion* is widely used among Ambedkerites, who regularly criticize those Buddhists whose break from Hinduism is incomplete. For histories of conversion in the subcontinent, see, in particular, Dube 1998; Kent 2004; Viswanath 2014; Viswanathan 1998; Zupanov 2005; and Fitzgerald 1999.

6.   In 2009 the High Court of Delhi declared Section 377 unconstitutional with respect to sex between consenting adults. In 2013 the Supreme Court of India overturned that decision, with the Court arguing that any change to Section 377 should be a matter of parliamentary decision. For a cautionary essay on the contemporary geopolitics of gay rights diplomacy in India, see Shah 2014.

7.   See www.oed.com.proxy.library.cornell.edu/view/Entry/198963?redirectedFrom =temporize#eid. See also Arondekar 2015.

8.   In a series of articles Lawrence Cohen has diagnosed backwardness as a mode of sexuality that is not female-male (forward) but male-male (backward). He argues that in Uttar Pradesh and Bihar over the twentieth century and into the present, male homosociality stands for the predatory nature of backward places (screw or get screwed) as well as the possibility—for those who master both sides of that equation—of a form of life that allows for pleasure and distance/difference from the violence from the modern and center. In particular, see Cohen 1995a and 2008.

9.   McDowell (2012: 8) writes, "In sum, three factors contribute to privileging caste as the most important aspect of backwardness for the Mandal Commission: a text-based understanding of caste hierarchy as a source of backwardness, caste's inher-

ited practicality as the unit of measure and a triple-weighting of social indicators. As we move from text to context, sociological assumptions embedded in hierarchies of backwardness—namely, that caste identities and their hierarchical positions are static—emerge as the key site of political work and the most flexible and inflexible aspect of backwardness."

10. This kind of relationship to the past is akin to what Heather Love (2009) calls for, a relation between history and those "backward others" who have been perforce left behind. She enjoins us to linger with the tragic past and present of homosexual existence rather than join the march of progress away from tragedy and toward liberation. Backwardness for Love is a queer "structure of feeling" as well as a model for queer historiography. The geopolitical distribution of backwardness is not a significant line of inquiry for Love, as it must be for me and other so-called area specialists. However, her question is generative: "how to make a future backward enough that even the most reluctant among us might want to live there" (163).

11. The ongoing efficacy of this threat was recently reported on in a widely read English-language daily paper in a piece that manages to situate *hijras* as both out of sync with the time of capital—threatening others "to extort money" rather than earning—and progressive upholders of national order, "heroic saviors" working for a "noble cause" when they are able to stop an armed mob from advancing on a predominately Muslim neighborhood. See Akram 2014. Backward futures indeed.

12. Within living memory the children of *devadasis* were registered in school as *devara-makalu* (god's child). This practice displaced the father, whose name is called for in all Indian documents. The documentation of patrilineage emerged in the colonial era in the context of changes in and challenges to property regimes, as Geeta Patel reminds me (pers. comm., June 9, 2015).

13. For a nuanced consideration of the position of sons of *devadasis* and their role in the Dalit politics and reform, see Epp 1997.

14. This is a paraphrase from Rubin 1975.

15. See Rawat 2001.

References

Akram, Maria. 2014. "Eunuchs Hold Off Trilokpuri Goons." *Times of India*, October 28. timesofindia.indiatimes.com/india/Eunuchs-hold-off-Trilokpuri-goons/articleshow /44954443.cms.

Ambedkar, Bimrao Ramji. 1956. "Why Nagpur Was Chosen." www.columbia.edu/itc /mealac/pritchett/00ambedkar/txt_ambedkar_conversion.html.

Arondekar, Anjali. 2009. *For the Record: On Sexuality and the Colonial Archive in India.* Durham, NC: Duke University Press.

———. 2010. "Time's Corpus." In *Comparatively Queer: Interrogating Identities across*

Time and Cultures, edited by William J. Spurlin, Jarrod Hayes, and Margaret Higgonet, 113–28. New York: Palgrave Macmillan.

———. 2012. "Subject to Sex: A Small History of the Gomantak Maratha Samaji." In *South Asian Feminisms: Contemporary Interventions*, edited by Ania Loomba and Ritty Lukose, 244–63. Durham, NC: Duke University Press.

———. 2015. "Time Pass: A (Queer) View from South Asia." In *The Writing Instructor*. parlormultimedia.com/twitest/arondekar-2015-03.

Asad, Talal. 2009. *Genealogies of Religion: Discipline and Reasons of Power in Christianity and Islam*. Baltimore: Johns Hopkins University Press.

Bacchetta, Paola. 1994. "Communal Property / Sexual Property: On Representations of Muslim Women in a Hindu Nationalist Discourse." In *Forging Identities: Gender, Communities, and the State*, edited by Zoya Hasan, 188–225. New Delhi: Kali for Women.

Boellstorff, Tom. 2005. *The Gay Archipelago: Sexuality and Nation in Indonesia*. Princeton: Princeton University Press.

Chakrabarty, Dipesh. 2009. *Provincializing Europe: Postcolonial Thought and Historical Difference*. Princeton: Princeton University Press.

Chatterijee, Indrani, ed. 2004. *Unfamiliar Relations: Family and History in South Asia*. New Brunswick, NJ: Rutgers University Press.

Cohen, Lawrence. 1995a. "Holi in Banaras and the Mahaland of Modernity." *GLQ* 2, no. 4: 399–424.

———. 1995b. "The Pleasures of Castration: The Postoperative Status of Hijras, Jankhas, and Academics." In Paul R. Abramson and Steven D. Pinkerton, ed., *Sexual Nature/Sexual Culture*. Chicago: University of Chicago Press.

———. 2008. "Science, Politics, and Dancing Boys: Propositions and Accounts." *Parallax* 14, no. 3: 34–47.

Dinshaw, Carolyn, Lee Edelman, Roderick A. Ferguson, Carla Freccero, Elizabeth Freeman, Judith Halberstam, Annamarie Jagose, Christopher S. Nealon, and Tan Hoang Nguyen. 2007. "Theorizing Queer Temporalities: A Roundtable Discussion." *GLQ* 13, no. 2: 177–95.

Dube, Saurabh. 1998. *Untouchable Pasts: Religion, Identity, and Power among a Central Indian Community, 1780–1950*. Albany: State University of New York Press.

Epp, Linda Joy. 1997. "The Social Reform of Devadasis among Dalits in Karnataka, India." PhD diss., York University.

Fabian, Johannes. 2014. *Time and the Other: How Anthropology Makes Its Object*. New York: Columbia University Press.

Fitzgerald, Timothy. 1999. "Ambedkar, Buddhism, and the Concept of Religion." In *Untouchable: Dalits in Modern India*, edited by S. M. Michael, 57–71. Boulder, CO: Lynne Rienner Publishers.

Kent, Eliza. 2004. *Converting Women: Gender and Protestant Christianity in Colonial South India*. New York: Oxford University Press.

Kshīrasāgara, Rāmacandra. 1994. *Dalit Movement in India and Its Leaders, 1857–1956.* New Delhi: MD Publications.

Kumar, Kirtana. 2000. *GUHYA.* Bangalore. Pad.ma/BVE/info.

Love, Heather. 2009. *Feeling Backward: Loss and the Politics of Queer History.* Cambridge, MA: Harvard University Press.

Mani, Lata. 1998. *Contentious Traditions: The Debate on Sati in Colonial India.* Berkeley: University of California Press.

McDowell, Andrew. 2012. "Echoing Silence: Backwardness, Governmentality, and Voice in Contemporary India." *Journal of Asian and African Studies* 47, no. 4: 348–62.

Muñoz, José Esteban. 2009. *Cruising Utopia: The Then and There of Queer Futurity.* New York: New York University Press.

Pak, Shailaji. 2014. *Dalit Women's Education in Modern India: Double Discrimination.* New York: Routledge.

Patel, Geeta. 2000. "Ghostly Appearances: Time Tales Tallied Up." *Social Text* 18, no. 3: 48–66.

Puar, Jasbir. 2007. *Terrorist Assemblages: Homonationalism in Queer Times.* Durham, NC: Duke University Press.

Rao, Anupama. 2009. *The Caste Question: Dalits and the Politics of Modern India.* Berkeley: University of California Press.

Ramberg, Lucinda. 2014. *Given to the Goddess: South Indian Devadasis and the Sexuality of Religion.* Durham, NC: Duke University Press.

———. 2009. "Magical Hair as Dirt: Ecstatic Bodies and Postcolonial Reform in South India." *Culture, Medicine, and Psychiatry* 33, no. 4: 501–22.

Rawat, Ramnarayan. 2001. *Reconsidering Untouchability: Chamars and Dalit History in North India.* Bloomington: Indiana University Press.

Reddy, Gayatri. 2010. *With Respect to Sex: Negotiating Hijra Identity in South India.* Chicago: University of Chicago Press.

Rege, Sharmila. 1995. "The Hegemonic Appropriation of Sexuality: The Case of the Lavani Performers of Maharashtra." *Contributions to Indian Sociology* 29, nos. 1–2: 23–38.

Rubin, Gayle. 1975. "The Traffic in Women: Towards a Political Economy of Sex." In *Towards an Anthropology of Women,* edited by Reina R. Reiter, 157–210. New York: Monthly Review Press.

Sarkar, Tanika. 1992. "The Hindu Wife and the Hindu Nation: Domesticity and Nationalism in Nineteenth Century Bengal." *Studies in History* 8, no. 2: 213–35.

Shah, Svati P. 2014. "Queering Diplomacy: Shifts in US Foreign Policy Reflect the Globalisation of LGBT Politics." *Caravan Magazine,* May 1. www.caravanmagazine.in /perspectives/queering-diplomacy#sthash.pPS4f9d9.dpuf.

Sreenivas, Mytheli. 2008. *Wives, Widows, and Concubines: The Conjugal Family Ideal in Colonial India.* Bloomington: Indiana University Press.

Uberoi, Patricia, ed. 1994. *Family, Kinship, and Marriage in India.* Delhi: Oxford University Press.

Viswanath, Rupa. 2014. *The Pariah Problem: Caste, Religion, and the Social in Modern India*. New York: Columbia University Press.

Viswanathan, Gauri. 1998. *Outside the Fold: Conversion, Modernity, and Belief*. Princeton: Princeton University Press.

Wakankar, M. Milind. 2010. *Subalternity and Religion: The Prehistory of Dalit Empowerment in South Asia*. New York: Routledge.

Weston, Kath. 1993. "Lesbian/Gay Studies in the House of Anthropology." *Annual Review of Anthropology* 22, no. 1: 339–67.

Zupanov, Ines G. 2005. *Missionary Tropics: The Catholic Frontier in India (Sixteenth–Seventeenth Centuries)*. Ann Arbor: University of Michigan Press.

VOYAGES ACROSS INDENTURE

From Ship Sister to Mannish Woman

Aliyah Khan

CARIBBEAN LESBIANS DO NOT EXIST. So we are told. . . . *Of course, Caribbean lesbians do exist.* As soon as I write this—as soon as I say it—I am attacked and dismissed: not my existence, but my authenticity as a Caribbean person and whether or not I have a legitimate claim on that identity. . . . How does a living, breathing, loving person prove her existence? And why should she have to?
—Rosamond King

$\mathscr{I}$n much of the Anglophone Caribbean, homosexuality is both legislatively illegal and viewed by the general public and government officials as a product of "colonial influence"—an antisocial import allegedly propagated by white tourists and foreign media—even as antigay colonial Anglican religiosity, imported US evangelical values, and British Victorian constitutional laws became naturalized postcolonially as "Caribbean." Many vociferous Caribbean cultural purists also conveniently forget that they and the Caribbean itself are in and of the West. In a typical Guyanese *Stabroek News* letter to the editor, one significantly named "Abu Bakr," speaking on behalf of Muslim Indo-Guyanese and by extension the whole country, wrote in 2010:

> We are assured that in India and Africa our folks were, before the Westerners imposed their alien laws, happily sodomising each other without let or hindrance. We are therefore to be persuaded of the liberating virtues of deviation from the natural order. The argumentation is false, the ethnology contrived. If anything at all the current advocates of gay rights are examples of a neo-colonialist tendency to mimic every fad and fashion that is born in the former metropoles. Gays soldered themselves onto the human

GLQ 22:2
DOI 10.1215/10642684-3428771
© 2016 by Duke University Press

rights wagon in the West. . . . We have got to ensure that we live in a clean world.[1]

As is necessary for the aspiring second coming of the caliph, Bakr is well versed in the rhetoric of imperial metropole and periphery. Homophobia in the Caribbean is rather more about citizenship and national belonging than it is about ignorance or even religiosity. Frantz Fanon (2008: 157–58n44) himself argued in 1967 that while male transvestites existed in Martinique and the Caribbean, "in Europe, on the other hand, I have known several Martinicans who became homosexuals, always passive." Colonialism and the inferiority complex of the colonized in Europe—Fanon says it is there that Martinicans are exposed to the Oedipus complex—thus create Caribbean homosexuals, who repeat history as "passive" partners to white men (ibid.). Nadia Ellis (2015: 896) shows that in this Fanonian moment at the end of colonialism, "any intersection in the analysis between race and homosexuality left the black queer figure shadowy, unformed, at just the moment when the white 'homosexual,' as a clearly defined subject, was coming into view." Afro-Caribbean men who migrated to postwar Britain were viewed as either heterosexual predators of white women or "vulnerable prey" who could be "swept away by the city streets and corrupted by decrepit, malingering English men" (ibid.: 896). The Caribbean's insistent transnationalism and paradoxical rooting in migrancy was a sexual and political danger for the colonial man aspiring to postcoloniality: if travel to the European metropole made one a homosexual, symbolically and bodily disciplined by yet another dominant white man, one had better stay put and focus on building a new nation an ocean away. Eudine Barriteau (2003: 11) rightly argues that the resulting "male marginalization thesis," which paints Caribbean men as eternal victims whose masculinity must be restored by the postcolonial state, is a particular stumbling block for Caribbean feminism and does a general disservice to the complexity of gender roles in the global south. The discursive weakness of positioning Caribbean male sexuality as dependent on European victimization is exploited on the conservative side of the political spectrum by Bakr and his bigoted cohorts, who echo the belief in the colonial creation of homosexuality but have also cottoned on to a fundamental truth of Joseph Massad's classic analysis of the insidiousness of the "Gay International": that LGBTQ issues are framed globally in terms of Western neoliberal human rights discourse, to the detriment of indigenous forms of self-expression and activism. Indo-Guyanese and Indo-Caribbean culture, though, are inherently hybridized discourses constructed through ongoing migration and encounter with the other, be it India or the Afro-Caribbean. In this shifting identitarian terrain, Caribbean denunciations of homosexuality devolve quickly, as demonstrated, into talk of cleanliness, purity, natural orders, and disgust. As usual, distaste for and disavowal of homosexuals is the one thing on which Indo- and Afro-Caribbeans, be they Hindu, Muslim, or Christian, agree.[2]

The 1838–1917 transoceanic indentured trade that brought laborers from India to work on British, French, and Dutch plantations in the Caribbean and elsewhere resulted in populations in Trinidad and Guyana that are demographically almost evenly split between the descendants of Indian indentured laborers and African slaves.[3] The subject of Indo-Caribbean scholarship and historical identity in this schema is usually the *jahaji bhai*. This fraternal "ship brother" relationship replaced the bonds of family and caste aboard the (indenture)ships of the British East India Company. Less than one-third of the migrants were women; they formed their own *jahaji bahin*, "ship sister," bonds, as demonstrated in the historical account of the 1885 rape and murder of one Maharani ("Princess"), whose female Indian friends acted as advocates for her case aboard ship and upon landing in British Guiana, in defiance of the lack of credibility given Indian men and all women under colonial British jurisprudence (Shepherd 2002).[4] The *jahaji bhai* narrative of survival gives Indo-Caribbean people their own heterosexual, transoceanic story of labor and racial oppression with which to parallel and counter the nationalist discourse of Afro-Caribbean slavery and postcolonial entitlement to land and rule. Indo-Caribbeans are thus maneuvered into the hybrid, ocean-crossing paradigms of Caribbean area studies because the *jahaji bhai* survived, as the Indo-Trinidadian historian Ron Ramdin (1994: 13) says, "the other Middle Passage," and as the British scholar Hugh Tinker (1993: 3) puts it, "a new system of slavery." This formulation is resisted or at least complicated by Verene Shepherd (2002: xviii) and some other Caribbean scholars, who argue—correctly—that while many of the material conditions of Indo-Caribbean indentureship were the same as slavery and indeed the indentured lived in the *logie* barracks vacated by African slaves, an individual bound by an indentureship contract with an end date did not have the same life experience as a chattel slave whose life was spent in and children were born into servitude. Mutual suffering during colonial transoceanic ship journeys has proved to be a relatively crude basis for ethnic affiliation and alliance in postcolonial Trinidad and Guyana, where many Indo-Caribbean people still embrace the Bhojpuri Hindi-Caribbean nationalist slogan "apan jaat," voting with one's race or caste. Nonetheless, Indo-Caribbean people's endurance of the *kala pani*, "black water," transatlantic voyage is enough to figure them as properly transoceanic and therefore properly Caribbean in national discourses characterized and limited by what M. Jacqui Alexander (1994: 6) deftly identifies in Trinidadian politics as the "heterosexual imperative of citizenship." Nineteenth-century Hindus believed that the metonymic *kala pani* crossing would cause them to lose caste status; their origin story begins with loss, and so postcolonial "recovery" of *jahaji bhai* stories has meshed well with what Anjali Arondekar (2015: 99) calls the archival "language of search and rescue" and its "attachments to loss." *Jahaji bhai* relationships are characterized as strictly fraternal and familial, a way to create a racial-cultural imagined community, finding suitable heterosexual marriage partners, and strengthening Hindu or Muslim religious ties. As Sean Lokaisingh-Meighoo (2000: 87) emphasizes, *"There is no homosexual subject in* jahaji bhai *culture."* The wearisome search for more hidden historical homosexuals should now be on; we must ferret and trot out queer aboriginal nonconforming genders and behaviors and identities to show Bakr that we were in fact "happily sodomising each other without let or hindrance" before the advent of the British and their perversions both political and sexual. What is the Indo-Caribbean addition to what Arondekar (2015: 101) calls the "veracity archive" of historical homosexuality, with its "salvific truths"? The possibility with which we must contend is that there may not be one; that while questing for queers in the historical record may uncover a few instances of interest, we may not find the ancestor we are looking for. Arondekar calls for reframing the hunt for historical homosexuals as a "return to a history of sexuality . . . not through a call to loss (of object and/or materials), but rather through radical abundance, through an archive that is incommensurable and quotidian, imaginative and ordinary." Perhaps the majority of the vast archive of Indian indentureship is made up of numbers: numbers of people, numbered people, numbers of goods, numbers of plantations, numbers of ships and sailors, numbers upon numbers of the mind-numbing bureaucratic minutiae of empire. Whether or not they speak to a history of sexuality, the individual stories of indentureship weave through and under these numbers while resisting their quantification.

In this essay I show, first, that the *jahaji bhai* narrative of community and cultural survival elides at least one documented case of Indian indentured men engaged in same-sex acts aboard ship. One case, though, is evidence of "radical abundance" rather than homosexual subjectivity. The details of this case were scrupulously recorded by the British, though that nation of shopkeepers and their meticulous accounts never acknowledged the possibility of women loving women aboard ship. There is no Indo-Caribbean equivalent of the Afro-Surinamese and Afro-Caribbean *mati* sexual and emotional relationship between female shipmates as described by Omise'eke Natasha Tinsley (2008: 192, 198). But as Rosanne Kanhai and Brinda Mehta show, Indian *matikor* female-only wedding dances aboard ships were rather queer—not because every homosocial space is queer but because Indian women simulated sex acts with each other's bodies under the guise of celebrating heterosexual marriage and procreation.[5]

Such same-sex shipboard stories are glossed over as aberrant behavior by Indo-Caribbean nationalist cultural discourse. It is not even a question of homosexual act versus queer identity; the *jahaji bhai* narrative blatantly denies the existence or possibility of either. As Arondekar (2009: 7) asserts, "Homosexuality emerges as the structural secret of the archive, without whose concealment the archive ceases to exist." The archive of Indo-Caribbean indentureship and the story of a people it generates, with its unending details of gender, class, religious, and racial suffering, is rendered curiously impersonal by the absence of the homosexual. I first focus on the archival recovery of the story of two indentured Indian men, Mohangoo and Nabi Baksh, caught in flagrante delicto in 1898 while being transported aboard the British ship *Mersey* to the cane fields of British Guiana. Both men disappear from the historical record upon disembarkation in British Guiana. But in the context of the never-ending Indo-Caribbean search for origins, where contemporary community members routinely comb colonial archives from Kingston to Kew for names of obscure ancestral villages and villagers in Bihar and Uttar Pradesh, we can claim Mohangoo and Baksh as perhaps not linear ancestors but kin. Who else will hear the postcolonial *dua* (supplication) of the few Indo-Caribbean youths struggling in 2015 to keep Sangam, the sole Indo-Caribbean queer community organization, afloat, while the World Health Organization simultaneously reports the abominable statistic that Indo-Guyanese men have the highest suicide rate in the world ("Desperate Measures" 2014: 44)?[6]

In the second part of this essay I read the *jahaji bahin*—ship sister—as a queer subject through the figure of the Indo-Caribbean "mannish woman," as illustrated by an Indo-Trinidadian-Canadian writer, Shani Mootoo, in her novel *Valmiki's Daughter* (2008). There are two pressing reasons for prefacing this contemporary reading with the archival *jahaji bhai* story of Mohangoo and Baksh: first, that Indo-Caribbean popular histories sometimes speak of the situational ribaldry of women participating in *matikor* but never of men who love men, as the latter relation is a fundamental threat to the imagined ethnic community in the New World, as it (re)constitutes its patriarchal structure. This archival attention to same-sex practices of women rather than men is perhaps not as unusual as it seems: the colonial historical record does focus on incidences of male-male "unnatural" behavior, whereas the *matikor* narratives recuperated by Kanhai and Mehta are derived from oral histories, travel journals, and family stories, the type of invaluable archival material eschewed by official British record keepers. Second, the deconstruction of *jahaji bhai* heterosexual masculine subjectivity and its relation to community and state is a necessary precursor to elaborating any queer model of the Indo-Caribbean. There appear to be no recorded instances of sexual relationships between women in the archival records of Indo-Caribbean indentureship, though many of these records are lost to time and environmental damage. Literature, I argue, is not only a supplement to the historicity of the queerless archive. Literature *is* queer archive, and its idiomatic digressions, vagaries, hailing, significations, and self-involvement challenge, as Arondekar (2015: 101) puts it, "the aura and/or seduction of 'resistance' . . . suturing subaltern archives to an oppositional imperative." It does not add to the archive; it opens it.

Valmiki's Daughter, the tale of a young Indo-Trinidadian woman and her cultural, familial, and personal struggle with her lesbian sexuality, is Mootoo's biomythographical "coming-out" novel: that is, the one in which the major Indo-Caribbean protagonists are unquestionably homosexual, and which is a story about homosexuality.[7] Most importantly, it appears to be the first novel written in which the main character, Viveka Krishnu, is an Indo-Caribbean lesbian and mannish woman. I read *Valmiki's Daughter* in the mode of autoethnography, or more properly, Audre Lorde's biomythography, a subaltern genre of simultaneously writing the self and story of one's people that originates in Lorde's resistance to the silencing of the queer Afro-Caribbean *zami* woman. *Zami* or *zanmi* is Lorde's (1982: 9) Grenadian and Carriacou term for *lesbian*, or perhaps more accurately, woman-loving-woman. That women *make*, rather than *are*, *zami* is one of Lorde's major concerns in her 1982 work *Zami: A New Spelling of My Name*. The text is a queer Caribbean feminist biomythography—Lorde was a New Yorker with parents from Grenada and Barbados, and identified as a black Caribbean *zami*. Here I wish to emphasize the Caribbeanness of a written form that is not so different from the call-and-response "Krik? Krak!," an Afro-Caribbean oral tale that involves both storyteller and audience as participants and subjects. A community storyteller like Lorde must ask "Krik?" and the community must respond "Krak!" for the story to begin. Biomythography is, in Lorde's and other Caribbean writers' conception, (auto)biography that heralds an imagined community through the mythicizing of one or a few individuals' personal stories. Her charge to create particularly queer black biomythography was notably taken up by the activist and academic Wesley Crichlow (2004b: 217n1), who begins his sociological accounts of being a gay Afro-Trinidadian man by reclaiming the homophobic insult "buller man," which he describes as "an indigenous derogatory epithet that I grew up with in Trinidad and Tobago, used to refer to men who have sex with other men. It is also widely used in some English-speaking Caribbean islands such as St Lucia, St Vincent and Barbados." Crichlow follows this reclamation by identifying himself as subaltern, "representing self and relating to other similar, yet unique experiences in a developmental exploration of other bullers' lives and identities . . . as a subaltern I speak from a contested place" (ibid.: 187). He is thus simultaneously and consciously native informant and subaltern, a positioning that allows him to merge academic theorizing and social justice work. This, Crichlow and Lorde show, is critical Caribbean praxis.

Like the Latin American subaltern genre *testimonio,* biomythography gives equal privilege to a speaker's locus of enunciation and to the content of her words, and invites the audience to engage. Biomythography sidesteps genre debates over the authenticity of fictionalized autobiographies, choosing a position outside that structure of narrative. It is not that author and text are indistinguishable but that they bleed into each other in a way that must be acknowledged, especially when the subject has been heretofore unspoken and the speaker's community voiceless. For Lorde, biomythography, the story of the self speaking its truth, is somewhere to begin queer representation. That her biomythography is also an Afro-Caribbean-descendant woman's story is emphasized in the narrative's opening lines after the prologue: "Grenadians and Barbadians walk like African peoples. Trinidadians do not. When I visited Grenada I saw the root of my mother's powers walking through the streets. I thought, this is the country of my foremothers, my forebearing mothers, those Black island women who defined themselves by what they did" (Lorde 1982: 9). The Trinidadian inability to "walk like African peoples" is a tantalizing detail that reminds one, first, that unlike Grenada and Barbados, almost half of the Trinidadian population is Indo-Trinidadian and, second, that biology is not Afro- or Indo-Caribbean destiny.

In her examination of the intersections of feminist and queer literary production in the Caribbean, Vera Kutzinski identifies Mootoo's fiction as indeed falling within the genre of queer Caribbean testimony. Writing about *Cereus Blooms at Night,* Kutzinski (2001: 194) calls it "a fictional autobiography that is also a biography . . . a variation on the form of the *testimonio.*" Excluding prologue and epilogue, each of the four parts of *Valmiki's Daughter* is titled "Your Journey: Part [section number]," with the final section titled "Your Journey Home." The address to the reader begs the question of the narrator's identity in this third-person narrative, a subtle indication that there is a storyteller to ask "Krik?" and an audience being taken on a journey who must reply "Krak!" Thus I read *Valmiki's Daughter* as a community story and argue that, though a privileged genre of literature, the novel is also archive. It is a work of origins, of queer Caribbean biomythography.

Ship Brothers

Biomythography is one way of telling a personal and communal story under the constrained circumstances of indentured migration. The *jahaji bhai*, "ship-brother," relationship that took the place of biological family for indentured Indian men during and after their sea voyages to the Caribbean is, says Lokaisingh-Meighoo, the general, male-privileging signifier of all Indo-Caribbean identity. It is also a signifier whose deployers are (suspiciously) quick to deny erotic subtext, possibilities, or origins:

> While *jahaji bahin* or "ship sister" is occasionally used in certain Indo-Caribbean cultural practices, it is the usual case that *jahaji bhai* func-tions as a "gender-neutral" term. Of course, so-called gender-neutral terms are always-already gendered as masculine, in the sense that "man" func-tions as the gender-neutral term for "humanity" . . . recuperation of the Indo-Caribbean homoerotic subtext within *jahaji bhai* culture threatens not only the entire *jahaji bhai* culture of Indo-Caribbean studies, but all Indo-Caribbean male homosocial spaces as somehow queer. (Lokaisingh-Meighoo 2000: 80, 91)

While it may seem logical to assume that some same-sex sexual relationships occurred in the stressful homosocial environment of the colonial ship, even histo-rians of the Indo-Caribbean generally give a wide berth to such a possibility.[8] The uncomfortable subtext of *jahaji bhai* Indo-Caribbean studies and literature is that the bonds between indentured male shipmates were probably sexual, but that is a problem: a problem for postcolonial formulations of Indo-Caribbean cultural iden-tity, and a notable difficulty for relatively nascent Indo-Caribbean feminism, which is often focused on addressing rampant domestic violence against Indian women. Same-sex shipboard relationships therefore tend to be dismissed and criminalized as situational, in the manner of relationships between emotionally and sexually lonely prison inmates. Such relationships are never discussed in terms of plea-sure, choice, or a persistent behavior or identity. But the colonial historical record does on occasion contradict its own supposition of necessity and desperation. As early as 1649, the British Royal Navy recorded a shipboard incident involv-ing a sixteen-year-old sailor, John Durrant of Stepney, and one "Abdul Rhyme, a 'Hindostan peon'":

> The feature of the case that seemed to irritate the captain who conducted the trial was not that buggery had been committed repeatedly or that it

had been done with the boy's consent. The horror of the event was that an English lad had allowed himself to be penetrated by a heathen, Abdul Rhyme, a "Hindostan peon." Numerous witnesses testified to having seen the two frequently involved in buggery and in mutual masturbation on the quarter deck as well as below . . . the rantings of the trial's presiding officer indicate he was more agitated by acts of miscegenation that disrupted the operation of the total institution than buggery, which was an ordinary part of the vessel's functioning. Indeed the tendency to regard interracial sex as far more serious than homosexuality was not a peculiarity of this particular captain or a feature of life aboard an individual ship. (Burg 1983: 159)

Though the sentence in Stuart England for buggery aboard ship was death, the accused here were each given forty lashes, wounds to be rubbed with saltwater, and an extended diet of bread and water. Triply damning "passive" intercourse with a same-sex member of a subject race was the concern of the long-deceased English captain, but the record of *consent* and the acknowledgment of the frequency of same-sex acts aboard ship are far more interesting. British colonial records are far more likely to refer to homosexuality in vague and situational terms, especially in the nineteenth-century era of Indian indenture. The historian of indenture Tinker (1993: 204–5) notes two reports in which same-sex acts among indentured Indian men were blamed on the dearth of indentured Indian women: in 1874 the British consul in Reunion claimed the lack of Indian women "gives rise to other acts of depravity of so disgusting a nature they cannot be referred to"; and former Malaya high commissioner Sir John Anderson testified to the 1909 Sanderson Committee that "not among the Tamils; [but] amongst the Northern Indians there is a good deal of unnatural crime." Unmentionable "acts of depravity" and "unnatural crime" were typically the beginning and end of Victorian and Edwardian descriptions of male homosexuality in the colonies—unless homosexual acts threatened British sovereignty and financial gain.

On October 31, 1898, the British "coolie ship" *Mersey*, having completed the September–December leg of its annual round-trip journey from Calcutta, docked in British Guiana with a cargo of rice and 673 Indian indentured contract laborers.[9] In duration it was a relatively typical oceanic journey, with favorable winds—it was even a bit shorter than usual, at 110 days, or about three and a half months. On December 7, 1898, the governor's office of British Guiana generated the usual official inspection report of the voyage to the Colonial Office in England (Sendall 2008).[10] But this report contained some unusual details: the proceedings of an investigation into an alleged act of sodomy that had occurred on board.

A. H. Alexander, the immigration agent-general of British Guiana, was charged with investigating the incident four days after the ship docked. He summarized the incident as follows:

> On the 25th: September, the Surgeon Superintendent made the following entry in regard to an alleged case of Sodomy: "No: 696 Nobibux m, 20 years, and No: 351 Mohangu, m. 22 years, were caught about midnight by a Sirdar named Rambocus committing sodomy.[11] When brought up before the captain and myself they both confessed their guilt. Nobibux stated for the last ten years he had allowed men to commit acts of beastliness: he had no doubt induced Mohangu to do this criminal act[.] Nobibux was put in irons and Mohangu, after blistering his penis, was made to holy stone from 6 a.m. to 6 p.m. daily . . . It would appear that Nobibux was kept in irons from the 25th: September to the end of the voyage. (Sendall 1898: 13–14)[12]

The surgeon superintendent of coolie ships was responsible for all doctoring and medical matters, but was contracted only for the length of the voyage. On this particular voyage of the *Mersey*, the surgeon—and penile blisterer—was one Dr. Arthur Harrison. Upon questioning by Alexander, Harrison corroborated his log entry, testifying that the *sirdar* "Rambocus" "stated that at about midnight he was on watch in between decks and saw something unusual between these two men, they being under one blanket; he pulled off the blanket and saw them committing Sodomy" (Sendall 1898: 31). Rambocus called the head *sirdar* Salikram to the scene, who then

> asked them why they were doing this wrong thing. . . . they at first denied it and afterwards they confessed they did it for pleasure. . . .
>
> The men were then questioned and asked if the charge was true. They both at once confessed. Nabibux said "I have done it" and Mohungu said the same as far as I can remember. . . .
>
> Nabibux was put in irons and fastened to a stanchion. Mohungu was placed in hospital and ordered to holystone from 6 a.m. to 6 p.m. I blistered the penis of Mohungu. I did so as a punishment as I thought he deserved it. I did so at once on concluding the enquiry. The Captain was aware of it. Mohungu was the man who committed the act on Nabibuccus. I blistered him as a preventative, as he might have attempted the act again. I have known cases where the penis has been blistered, as a preventative treatment, in case of Masturbation with boys.
>
> I have power of punishment on board, subject to a consultation with

the Captain, and entry in the ships log, I did consult in this case, and it was logged.

At the time I blistered the man I did not think of the crime he had committed against the criminal law of England. I did not look on it in that light, but as a matter of discipline on board ship. I made no special examination of the private parts of either of the men, I cannot say if the act was committed or not. (ibid.: 32)

Alexander later questioned Rambocus, and the latter gave contradictory testimony, alternately reaffirming and recanting details of what he believed that he had seen. The archive records each iteration of Rambocus's testimony, presenting the researcher with the interesting dilemma of which of the stories to believe. In light of the "confession" of the two men (obtained under unknown conditions), Alexander chose to believe the story in which Rambocus saw them engaging in sodomy. Alexander's choice of story becomes the fact of the archival record, and it is conveniently the story that best lends itself to a recuperative search for a history of Indo-Caribbean homosexuality. Though the preponderance of evidence and testimony points to the two indentured men having spent some time one night in some sort of physical contact, it must be acknowledged that no one other than they could say "what really happened." The confused—or defiant!—Rambocus's thwarting of a contemporary desire for queer "salvific truths" is, however, no reason to be disappointed with the archive's refusal to produce definitively homosexual subjects. There is still a story worth telling.

In Harrison's reckoning, the *presumption* of sodomy was enough to assume guilt and enact punishment, though the degree of punishment depended, as it often does, on position as active or passive partner. Counter to discourses in which the penetrated partner is adjudged the true homosexual in need of sanction, Mohangoo, the twenty-two-year-old man who "committed the act," was treated— tortured—more harshly than Baksh, the twenty-year-old man who admitted to multiple offenses: being penetrated, "inducing" the other to commit the act, and having a ten-year history of sexual relationships with other men in colonial India.[13] In burning Mohangoo's penis as a "preventative," the power-mad Harrison was perhaps suggesting that Mohangoo at least was a morally salvageable Victorian colonial subject, whereas Baksh may have been too far gone into Asiatic homosexual debauchery to warrant more than the token chaining-up afforded those found guilty of any crime aboard ship. In his testimony Harrison also reaffirmed the space of the ship upon the sea as outside the legal boundaries of the state: colonial shipboard law was unto itself, and the captain and doctor ruled together as

sovereigns. In the end, Harrison was punished with the deduction of £100 of his
£673 voyage pay and Alexander's notification to the colonial government that "he
is not to be employed again" (underlined in the original report) (Sendall 1898: 3).
Harris was sanctioned not because sodomy—a criminal offense—did not warrant medicalized investigation and correction of assumed underlying pathology but
because the colonial government required that maritime incidents be adjudicated
under British law rather than through vigilante shipboard justice. Alexander noted
that the men should have been tried in court in British Guiana and that Harrison
"acted in violation of Rule No 165, relating to colonial Emigration, which strictly
prohibits harsh treatment of the people" (Sendall 1898: 2–3, 17). Underlying this
seeming concern for the health and safety of the indentured, I read the strong sug-
gestion that the hapless Harrison should be denied his birthright of participation
in the English project because he injured a subject body under a labor contract,
akin to committing property damage.

This footnote in the history of Indo-Caribbean indentureship is tantalizing for several reasons: first, because of the rarity of the legal charge of sodomy
between Indian *jahaji bhai*, not even involving wayward English sailors like John
Durrant; second, because after the investigation, the colonial government held an
Englishman—the surgeon—responsible for punishing the men without the permission of either the Indian or the colonial Guiana government, symbolically dock-
ing his pay for the voyage; third, because in addition to the testimony of the white
British officers, the investigator also asked for and documented the testimony of
some of the Indians involved, notably the *sirdar* Rambocus who had found the men;
fourth, as noted above, because of the difference in the two indentured men's pun-
ishments; and fifth, because Baksh named himself a habitual participant in sexual
activities with other men in India, and the men said that they had committed the
act for reasons of will and pleasure. The historical record suggests that these men
were not heterosexuals who engaged in same-sex acts because they were isolated
from women and desperate; they chose to do so because they derived pleasure from
it, and Baksh at least had had sex with men when women had been available to
him. Any claim that either of the two men had some sort of gay or queer *identity*
would be improbable and anachronistic; what is worth noting, though, is that these
Indo-Caribbean *kala pani* ancestors construed sex with each other as affectively
positive.[14] Tinsley argues for this possibility in the case of same-sex sexual contact
between enslaved Africans, as

> relationships between shipmates read as queer relationships. *Queer* not in
> the sense of a "gay" or same-sex-loving identity waiting to be excavated from
> the ocean floor but as a praxis of resistance. *Queer* in the sense of marking

disruption to the violence of normative order and powerfully so: connecting in ways that commodified flesh was never supposed to, loving your own kind when your kind was supposed to cease to exist, forging interpersonal connections that counteract imperial desires for Africans' living deaths. Reading for shipmates does not offer to clarify, to tell a documentable story of Atlantic, Caribbean, immigrant, or "gay" pasts. Instead it disrupts provocatively. Fomented in Atlantic crosscurrents, black queerness itself becomes a crosscurrent through which to view hybrid, resistant subjectivities— opaquely, not transparently. (Tinsley 2008: 199)

While Mohangoo and Baksh certainly committed a provocative disruption to the normative order, their case is also a documentable story, though not one that necessarily documents the preexistence of a queer identity. This incident is too rare to claim it as part of a heretofore-unidentified queer *jahaji bhai* praxis of resistance, except in an individualistic affective sense: the men did what they thought would feel good, British and Indians be damned.[15] Copies of the two men's original indentureship passes are included with Alexander's report and give some indication of their fates: they were sent to British Guianese sugar plantations that were very far apart, Mohangoo to an estate named Rose Hall on the east coast and his alleged victim Baksh to another called Vergenoegen on the west coast of British Guiana (Sendall 1898: 38–39). As noted by an unknown hand on the side of the passes, Mohangoo was a Seetapore Hindu of the Ahir cow-herding caste, and Baksh was a Muslim from Faizabad. This religious difference ironically echoes the fact that in the colonial period, it was not just Hindu caste barriers that broke down but also interreligious social and marital divisions between Muslims and Hindus—it was and is race that is the defining element of Indian community membership in the Caribbean. Once there was a large enough stable population, however, interreligious barriers, though not Hindu caste ones, were to some extent reestablished. Indian community survival and cultural perpetuation demanded denial of early colonial sexual freedoms and a speedy return to visible heterosexual, patriarchal, and reproductive orthodoxy.

Queer Exilic Biomythography

Caribbean studies has always been formulated as a transnational and transoceanic arm of area studies. The Caribbean is Antonio Benítez-Rojo's (1992: 3) "repeating island," Stuart Hall's (2003: 240) triple "presences," Roberto Fernández Retamar's (1979) Caliban in the encounter with Europe, Fernando Ortíz's (2001) transculturative mestizo, and a rhizomatic node of Paul Gilroy's (1993) *Black Atlantic*, populated by paradigmatic cultural and bodily hybrids that are obscenely quotidian. In 1891 José Martí (2005) himself tells us that in Nuestra América, Our America, "no hay razas." There are no races, because in the Caribbean there is only the unraced, all-raced Creole. This Caribbean master narrative of hybridity stipulates the normativity of the hybrid and the creolized; as Viranjini Munasinghe (2002: 679) argues, racial mixing and "impurity" is reconstructed as racial purity in the nationalist production of race in postindependence Trinidad and other Caribbean locales. By dint of defining themselves as discretely Indo-Caribbean, and not simply Caribbean, the descendants of Indian indentured laborers were and are deemed "unmixables," ironically unfit for participation in the postcolonial Caribbean nationalist project (ibid.: 682). The imperfectly assimilated Indo-Caribbean is thus excluded from Caribbean area studies in its traditional guise of hybridity studies.

In Caribbean studies, oceanic area is stabilized first by hybridity and then by exile. The historical subject of the archive and the self/subject of queer biomythographical fiction work in tandem to disrupt this iteration of area studies, demanding recognition of the particularity of the Indo-Caribbean story while illustrating, as Arondekar (2009: 5) says, "area studies as vitally constitutive of the histories of sexuality, and vice versa." Sexuality is a newer discussion for both Indo-Caribbean-specific and general Caribbean area studies, though after the mid-twentieth-century first generation of (male) Indo-Caribbean writers like V. S. Naipaul and Samuel Selvon, gender was not absent from the discourse. As Gabrielle Hosein and Lisa Outar (2012: 3) note, through the work of Indo-Caribbean women writers like Mahadai Das and artists like Rajkumari Singh, "the image of the coolie woman, in particular, is one that continues to be iconic in any discussion of Indo-Caribbean femininity. . . . The harnessing of those ancestors to narratives of self-sacrifice and familial commitment, however, sometimes downplays the revolutionary nature of the choices some of those early women made." In such narratives the term *coolie* is rehabilitated from its racialized labor history, but in the service of a politics of respectability. After an indentureship period featuring a severe gender imbalance, unprecedented freedom of mate choice for women, and resulting extreme relationship violence, a structure of extended patriarchal family—defined here as the eldest man and father as head of household, with ultimate say over the schooling, employment, marital choices, religious and social interactions of all other family members, including and especially adult women—reasserted itself. "The institution of family was reconstructed from the ruins it was in during indenture," says Gaiutra Bahadur (2014: 205–6), with "the retreat of women into the domestic sphere. This was done for survival's sake: the family was a collective economic unit, based on a division of labor by sex, with women working unpaid at home." Postindenture, women lost the wages they had earned as weeders on sugar plantations. Moving from a *logie*, the converted slave barracks in which the indentured lived, to even a small house, also required significantly more domestic labor. The Rāmāyana Sita narrative of the virtues of domesticity— beloved above all other Hindu epic texts in the Caribbean, as documented by Paul Younger (2010) and Steven Vertovec (2000) —mutually reinforced the economics of postindenture until Indo-Caribbean feminine respectability became synonymous with being the homemaking wife of a man.

Indo-Caribbean feminism—as theorized by Patricia Mohamed (1998), Kamala Kempadoo (2004), Rhoda Reddock (2008), and others—was until recently so busy defining itself against Afro-Caribbean feminism and addressing the dreadfully high rates of domestic violence against Indo-Caribbean women that same-sex sexuality was ignored or, worse, dismissed as antithetical to feminist credibility. Kutzinski writes in 2001 that "even feminist critics . . . are still 'searching for safe spaces,' ideologically speaking, when it comes to approaching literary representations of gender and especially of female sexuality. What spells ideological safety, to today's feminist scholars of Caribbean extraction, is heteronormativity" (168). As a rule, this Caribbean feminist attachment to heteronormativity is no longer the case: scholars like Yasmin Tambiah (2009), Gabrielle Hosein (2012) , Andil Gosine (2009), and Amar Wahab (2012), inspired by M. Jacqui Alexander's pioneering work, have in recent years insisted on sexuality as part of Indo-Caribbean feminist discourse. But in community practice, for example, at Indian Arrival Day celebrations in Trinidad and Guyana, and at Diwali, Phagwah, and Eid parades and celebrations in the Indo-Caribbean immigrant overseas *département* of Richmond Hill, Queens, in New York City, historical memorialization tends to omit mention of the real origins and histories of many indentured women: as widows, runaways, prostitutes, bazaar girls, the unwanteds of colonial Anglo-India. Also ignored is that the dearth of women on the plantation led to a decades-long period of relaxation of Indian sexual mores, one early cause of the "coolie wife murders" of late nineteenth-century British Guiana.[16] While domestic violence in marital relationships is a remembered source of sorrow, the community much prefers to forget the colonial period of sexual license and very occasional polyandry. The *jahaji bahin* is instead memorialized as *mata-ji*, mother to a nation in exile.

Mariam Pirbhai (2010: 39) argues that there are other possibilities for the *"jahaji-bhain* principle" of feminine shipboard affiliation, where it can provide a "platform for a cross-racial feminist alliance against gender, class and other forms of oppression in contemporary Caribbean societies. In these terms, the *jahaji-bhain* (or *jahaji bahin*) functions as a newly conceptualized ethics of inter-relation that includes the racial other as well as a more fluid conception of Indo-Caribbeanness itself." Even in the grand scheme of poverty, corruption, neoliberal globalization, tourism exploitation, domestic violence, racial violence, and any number of social ills plaguing sectors of the Anglophone Caribbean, there is no more present form of oppression than that surrounding homosexuality, because it is, as Crichlow (2004a: 55) repeats in his queer Afro-Trinidadian "buller" biomythography, the only circumstance under which all entities—state, school, community, biological family—are likely to violently reject the individual.

There are novels that treat Afro-Caribbean queer female sexuality, including much of the work of Paule Marshall and Patricia Powell. In Caribbean queer studies, it is often implicitly permissible to set aside postcolonial debates over linguistic and racial identity because of the temporal *urgency* of the cause of queer sexuality, which at the very least involves mutual recognition of queer self and others, and with luck the cohesion of a queer Caribbean imagined community. Indo-Caribbean religious and ethnic community-specific queer concerns are subsumed and framed through the discourse of majority Afro-Caribbean Creole issues.

Gender normativity is crucial to the survival and perpetuation of the Indo-Caribbean minority community, which enforces common racial mores and rigid structures of public and private gender behavior to maintain cohesion. As a result, the queers of the Indo-Caribbean community require their own mythical stories to prove their very existence against the dominant *jahaji bhai* narrative of Indo-Caribbean history. In Trinidad and Guyana, homosexuality disrupts the ethno-nationalist project of Indo-Caribbean social and political inclusion that hinges on particular conceptions of Indian gender normativity, which includes the cultural importance of *jahaji bahin* marriage compliance as a value that ensures community survival. Queerness also troubles the Hindu and Muslim religious identities to which Indians clung as markers of their discreteness even as they lost their ancestral languages in a mere generation or two in the Caribbean.

The protagonist of *Valmiki's Daughter*, Viveka Krishnu, self-identifies not as queer but as a lesbian, or as Tinsley (2010: 8) prefers in her discussion of the links between Afro-Caribbean female lesbian attraction and labor, a Caribbean woman who loves women. The terms *queer, homosexual, gay,* and *lesbian* do have their own contextual Caribbean specificity—Tinsley acknowledges, for instance, that *lesbian* has entered the Caribbean lexicon and is linked to Massad's Gay International in both strategically useful and potentially harmful ways. There are other woman-loving-woman-specific signifiers in the Caribbean, including *zanmi* (Grenada/Carriacou), *madivine* (Haiti), *mati* (Suriname and the Dutch Caribbean), and the derogatory Jamaican "Man Royal" and "sodomite." I adopt Tinsley's (2010: 8) theoretical strategy of refusing to "crown any one noun or adjective 'most' emancipatory." As Tinsley says, the tensions are simply too productive.

Kutzinski (2001) notes that Mootoo herself is an Indo-Trinidadian-Canadian lesbian writing her own experience, or at least extrapolating it into a community experience. In this vein, *Valmiki's Daughter*, the first Indo-Caribbean novel to feature a lesbian protagonist, is also biomythography. The female protagonist's attempts to come to terms with her sexual attraction to women is mythologically familial—her father, Valmiki, is a closeted homosexual man who watches her progressively increasing visibility in Trinidad with alternating dismay and pride. Viveka inherits her father's failed struggle, the futile attempt of most Caribbean homosexuals before her to live openly in their native lands. She attempts to transform it into something else by metamorphosing into something new: a visible lesbian. But there are as yet no models for her to follow in the Caribbean, and her knowledge of women like herself is confined to derogatory rumors, whispers, and insults.

Viveka is seemingly excluded from *jahaji bahin*, "ship sister," bonds of solidarity with other Indo-Caribbean women (including her own sister and mother) by dint of her sexuality. This is particularly lonely, as it gives her no recourse from an Indo-Caribbean patriarchal familial and societal structure that still makes space for her father, a closeted man who has sex with other men. She is more invisible than a man who hides in plain sight, as Valmiki does, under the guise of societally legitimized heterosexual extramarital affairs. This is true even though she is a "mannish woman," which in Trinidad refers, most often, to a woman who presents as masculine in dress or appearance. But as Crichlow (2004a: 52–53) notes, while the Trinidadian men of his childhood performed heterosexuality in appearance and behavior as a matter of survival,

> anger toward *zami* queens seldom surfaced because most people expected women to carry themselves in traditional ways. Women played highly feminized gender roles, raising children, cleaning house, cooking, washing, dressing, and behaving in ways that excluded labels such as "lesbian," "butch," "zami," or "man royal." . . . Within a Trinidadian community, some codes of behaviour allowed women to go unmarked, less rigorously policed in terms of regulated notions of gender behaviour and their connections to sexuality. Notions of what it meant to look and act *zami* were not

as overtly marked as notions of what it meant to look and act like a buller
man. (52–53)

In essence, unless women like Viveka actually *speak* their sexuality, the neighbors gossip but never act, so unfathomable is the idea that a Caribbean woman
might voluntarily decline the very real social and financial status brought her by a
man. Her father, by contrast, works so hard in his ideally masculine roles as doctor, father, provider, and straight Romeo that he does manage to hide his sexual
relationships with other men from everyone but his wife. He can live a double life
because he is the Indo-Caribbean patriarch, with the freedom of movement and
choice his lesbian daughter could never have.

    While there is some tolerated space for Indo-Caribbean male homosexual-
ity in the arts—particularly and ironically in the propagation of Hindu Indian
dance forms as evidence of community survival (Puar 2001)—Indo-Caribbean
lesbians remain without voice, except in literary and scholarly realms. Alexander's
(1994) study of the revision of sodomy laws in 1986 Trinidad provides the legal
context for *Valmiki's Daughter*. In sum, Victorian laws relating to "buggery" and
rape were reformulated under the rhetoric of "protecting women"; the end result
was the 1986 "Sexual Offenses Act" under which *all* anal sex between persons
of any sex or gender was criminalized (adults over sixteen were to receive twenty-
five years in prison), and lesbian sex was criminalized for the first time under the
rubric of "serious indecency" (adults over sixteen receive five years in prison).
In addition, all "prostitutes and homosexuals" were legally barred from entering
the country. The term *serious indecency* should remind one of the aforementioned
euphemistic colonial phrases "acts of depravity" and "unnatural crime"; constitutional law in the Caribbean Commonwealth draws heavily from imperial British
common law. The 1986 legal provisions were upheld in 2000, though they are
rarely, if ever, enforced. *Valmiki's Daughter* describes a cultural milieu after 1986
and takes place over two years. The exact two years are not specified, suggesting
that postcolonial homophobia in Trinidad is an ongoing story.

    Mootoo takes on the classic trope of the postcolonial Caribbean exile as
promulgated by the earlier work of Naipaul, Selvon, and the first generation of
Indo-Caribbean writer-exiles in Britain and Canada, but renders that figure truly
*post*colonial by queering it: first, the politics of independence are past, and the
Indian has already become Indo-Caribbean; and second, the Great White North(s)
beckons Viveka with the promise of ostensibly queer-liberated Canada, but it has
become just another transoceanic node to which she might travel, always bearing
in mind that the return to Trinidad is a mere six-hour plane ride away. As Gayatri

Gopinath (2005: 165–66) says, Mootoo's writing complicates exile by "trac[ing] the various forms of travel and motion undertaken by sexual subjects both within the home and away from it." Exile, for this younger Indo-Caribbean generation, is not permanent, even when the exile is queer. Canada is framed in the novel as an anonymous respite from overbearing family; for the savvy postcolonial woman, foreign queer acceptance has temporary use-value that outweighs the burden of white anti-immigrant racism abroad. The biomythographer Crichlow (2004a: 69) pragmatically admits:

> While coming out at white gay and lesbian clubs, I already knew about racial harassment and the sexualization of racism within gay and lesbian communities. Even so, I felt great being in a dance club with other "gay people." Race and racism did not preoccupy me—I just wanted to be free, to be a buller, to leave behind the frightening starkness of life under Black heterosexism and violence. At moments like these, I deliberately avoided invoking or adopting any type of race or political consciousness; I simply wanted to have fun, be a buller, without trying to justify it. In the absence of Black same-sex support groups, spaces, and agencies, Black people need white spaces in order to support and affirm their same-sex identity.

Migrating north or west to white queer spaces, Crichlow argues, is a valid physical and psychological survival strategy in the absence of any natal community support—at least at first. Then, as Lorde (1982: 176, 179) says in her biomythography, racial and other differences reassert themselves: "I remember how being young and Black and gay and lonely felt. . . . There were no mothers, no sisters, no heroes. . . . Downtown in the gay bars I was a closet student and an invisible Black." This is a cruel logic of scarcity for lesbian women of color like Viveka, who decides in the end to leave her home country for Canada.

As migrants, though, Crichlow and Viveka are different from the traditional literary figure of the postcolonial exile typical of the Caribbean (and Caribbean studies) nationalist framework of hybridity. The traditional Caribbean exile is he or she who has failed or refuses to hybridize at the moment of colonial independence, retreating from the barrenness of a postcolony teeming with Bhabhian and Naipaulian mimic men to the cultural wholeness of the "Mother Country." Crichlow and Viveka also leave or want to leave, but not because they refuse Caribbean subjectivity or have any doubt about their particularly Trinidadian cultural or even national identity. What they refuse is a contemporary construct of postcolonial *citizenship*. The antithesis of the postcolonial Caribbean citizen is the Caribbean exile, but also, now, the Caribbean queer, figured as Munasinghe's impure hybrid in a rebuke to the madly ironic notion of a postcolonial hybridity that with the complicity of *jahaji bhai* transnational Indo-Caribbean studies denies its constitutive queerness.

Ship Sisters

Valmiki's Daughter posits from its very title onward that this daughter, Viveka Krishnu, is no queer Indo-European Lakshmi-Aphrodite, springing from the ocean to bless the world with divine feminine *shakti*. Viveka has a clear lineage. Her father, Valmiki, the masculine Indo-Caribbean *jahaji bhai* subject, opens the way—but it is Viveka, a woman who speaks her lesbian identity, who is brave and bright enough to morph herself in order to pass through. After all, in Sanskrit the name "Viveka" means no less than "wisdom" itself, with connotations of a higher human ethical ability to discern right from wrong. Names are important in the novel; Valmiki is named after *the* Vālmīki, the sage who is said to have transcended his origins as an *adivasi* (indigenous person) and as a *dacoit* (brigand) to author the ancient Hindu epic the Rāmāyana. The ancient Vālmīki's transformation happens when he meets sages who ask him if his wife and children have a moral share in his sinning, since they survive on his thievery. He says yes; his wife and children say no. Shocked, he leaves them and falls into meditation for years, until an anthill grows up and covers him. The sages eventually return, whereupon Vālmīki emerges from the anthill (*vālmīk*) an enlightened man, and they rename him after it (Leslie 2003: 186, 14–15). In Vālmīkish fashion, the novel's Valmiki believes that his daughter should share the wages of sin. When he realizes that Viveka has begun a carelessly visible relationship with a woman, he says to himself, "She was beginning to live the life he had made choices to avoid. It was his doing. His fault. But how dare she? How dare she think only of herself. Had she no good sense after all? No sense of loyalty—if not loyalty, then responsibility—to her family, to society? To him?" (Mootoo 2010: 342–43). Unlike Vālmīki the sage, who transcends his caste origins, the Trinidadian Valmiki never escapes the anthill of the closet and normative Hindu masculine destiny.

State ideology is perpetuated by the normativization of certain social mores, such that communities can police their own members on behalf of the nation. In Trinidad parlance, at the age of twenty or so Viveka is "mannish." Being called mannish by her younger sister Vashti early in the novel is the jolting catalyst for Viveka's feelings of same-sex attraction to rise to the surface of her consciousness. Her sister looks at her critically and says

you do look kind of tough for a female . . . you have a tendency to be muscular. I mean, really: do you want big calves and harder arms—which you
will get if you play sports? That's so ugly on a . . . whatever. It makes us
look mannish. Mom says *you're* sort of mannish." That was enough. The
word *mannish* was unacceptable. . . . Later on, in the limbo of taxi travel,
the dreaded word came to her again. *Mannish*. An onomatopoeic word that
sounded as disgusting as what it suggested. (ibid.: 89–90, 114)

Viveka does not yet know what she is, but she dreads what "mannish" signifies,
and she walks around feeling strangely bound, harboring "the sensation that her
arms were tightly bound to her body with yards and yards of clear Scotch tape"
(ibid.: 98–99). Viveka and all the members of her family know that "something" is
amiss with her, but no one dares say it aloud.

"Mannish" in the Caribbean can refer to a masculine woman, an exces-
sively patriarchal man, or a boy who acts older than his age. In all cases, there is a
connotation of behavior that is so hypermasculine as to be socially unacceptable,
an intriguing policing of the bounds of masculinity that can implicate men and
women, adults and children. The mannish aspire to a masculinity that is imbued
with societally destabilizing violence: mannish men are testosterone-charged
potential perpetrators of violence, mannish boys come too early to violence, and
mannish women demand violence from society as punishment for transgressing
gender norms—they are "asking" for it. Being a mannish woman is particularly
dangerous—not just for her physical safety but for the postcolonial national project. Viveka's mannish appearance suggests that she might not reproduce. As Alexander (1994: 20) notes, "The archetypal source of state legitimation is anchored in
the heterosexual family, the form of family crucial in the state's view to the founding of the nation." There is typically no place for the mannish lesbian woman in the
family that is the microcosm of the nation; but the specter of the Indo-Caribbean
mannish woman is a relatively new one in a region where gendered perceptions of
Indo-Caribbean women begin with their figuration in colonial literature as particularly feminine, docile, and domestic in comparison with Afro-Caribbean women.[17]

Viveka is an Indo-Caribbean mannish woman. As a child, she is a stereo-
typical tomboy who loves sports and dismisses girls and women who primp and
scheme for male attention. She sometimes imagines herself to be her brother,
Anand, who died in infancy, and at other times believes herself to be a blond-
haired white boy named Vince. Young Viveka imagines herself to be her brother
for two reasons: first, because she mistakenly believes that as an eldest sibling she
should somehow have been able to protect him from death, and second, she is sub-

consciously aware of her father, Valmiki, thinking that if his son had lived, the two children, particularly because of Viveka's angular facial features, her lankiness, and her short hair, would have been unmistakable as siblings—and perhaps mis-identified as brothers (Mootoo 2010: 62). Viveka understands she is not feminine enough to be an acceptable daughter to her parents, so, she imagines, she might as well be their son.

Her second masculine alter ego, Vince, was "strong, powerful, peaceful, and could do anything and everything. He had a horse he could ride. He didn't speak much. He was kind. His name was Vince, short for 'invincible.' He was not in the least the bastard her father said all men were. Vince loved being outdoors" (ibid.: 110). Vince is a protective identity—he is perhaps even a mannish boy in his precociousness. At seven, it is Vince, not Viveka, who observes her father in the act of committing adultery with a white female neighbor—his closet cover is multiple affairs with women. She does not understand what she sees, so her Viveka self goes away, and Vince takes over. After witnessing this adulterous adult incident, the child "did not go straight home, but ran around and around the neigh-bourhood until, dripping with sweat, he limped, feet swollen, blistered, and bleeding, through the front gates of his parents' house" (ibid.: 114). Vince, of course, is curiously white, though the child Viveka has no particular ideas about race or interaction with anyone who is white. She lives in the Trinidadian postcolony where colorism is no stranger, but whiteness is literary and foreign. Vince is modeled on the sporty, adventuresome English schoolboys of her storybooks.

As an adult, Viveka does not consider herself other than female and attracted to women; she is not trans* and she is not bisexual. She is physically capable of having sex with a man, as her father is capable of having sex with women, but she derives no physical or emotional feeling from it and is merely a spectator. She is a masculine lesbian, and her style of lovemaking with the extremely feminine Anick, her foreign French lover who is married to an Indo-Trinidadian man, is almost stereotypically dominant—she realizes this predilection immediately during their first, much-anticipated sexual encounter. Making love to another woman for the first time as a young adult is what purges Viveka of both masculine alter egos, her brother and the white boy. She imagines that Anand and Vince grow up into discrete young men and leave her:

> Tears suddenly ran down Viveka's cheeks and she wiped them fast so that Anick wouldn't know. She had felt, during the initial moments of their love-making, a sense of having taken on the form of a young man's body. Her body had become, albeit briefly, Vince's body, and in other moments [her

dead baby brother] Anand's. These two were suddenly young men: sturdy, muscled, handsome. As handsome as Anick was beautiful. It was strange how Vince and Anand had grown into such young men; this was the strongest sensation of that sort Viveka had ever had—of not being what she looked like, female. And yet, she knew now more than ever that her feelings and her way with Anick were hers and hers alone. Not a boy's. Not a man's. Whatever she was, these feelings were hers. . . . Perhaps she could be finished with Anand now. And with Vince. (ibid.: 322–23)

Viveka in this moment realizes, quite simply, that she need not be a boy or man to desire women, and that perhaps this desire was, all along, the fundamental reason for the existence of Anand and Vince. Though the relationship with the Frenchwoman is doomed, engaging in it gives Viveka the courage to live visibly as a mannish woman—to cut her hair short and begin dressing in a more gender-neutral way, in defiance of her mother's wishes. But the novel leaves undetermined what else an Indo-Trinidadian mannish woman identity might involve, implying that in the Indo-Caribbean, as anywhere else, queer identifications are simultaneously particular, fluid, and perpetually under construction. Similarly, Crichlow (2004a: 53) points out that the sartorial appearance of masculinity is not always enough to label a woman as lesbian in Trinidad:

> Women wearing men's overalls or doing physical work traditionally constructed as masculine did not challenge women's traditional gender roles. If anything, some of the clothes women wore reflected poverty, and it was acceptable for them to wear such clothing until they could afford something new. Clothes functioned as visible signs of identity that were subject to disruption and symbolic theft, and this challenged the role of clothes as grounds for gender. Furthermore, acts such as physical aggressiveness, when a woman was fighting for her "male partner, children, girl friend, or a good friend," were reconfigured and represented as very womanly—the act of a strong woman and at the same time a girlish thing to do. Observers never assumed that a woman protecting another woman from male violence had a sexual interest in her or that women who listened to one another's problems had a same-sex attraction. Rather, women supported one another in response to violence and shared communal experiences.

Alexander calls this a "gendered call to patriotic duty" (quoted in Crichlow 2004a: 53).

Though Adam Geczy and Vicki Karaminas (2013: 25) (following Colette) find specifically "mannish" lesbians in the middle-class female dandies of Victorian and Edwardian London and Paris, Jack Halberstam (1998) and others show that "female masculinity," as typified here by racialized working-class and poor women wearing traditionally masculine clothing, is not a phenomenon limited to the Caribbean. Halberstam suggests that normative feminine and masculine appearances in the same society take turns being "approximate" and "precise" (28), which leaves gendered dress simply relational. Class is an understated factor in Viveka's narrative; as the daughter of a doctor, she is very comfortably upper middle class. Her masculine dress is more visible and open to sexualized interpretation than the masculine dress of a poor woman. Viveka's responsibility to present herself as gender-normative extends beyond service to generalized postcolonial Caribbeanness and to the nation of Trinidad. She is also tasked with perpetuating the cultural and physical survival of her specific upper-middle-class Indo-Trinidadian community by being properly feminine. This is a duty that her traditional and marriage-minded Indian mother Devika understands and embraces:

> Educated women, [Devika] said, were aggressive, unladylike. The only professions she could imagine for either of her daughters in an age, she conceded, when women were demanding to spend time outside of the home, were catering, flower arranging . . . and teaching. . . . What she understood was preparing oneself for marriage. But marriage had never interested Viveka. (Mootoo 2010: 100–101)

Unlike her daughter, Devika is highly concerned with the gender and class proprieties of being an upper-middle-class Indo-Caribbean woman (this is the family's class location, as the patriarch Valmiki is a doctor). Devika perceives herself as a traditionally strong Indo-Caribbean woman because she can bear heavy burdens. That is the acceptable kind of martyred strength for an Indian woman, a strength that echoes colonial British representations of Indian indentured women as simultaneously docile, submissive, and hard workers. As Devika understands it, her familial role is as head of household. But her husband and daughter are willful and unmanageable, refusing to conform to their own apportioned roles in the nuclear family in any more than superficial ways. Their homosexuality is unthinkable, the greatest threat she could ever imagine to the sanctity of family and state, especially as it suggests a terrifying postcolonial community scenario where the Indo-Caribbean child is cursed with the sins of the Indian father—the aspiring upright citizen haunted by a motley ancestral collection of homosexuals, prostitutes, and runaways. But it is Viveka in her queerness and defiance who is the real *jahaji bahin*, a member of the sorority who had the courage to leave Trinidad.

The literary trope of the Caribbean exile as promulgated by George Lamming, Selvon, Naipaul, and other (overwhelmingly male) writers of the first post-colonial Caribbean generation is omnipresent in *Valmiki's Daughter*, but the object and agent of struggle have shifted beyond a concern for the geopolitical that is rooted in mourning, nostalgia, and loss. No longer must the male postcolonial, scion of the *jahaji bhai*, escape becoming a mere mimic man by exiling himself in the British motherland. The independence question of Britishness or Indianness is reconciled in the generations after colonialism: Viveka is born an Indo-Caribbean woman, an identity with unique cultural substance. As a literary scholar, aspiring writer, and Indo-Trinidadian, she is rather irked by Naipaul, complaining that

> he makes Indians out to be ugly, stupid, concerned only with their narrow knife-edged slice of life. He's criticizing his ancestors, but these are my ancestors too, and by implication he is criticizing me. And yet, I keep wanting to read on. He gets it right, but so what? . . . I don't think he really hates us so much as he is gravely disappointed in what we have not become. (ibid.: 104–5)

Viveka suggests, as other Caribbean writers and critics including even Derek Walcott have said, that there is no satisfying Naipaul, to whose literary genius and community representation all Indo-Caribbean people are beholden.[18] The novel pays its dues to Naipaul, acknowledging him as the godfather of Indo-Caribbean literature. But in a nod to the postindependence goal of racialized national unity, it is in Afro-Caribbean literature that Viveka sees a way out of the stultifying calcifications of Indo-Caribbean culture: "The writings of Jamaica Kincaid, Dionne Brand, Jean Rhys, Derek Walcott, and Earl Lovelace provoked her to want to experience a Caribbean-ness, and a Trinidadian-ness more specifically, that was antithetical to her mother's tie to all things Indian and Hindu" (Mootoo 2010: 100–101). These writers' works are her biomythographies of being Caribbean: they illustrate for Viveka her regional identity and indirectly suggest a nonracialized way to conceptualize Caribbean queerness.

Viveka is meant to escape the destiny of the "bound coolie" who reindentured or remained on the sugar estate even after the initial indentureship contract had expired. Realizing that she has no future with her married female lover in Trinidad, as the woman refuses to leave her husband and societal and familial condemnation is too much to bear at a young age, Viveka goes about her freedom in the same practical way as does Crichlow: she looks north to Canada. Her father, Valmiki, has found a way to live in Trinidad and have a clandestine male lover. But he is able to do this because he is a man, and a well-off doctor, and neither his wife nor society questions him when he goes off on his own to meet his male lover in secret. Indo-Caribbean women's traditional relegation to the domestic sphere simply does not permit such freedom of movement and visibility for a woman or a lesbian. The novel suggests that now it is the Indo-Caribbean woman who must take up the mantle of the Caribbean *jahaji*, the voyager who is not, however, a permanent exile. As such, Viveka agrees to marry a man who will take her to Toronto. Her future husband knows of her sexual past and is accepting. She does not rule out the possibility of returning to Trinidad; she is concerned with *now*.

This is a realistic ending for a novel set in the rather more than less homophobic contemporary Anglophone Caribbean, mired as it is in a stew of Victorian sexual mores and hypocrisies, colonial law and US expansionism, neoliberal and neocolonial foreign economic exploitation, evangelical religious fervor, and the foundational uncertainty and, to many, shame of unknown ancestors, lost languages, and hybrid identities. In this milieu, queerness is a liminal area. What will preserve your life and sanity is what you should first do.[19] We are left with the understanding that Viveka lives her life only as she chooses when she says, in the novel's final line, "You'd be surprised at my courage right now" (Mootoo 2010: 395). Marrying a man is less capitulation than clever strategic planning. Like Mohangoo and Baksh and even Abdul Rhyme, the peon of Hindostan, she operates on the principle of pleasure: her own. This affective temporal relation, pleasure across time, is a lateral kinship that eludes and elides the desire for the ancestral homosexual in the archive who will legitimate and save the queer Caribbean. Viveka refuses to be a queer Indo-Trinidadian victim of society and circumstance, hybridized into a collection of cultural and personal fragments characterized by loss. She holds in reserve the daunting (to area studies) option of leading a truly transnational life with the equally tendentious (to queer studies) possibility of location-dependent queer code switching. In this traditionally protean yet multiply localized biomythography of the Caribbean, there is no geographic or temporal need for Viveka or any Caribbean queer to invest in a one-way ticket for the ship sailing into exile.

Notes

1. The father-in-law and close companion of the Prophet Muhammad, Abu Bakr became the first caliph and leader of the Muslims after the Prophet's death. *Stabroek News* is one of Guyana's major daily newspapers.

2. The Indo-Caribbean population is about 10 percent Sunni Muslim, with the rest mostly Hindu. Unlike Guyana, Trinidad has a sizable Indian Christian (mostly Presbyterian) population, dating from nineteenth-century Canadian missionary activities that were sanctioned by the British as a way to reduce crime, drunkenness, and "coolie wife murders" on the sugar estate. Conversion was attractive to migrants because missionaries also offered education—Bible in one hand and Children's Primer in the other—to the formerly indentured, and Christianity became the major Indo-Trinidadian road to the middle class. By contrast, the rise of the Indian middle class in British Guiana is associated with former indentured laborers growing rice as a cash crop, that is, with the former indentured becoming small-scale farmers in their own right.

3. Between 1838 and 1917, Indian indentured contract laborers departed from either the port of Calcutta in the north or the port of Madras in the south, bound for the Caribbean islands, the Guianas in South America, Belize in Central America, Mauritius, Fiji, and South and East Africa. Altogether, the Anglophone Caribbean, including Guyana, received 543,700 indentured laborers, about half a million people to replace emancipated African slaves on British sugar plantations (Ramdin 2000).

4. The term *jahaji bahin*, with variant spellings, has been used by scholars of the Indo-Caribbean including Peggy Mohan (2007), Niranjana Tejaswini (2006), and Mariam Pirbhai (2010: 39) but is newer to popular usage, having been recently embraced by the Indo-Caribbean feminist organization Jahajee Sisters, founded in New York City in 2007 to address domestic violence and other social issues affecting women in the large diaspora community. According to its founders, Suzanne Persard and Simone Devi Jhingoor, "During the period of Indian indentureship (1838–1917), *Jahajee Bhai* and *Jahajee Bahen* (ship brother and ship sister) were terms used by our ancestors to unify and support each other in the midst of the tumultuous voyage by sea from India to the Caribbean. Despite adversity, our ancestors who arrived in the Caribbean were able to forge bonds, survive, and thrive. In this spirit, Jahajee Sisters seeks to build community and power to address critical issues challenging Indo-Caribbean women. Crossing the Kala Pani from India and coming to the Caribbean was a deeply traumatic experience for Indo-Caribbean people. Yet, the fact that we were able to survive the Indian middle passage and the harsh system of indentureship, which attempted to strip us of our identity and culture, is an example of how resilient our people are. It especially shows the strength of our women, who played an integral role in preserving and carrying on the culture in the Caribbean and again in the US.

Reclaiming the word 'Jahajee' in our name and in our work is the way we have chosen to honor our history and live into our resiliency" (quoted in Outar 2012: 2–3).

5. For a detailed assessment of Mehta's and Kanhai's writings on *matikor* and its queer potentialities, see Pragg 2012.

6. To my knowledge there are no specifically Indo-Caribbean queer groups or organizations in the Caribbean itself. There is one in the United States: Sangam, which is based in Richmond Hill, Queens, New York, and was founded in February 2012 by Indo-Caribbean activists earlier affiliated with SALGA, the South Asian Lesbian and Gay Association of New York City, established in 1991. This origin is particularly salient, as it shows that Indo-Caribbean community organizers felt more kinship with the diasporic Indian queer community than they did with the queer Afro-Caribbean diaspora. The shared queer Indian kinship is largely a result of shared Hindu and Muslim religious upbringings, and common first- and second-generation immigrant Indian family mores. Sangam has not faced much *open* prejudice in the extremely large Indo-Caribbean community in New York but has suffered from a lack of financial community support and reluctance on the part of queer community members who seek out organizational counseling and support services but refuse to be visible or "out" (Sooklall 2014). Rampant suicide has a long history in the Indo-Caribbean. Along with addiction to rum and narcotics, "for numerous indentured men and women, the ultimate escape from the drabness and brutality of estate life was through suicide. Some hung themselves because they were unable or unwilling to submit to the degrading or severe manual labour expected of them. The vulnerability of women placed many tensions on indentured families and were another cause of suicides much discussed by officials" (Carter and Torabully 2002: 100).

7. The titular short story of Mootoo's collection *Out on Main Street* (1993) does feature an Indo-Trinidadian-Canadian lesbian protagonist faced with the intersections of racial, gender, sexual, and immigration issues. Mootoo's first novel, *Cereus Blooms at Midnight* (1996), features two minor lesbian characters and one, more important, trans* character, but the main characters are heterosexual in deed and by implication.

8. The *Mersey* incident is mentioned briefly by Bahadur (2014), who discovered the story in the archives during her *Coolie Woman* research.

9. For the particulars of the *Mersey*'s rigging, tonnage, and (indenture)ship role, see Richardson 1901.

10. The original colonial inspection report is archived at "Indian Immigrants for 'Mersey': Report of Arrival and Inspection 31 Oct.," December 7, 1898, File No. 25575, CO 111/506, Colonial Office Correspondence, Public Record Office, The National Archives of the UK, Kew.

11. *Sirdar*: in colonial India this term was originally a title of nobility, then a night watchman or the Indian man in charge of keeping order among the indentured.

12. *Holy stone* is an archaic naval term meaning to scrub the decks with sandstone.

13. The names of the two indentured men were more accurately transliterated as "Nabi Baksh" and "Mohangoo" on their indentureship passes (Sendall 1898: 38–39).

14. In his study of contact between aboriginal Andamanese and convicted Indian men imprisoned on the Andaman Islands during British colonialism, Satadru Sen (2010: 179) also raises the specter of jealousy in British descriptions of same-sex sexual contact between "natives," in this case Andamanese and Indians: "Who would the aborigine choose: the sahib or the convict? The sexualized savage in the clearing thus emerged as a feminized and juvenilized victim of civilized lust, but also as a trap that lured Indians out from the clarity of the colony into a shadow world of quarrels and intimacies that Britons could not penetrate." If two indentured Indian men on the *Mersey* chose each other, they were not choosing Dr. Harrison or any other white man on board.

15. Bahadur notes that the colonial record includes one other case of "unnatural crime" that occurred between indentured men aboard the ship *Brenda*. This case was brought to the British Guiana High Court in 1892. Other information is derived from anecdotes by European visitors horrified by the "uncleanliness and Sodomy" allegedly rife among male-majority Indian and Chinese indentured laborers (Bahadur 2014: 88).

16. For extensive and thorough auto-ethnographic documentation of Indo-Guyanese gender relations on the plantation, see Bahadur 2014.

17. The British orientalist Charles Kingsley infamously wrote of the contrast in the Caribbean colonies between the masculine, "superabundant animal vigour and the perfect independence of the younger [African] women" and "the young Indian woman 'hung all over with bangles, in a white muslin petticoat . . . and gauze green veil; a clever, smiling, delicate little woman, who is quite aware of the brightness of her own eyes.'" See Tejaswini 2006: 82.

18. Walcott and Naipaul, the two living Caribbean Nobel laureates in literature, have had a long-standing literary, philosophical, and rather personal rivalry. Insight into their disagreements may be gleaned from Walcott 1974.

19. In the sociopolitical context of the Caribbean and the Black Atlantic, says Tinsley (2008: 209), "I am compelled by [Judith] Butler's growing insistence, from the 1999 preface to *Gender Trouble* to the engaging *Undoing Gender*, that gender theory should address more material concerns—issues of survival for the transgendered and others whose 'unintelligible' bodies threaten their very lives."

References

Alexander, M. Jacqui. 1994. "Not Just (Any) Body Can Be a Citizen: The Politics of Law, Sexuality, and Postcoloniality in Trinidad and Tobago and the Bahamas." *Feminist Review* 48: 5-23.

Arondekar, Anjali. 2009. *For the Record: On Sexuality and the Colonial Archive in India.* Durham, NC: Duke University Press.

———. 2015. "In the Absence of Reliable Ghosts: Sexuality, Historiography, South Asia." *differences: A Journal of Feminist Cultural Studies* 25, no. 3: 98–122.

Bahadur, Gaiutra. 2014. *Coolie Woman: The Odyssey of Indenture.* Chicago: University of Chicago Press.

Bakr, Abu. 2010. "The Current Advocates of Gay Rights Are Examples of a Neo-Colonialist Tendency." *Stabroek News*, March 5.

Barriteau, Eudine. 2003. *Confronting Power, Theorizing Gender: Interdisciplinary Perspectives in the Caribbean.* Kingston, Jamaica: University of the West Indies Press.

Benítez-Rojo, Antonio. 1992. *The Repeating Island: The Caribbean and the Postmodern Perspective*, translated by James Maraniss. Durham, NC: Duke University Press.

Burg, B. R. 1983. *Sodomy and the Perception of Evil: English Sea Rovers in the Seventeenth Century Caribbean.* New York: New York University Press.

Carter, Marina, and Khal Torabully. 2002. *Coolitude: An Anthology of the Indian Labour Diaspora.* London: Anthem.

Crichlow, Wesley. 2004a. *Buller Men and Batty Bwoys: Hidden Men in Toronto and Halifax Black Communities.* Toronto: University of Toronto Press.

———. 2004b. "History, (Re)Memory, Testimony, and Biomythography: Charting a Buller Man's Trinidadian Past." In *Interrogating Caribbean Masculinities: Theoretical and Empirical Analyses*, edited by Rhoda Rheddock, 185–222. Kingston, Jamaica: University of the West Indies Press.

"Desperate Measures: When It Comes to People Taking Their Own Lives, Guyana Leads the World." 2014. *Economist*, September 13.

Ellis, Nadia. 2015. "Black Migrants, White Queers, and the Archive of Inclusion in Postwar London." *Interventions* 17, no. 6: 893–915.

Fanon, Frantz. 2008. *Black Skin, White Masks.* Translated by Richard Philcox. New York: Grove.

Geczy, Adam, and Vicki Karaminas. 2013. *Queer Style.* New York: Bloomsbury.

Gilroy, Paul. 1993. *The Black Atlantic: Modernity and Double Consciousness.* Cambridge, MA: Harvard University Press.

Gopinath, Gayatri. 2005. *Impossible Desires: Queer Diasporas and South Asian Public Cultures.* Durham, NC: Duke University Press.

Gosine, Andil. 2009. "Sexual Desires, Rights and Regulation." *Caribbean Review of Gender Studies* 3: 1–4.

Halberstam, Judith. 1998. *Female Masculinity.* Durham, NC: Duke University Press.

Hall, Stuart. 2003. "Cultural Identity and Diaspora." In *Theorizing Diaspora: A Reader*, edited by Jana Evans Braziel and Anita Mannur, 233–46. Malden, MA: Blackwell.

Hosein, Gabrielle. 2012. "Modern Navigations: Indo-Trinidadian Girlhood and Gender-Differential Creolization." *Caribbean Review of Gender Studies* 6: 1–24.

Hosein, Gabrielle, and Lisa Outar. 2012. "Indo-Caribbean Feminisms: Charting Cross-ings in Geography, Discourse, and Politics." *Caribbean Review of Gender Studies* 6: 1–10.

Kempadoo, Kamala. 2004. *Sexing the Caribbean: Gender, Race, and Sexual Labor.* New York: Routledge.

King, Rosamond S. 2008. "More Notes on the Invisibility of Caribbean Lesbians (2005)." In *Our Caribbean: A Gathering of Lesbian and Gay Writing from the Antilles*, edited by Thomas Glave, 191–96. Durham, NC: Duke University Press.

Kutzinski, Vera M. 2001. "Improprieties: Feminism, Queerness, and Caribbean Litera-ture." *Macalester International* 10, no. 18: 165–206.

Leslie, Julia. 2003. *Authority and Meaning in Indian Religions: Hinduism and the Case of Vālmīki.* Hants, UK: Ashgate.

Lokaisingh-Meighoo, Sean. 2000. "Jahaji Bhai: Notes on the Masculine Subject and Homoerotic Subtext of Indo-Caribbean Identity." *Small Axe* 7: 77–92.

Lorde, Audre. 1982. *Zami: A New Spelling of My Name.* Berkeley, CA: Crossing.

Martí, José. 2005. "Nuestra América." In *Nuestra América*, edited by Hugo Achúgar, 31–39. Caracas: Fundación Biblioteca Ayacucho.

Massad, Joseph. 2002. "Re-Orienting Desire: The Gay International and the Arab World." *Public Culture* 14, no. 2: 361–85.

Mohammed, Patricia. 1998. "Towards Indigenous Feminist Theorizing in the Caribbean." *Feminist Review* 59: 6–33.

Mohan, Peggy. 2007. *Jahajin.* Noida, Uttar Pradesh: HarperCollins India.

Mootoo, Shani. 2008. *Valmiki's Daughter.* Toronto: House of Anansi.

Munasinghe, Viranjini. 2002. "Nationalism in Hybrid Spaces: The Production of Impurity out of Purity." *American Ethnologist* 29, no. 3: 663–92.

Ortíz, Fernando. 2001. *Cuban Counterpoint: Tobacco and Sugar*, translated by Harriet de Onis. Durham, NC: Duke University Press.

Outar, Lisa. 2012. "'Breaking Silences': An Interview with Jahajee Sisters." *Caribbean Review of Gender Studies*, no. 6: 1–11.

Pirbhai, Mariam. 2010. "The *Jahaji-Bhain* Principle: A Critical Survey of the Indo-Caribbean Women's Novel, 1990–2009." *Journal of Commonwealth Literature* 45, no. 1: 37–56.

Pragg, Lauren. 2012. "The Queer Potential: (Indo)Caribbean Feminisms and Heteronor-mativity." *Caribbean Review of Gender Studies* 6: 1–14.

Puar, Jasbir. 2001. "Global Circuits: Transnational Sexualities and Trinidad." *Signs* 26, no. 4: 1039–65.

Ramdin, Ron. 2000. *Arising from Bondage: A History of the Indo-Caribbean People.* New York: New York University Press.

———. 1994. *The Other Middle Passage: Journal of a Voyage from Calcutta to Trini-dad, 1858.* London: Hansib.

Reddock, Rhoda. 2008. "Indian Women and Indentureship in Trinidad and Tobago: 1845–1917: Freedom Denied." *Caribbean Quarterly* 54, no. 4: 41–68.

Retamar, Roberto Fernández. 1979. *Calibán y otros ensayos: nuestra américa y el mundo.* La Habana: Editorial Arte y Literatura.

Richardson, T. F. 1901. "History of the British Ship Mersey, Which Arrived at Reedy Island Quarantine from Calcutta, Having Had Cholera on Board." *Public Health Reports (1896–1970),* 16n11: 501–2.

Sen, Satadru. 2010. *Savagery and Colonialism in the Indian Ocean: Power, Pleasure, and the Andaman Islanders.* New York: Routledge.

Sendall, Walter. 1898. "British Guiana 1898: Punishment for Sodomy Meted out to Nabi Baksh and Mohangoo on the Mersey." Digital Library of the Caribbean, AA00007501/00001.

Shepherd, Verene A. 2002. *Maharani's Misery: Narratives of a Passage from India to the Caribbean.* Kingston, Jamaica: University of the West Indies Press.

Sooklall, Rohan. 2014. Author interview, Flushing, NY, July 27.

Tambiah, Yasmin. 2009. "Creating (Im)moral Citizens: Gender, Sexuality and Lawmaking in Trinidad and Tobago, 1986." *Caribbean Review of Gender Studies* 3: 1–19.

Tejaswini, Niranjana. 2006. *Mobilizing India: Women, Music, and Migration between India and Trinidad.* Durham, NC: Duke University Press.

Tinker, Hugh. 1993. *A New System of Slavery: The Export of Indian Labour Overseas, 1830–1920.* London: Hansib.

Tinsley, Omise'eke Natasha. 2008. "Black Atlantic, Queer Atlantic: Queer Imaginings of the Middle Passage." *GLQ* 14, nos. 2–3: 191–215.

———. 2010. *Thiefing Sugar: Eroticism between Women in Caribbean Literature.* Durham, NC: Duke University Press.

Vertovec, Steven. 2000. *The Hindu Diaspora: Comparative Patterns.* New York: Routledge.

Wahab, Amar. 2012. "Homophobia as the State of Reason: The Case of Postcolonial Trinidad and Tobago." *GLQ* 18, no. 4: 481–505.

Walcott, Derek. 1974. "The Caribbean: Culture or Mimicry?" In *Journal of Interamerican Studies and World Affairs* 16, no. 1: 3–13.

Younger, Paul. 2010. *New Homelands: Hindu Communities in Mauritius, Guyana, Trinidad, South Africa, Fiji, and East Africa.* Oxford: Oxford University Press.

QUEER STUDIES / AFRICAN STUDIES

An (Im)possible Transaction?

Ashley Currier and Thérèse Migraine-George

$\mathcal{T}$he colonialist and Cold War consolidation of area studies and African studies in the United States has been well documented, although alternative origin stories of the rise of African studies circulate (Martin 2011). Area studies emerged to "manage and negotiate the tensions that arose after the Second World War and during decolonization worldwide" (Grewal and Kaplan 2001: 668). Despite questions that persist about the scholarly significance of African studies, the field has experienced resurgence in the last fifteen years because of sociopolitical anxieties about terrorism in Africa and around the world, the new avatar of Cold War geopolitics (Melber 2005: 371). African studies' renewed prominence comes at a time when scholars are also grappling with the present-day effects of neoliberal structural adjustment policies that weakened national economies throughout Africa, continuing a pattern of impoverishment that began with European colonialism. These conditions fuel theories of "Afro-pessimism" that lament political corruption, violent conflict, pervasive indigence, and worsening health outcomes experienced by Africans. By emphasizing social problems in African countries, the Afro-pessimist perspective regards the continent as unredeemable, perpetuating a colonialist, racist tradition of imagining the area: "Africa" as a continent in crisis that lags far behind "progressive," industrialized nations in the global north (Mudimbe 1988).

Queer African subjects, if we can invoke this category as a way to meld area and sexuality, may strike some observers as suffering the injustices outlined by Afro-pessimism. Images and stories of queer African "victimage," including stories of antiqueer rape in South Africa and the murders of LGBTI activists in

GLQ 22:2

DOI 10.1215/10642684-3428783

© 2016 by Duke University Press

Cameroon and Uganda, circulate transnationally (Carter 2013; Corey-Boulet 2013; Gettleman 2011; Hoad 2007: 69). A recent example is the international fascination with "African homophobia," around which Western and African sympathizers have called for African political leaders to abandon antisodomy laws and to stop antiqueer harassment and violence (Nyong'o 2012: 41). Indeed, some European governments, such as Great Britain, promised to withdraw development assistance from African countries that persecute LGBTI persons (Martin 2011). Antiqueer prejudice and violence on the African continent have not attracted much attention in US queer studies, even as US LGBTI activist organizations seek to intervene in African LGBTI organizing. In 2013 the Human Rights Campaign announced its foray into international LGBTI rights advocacy, which worried Wanja Muguongo, who leads UHAI, the East African Sexual Health and Rights Initiative, as this foray could jeopardize the work of African LGBTI activists. Muguongo stated, "We are not sitting down somewhere waiting for salvation to come from the North. . . . There are organizations that are working locally and they have their own ideas about what the struggle means" (quoted in Feder 2013). The "victimage" produced by discourses of "African homophobia" stems from a particular intersection of area and sexuality studies: cynicism about African sociopolitical conditions and confining portrayals of lived gender and sexual diversity. Queer studies' disengagement with queer African studies in the example of African homophobia illustrates the unproductive polarities in gender, sexuality, and queer studies that US area studies helped create. Despite its own limitations, queer of color analysis offers one corrective to this tendency by debunking "ideologies of discreteness" that posit race, class, gender, and sexuality as transparent formations "apparently insulated from one another" (Ferguson 2004: 4).

Queer studies scholarship often assumes the United States as a referent, although anthropological investigations of lived gender and sexual diversity in the global south have nourished US queer studies (Boellstorff 2007; Swarr 2012). One way to deprivilege the United States as a geopolitical referent is to embrace and deploy a logic of "queer comparison," which, as Tom Boellstorff (2007: 209) explains, based on his research on gender and sexual diversity in Indonesia, involves "not a form of law making but rather a form of critique and sensitivity to coincidence that complements ethnography; it does not set itself up as a transcendent critique that passes judgment on such work, but instead as an immanent critique that opens up new possibilities for scholarship and activism." Instead of invoking "queer theory" in this essay as a finite collection of ideas about destabilizing gender and sexual norms, we turn to "queer studies," "the open mesh of possibilities" theorized by Eve Kosofsky Sedgwick (1993: 8), as a dynamic, trans-disciplinary field that scavenges and repurposes ideas from diverse disciplines for promising, unpredictable ends (Eng, Halberstam, and Muñoz 2005: 3–4; Halberstam 1998: 13). Given the regional, ethnic, cultural, national, and historical complexity that forms "African studies," we treat the field as a dynamic body of knowledge informed by comparison and innovation.[1] At the confluence of two unruly discourses fostered by postmodern, postcolonial, and feminist thinking, African queer studies interpellates the Anglo-American policing of disciplinary boundaries and its persistent effort to control and neutralize the politics of knowledge production. A renewed attention to diasporic formations, migratory patterns, and transnational communities, both real and virtual, can challenge the disciplinary confinement of African studies to transatlantic frameworks, inciting engagement with pan-African, "outernational" formulations that escape pedestrian nationalist articulations (Walcott 2012: 30).

By putting the field formations of African studies and queer studies into new dialogic relations, we exploit the geopolitical dissidence of African studies to question the imperialist grounding of queer studies in the US academy. We also marshal the porosity and flexibility of queer studies' comparative logics to re-form queer African studies into a shifting site of cross-disciplinary turbulence, a discursive vortex in which the institutional constitutionality of theoretical formations is uncovered and productively ruptured.[2] Despite the iconoclastic and cross-cultural impetus of African and queer studies, their disciplinary borders have been policed by scholars eager to consolidate their own academic raison d'être and legitimacy, thereby illustrating Gayatri Spivak's warning that as a "margin" or "outside" infiltrates an institution or "teaching machine," its very "contours" become determined by this new context.[3] Probing the (im)possible transactions between African studies and queer studies allows us to retrace the sinuous contours of two ever-shifting field formations as they touch and rub off on each other and to question our own "epistemological will to knowledge" (Puar 2005: 122) by imagining another discourse that "generates its own archives and methods attentive to African histories and, more crucially, to the lives and bodies it seeks to make more possible" (Macharia 2015: 140).

Field Formations: Queer + African Studies

Until recently, many African studies scholars have avoided theoretical developments in queer studies. Similarly, lesbian, gay, and queer studies practitioners have largely overlooked gender and sexual diversity in African societies, with the exception of scholars who engage in "cherry-picking obscure references" to bolster arguments about the ubiquity of queerness (Epprecht 2008: 15). Notable exceptions include scholars such as Neville Hoad (2007) and Dagmawi Woubshet (2010), who privilege African perspectives in their work, modeling how queer African subjects can enliven US queer studies. Although the relationship between queer studies and African studies has been ambivalent since the emergence of queer studies as a "field" in the early 1990s, there has been affection and exchange between these camps at times, punctuated by periods of withdrawal and suspicion (Dynes 1983; Kendall 1999; Murray and Roscoe 1998; Pincheon 2000). Despite such scholarly wariness, circumspection toward conventional methods—"arrangement, hierarchy, taxonomy, and erasure"—functions "as a shared feature of queer studies, African studies, and postcolonial studies" (Macharia 2014). Consensus about interrogating prevailing methodological traditions indicates ways forward in a proposed conjoining of queer studies and African studies. Persistent questioning requires scholars to pay attention to how "we *go about* finding out about sexuality"—and area—"rather than deciding what our object of inquiry is in advance, or expecting it spontaneously to reveal itself" (Hemmings 2007: 27).

The tentative exchange between queer studies and African studies becomes apparent in historic moments of scholarly transaction. In the US academy, queer scholars launched Gays and Lesbians in African Studies (GLAS) in the African Studies Association (ASA) in 1995, the same year in which the first queer studies symposium, "Queers in Africa: A White Man's Disease," took place on "African soil" in South Africa (Reddy 2000: 163). In 1996 the ASA recognized GLAS as an "ASA-sponsored organization," although, as Deborah Amory (1997b: 5, 6) observes, other disciplinary associations in the United States had had LGBT or queer caucuses for more than twenty years. At the time, "GLAS, like other lesbian and gay professional caucuses, [was] overwhelmingly white, with many more men than women as members" (ibid.: 8). Whiteness and white supremacy haunt both African studies and queer studies.[4] Reminiscing about her entry into African studies in the 1980s, Amory (1997a: 102) notes a "racial division of labor between African studies and Afro-American studies. Put in the crudest terms, white people did African studies, while black people did Afro-Am." Amory's depiction reflects the influence of African national liberation movements and US civil rights organizing on a reimagined field of African studies in which African and Africanist scholars sought to reconfigure the intellectual division of labor.[5] The diagnosis of the white-dominated disciplinary formulation of African studies illustrates the territorial specificity of articulations of race, gender, sexuality, and area, which some scholars erroneously treat as interchangeable analogies.

The US system of racialization and racism produced an African studies confined to the "continent of Africa," whereas Africana and black studies metamorphosed into a "more symbolic field of diaspora and transnational processes and longings" (Amory 1997a: 111). Divisions between African and Africanist scholars over the ascendancy of an Afro-pessimist paradigm gripped US African studies in the 1990s, to which some scholars responded with studies that emphasize ingenuity and agency in African social practices, charting a new Afro-optimism that African scholars can deploy (Chabal 2008: 603).[6] Yet regional, linguistic, and disciplinary divisions in African studies keep scholars from speaking directly to one another, resulting in competing versions of "Africa," "Africans," and "Africanness." Recall the "plethora of Africas available" to the world in 1968, a year of global social and political revolution: "Africa proud mother of dozens of glittering civilizations, Africa the victim of colonialism, Africa origin of 'Western' civilization, Africa center of revolution, Africa emergent" (Pierce 2009: 133–34). The revolutionary potential of African politics, which Kwaku Larbi Korang (2006: 463) posits as "Africa-for-itself," falls away in dominant narratives formulated about "Africa-for-the-world."

Just as white scholars have occupied esteemed positions in an African studies canon, white scholars have determined the direction of queer studies. As Phillip Brian Harper (2005: 110) argues, the content of queer studies is "unacceptably Euro-American in orientation," influenced partly by queer studies' contested installation in the US academy. US-based academics have diagnosed the inadequacies of queer studies, specifically to account for the co-constructedness of race, gender, sexuality, and class, resulting in queer of color critiques. Queer of color critics, anthropologists, and feminists of color engage with the global south by working at the crossroads of race, gender, sexuality, and nationalism and by challenging the narrow parameters of Western-based identity politics (Arondekar 2005; Boellstorff 2007; Hong and Ferguson 2011).

However, African perspectives remain largely excluded from queer of color critiques and black queer studies.[7] This exclusion points out the problematic geopolitical orientation of queer of color critiques, which, despite their efforts to counteract provincial "conflations of race and sex" and to criticize "the epistemic violence of such analogical gestures," remain tethered to their academic origins (Arondekar 2005: 245). The interdisciplinary theorization of intersectionality undertaken by such critiques not only has remained largely embedded in certain cultural norms but has even, at times, resolidified "other"—that is, "ethnic" and "queer"—identities as necessarily "intersectional" in contrast to white, heterosexual identities assumed to be central and homogeneous. While positing the United States as the primary matrix for the deployment of intersectional analysis, such critiques also privilege a "gridlike model" that fails to account for the unstable and shifting dynamics of identity formation (Grosz 1994: 19; see also Puar 2011). Our diagnosis of exclusion is not premised on a call for analogical inclusion, whereby scholars make overtures to different geopolitical areas, overtures that can resemble neocolonial annexation. It is not enough to make space to add African examples in black queer studies or queer of color critiques, just as it is insufficient to suppose that adding South Asian or Middle Eastern examples will enrich such critiques. Such additions to critical queer/sexuality studies suggest that all areas in the global south are transposable, equivalent, and commensurable, a misleading notion (Arondekar 2005).

Documenting and contesting how "Africa" circulates in sociopolitical imaginaries constitute important key contributions by scholars, such as Hoad, working at the intersection of queer studies and African studies. Describing how his book *African Intimacies* "investigates the place of an entity that comes to be called 'homosexuality' in the production (discursive, material, imaginary) of a place called 'Africa,'" Hoad (2007: xvi) argues that "'homosexuality' is one of the many imaginary contents, fantasies, or significations . . . that circulate in the production of African sovereignties and identities in their representation by Africans and others." The "Africas" invoked in episodes of local homophobia diverge in the service of specific elite interests. In the 1990s and early 2000s, leaders of the South West African People's Organisation (SWAPO), the ruling party in Namibia, claimed that homosexuality did not exist before independence and was therefore "un-African." SWAPO leaders charged that queer Namibians' invisibility before independence disqualified them from demanding equality after independence, implying that queer Namibians did not contribute to national liberation (Currier 2012a). This view of the "un-Africanness" of homosexuality differed from recent claims in Liberia, where the Liberian Council of Churches interpreted the 2014 Ebola virus outbreak as evidence that "God is angry with Liberia" and that "Liberians have to pray and seek God's forgiveness [for] . . . corruption and immoral acts (such as homosexualism, etc.)" (*Daily Observer* 2014). The "Africanness" in this example evokes desperation, as religious leaders search for ways to remain relevant politically in efforts to eradicate Ebola.

Although the geopolitical "center" of our analysis is the African continent, especially to resist dilution of local LGBTI activism in the virtual global world of traveling queerness or, in its extreme, queer armchair tourism, Africa can also be productively understood as "people" within the diasporic perspectives of writers, artists, and critics (Achebe 2009). Problematizing the dichotomous relation of Africa's status as the "real" to the symbolic field of African diaspora as its "simulacrum" allows us to imagine new forms of African/queer transnational agency that not only eschew the problematic divide between the continent and the diaspora(s) but also subvert narrowly Afrocentric politics of homophobia deployed in various parts of the African continent. In our analysis, "Africa" breaks away from any fantasized spatiotemporal unity or stability and, following Achille Mbembe's (2001: 242) description of the "postcolony," is instead "a period of embedding, a space of proliferation" that escapes historical and geopolitical confinement.

If "Africa" and "queerness" are largely manufactured or "invented" to both provoke and satisfy Western normative fantasies, then African queerness can be similarly described as an orientalist construction in which "other" bodies become imagined and simultaneously erased as that obscure object of (Western) desire. By drawing attention to how Eurocentric modes of representation exclude and confine "others" to the exotic margins of representation, the queer African body also displays the biopolitical violence of dominant inscriptions intent on disciplining and punishing both its racial and its sexual existence. Some Western academics, activists, and diplomats characterize antigay threats and legislation as making different African nations inhospitable to queer life (DeJong and Long 2014; Spivey and Robinson 2010). Intended to defend African gender and sexual minorities from harm, such characterizations, as Marc Epprecht (2008: 16) argues, can actually put queer Africans at risk, as local elites blame them for bringing negative attention to the government, igniting a cycle of antiqueer mobilization. The emergence of well-resourced, African LGBTI activist organizations also raises questions about activist organizations' role in producing new categories of vulnerable people, who become potential targets of Western intervention, leaving behind queers unassimilable as LGBTI constituents (Currier 2012b; Thomann 2014). This situation can engender the potential depoliticization and co-optation of LGBTI movements by foreign donors.

Retracing Linkages between African Studies and Queer Studies

In light of problematic representations of "African homophobia" and sexualities, queer investigations have a place in African studies (Biruk 2014). Nonetheless, persisting, trenchant critiques of queer studies' ethnocentric arrogance point to a gulf between African studies and queer studies (Epprecht 2004). Scholars claim that queer studies' elitist register excludes African and Africanist researchers and activists (Clarke 2013). Although queer studies perspectives might not resonate with all African studies scholars, historians and ethnographers have documented Africans' same-sex sexual practices before, during, and after colonialism, research that discredits the notion that homosexuality is un-African (Epprecht 2004, 2008). In other words, and as Michel Foucault (1978) makes clear in his *History of Sexu-*

ality, contemporary normative categories, including sexual categories, have been historically constituted by the knowledge/power dyad. As Foucault points out, in premodern Europe, people's sexual acts did not automatically entail specific categorizations. Foucault's (1978: 10) "repressive hypothesis" can therefore be seen as applicable to modern African contexts as well.

In addition to scholars' substantive opposition to queer studies, adopting queer studies perspectives would likely result in negative consequences for daring scholars in the African academy. Amina Mama (1996: 39), a prominent African feminist theorist, affirms this point when querying the absence of studies about sexuality in African women's and gender studies. "Modern African societies, while displaying great diversity of sexual politics, seem to me to be more often repressed than liberated: homophobia is rampant, lesbianism hardly enters public discussion." Given the opprobrium toward homosexuality in some African nations, many scholars, with the exception of some in South Africa, have shied away from studying gender and sexual diversity because doing so would not be a "wise career move" (Epprecht 2013: 44).

Conversely, a growing number of African and Africanist activists and scholars embrace queer perspectives in their work (Ekine and Abbas 2013: 3–4; Gunkel 2010; Hoad 2007; Massaquoi 2008). Defending his use of the term *queer* in his research on "black queer visibilities" in South Africa, Xavier Livermon (2012: 298, 316) describes "queer" as an "analytic" optic through which to understand how black gender and sexually variant persons rework national, racial, gender, and sexual identities in urban South Africa. Acknowledging criticisms that queer theory is tainted by "academic neoimperialism," Brenna Munro (2012: xix) embraces queer studies in diagnosing and explicating national, racial, and sexual inequalities in her research on literary and cultural representations of gender and sexual variance in South Africa. Stella Nyanzi, a Ugandan medical anthropologist, uses *queer* as a label in her work without question. She cites the presence of accepted and celebrated "queerness," understood here as gender and sexual dissidence in indigenous cultural practices. Nyanzi (2014: 66) writes, "Queer Africa must reclaim . . . African modes of blending, bending, and breaking gender boundaries." "Queer" Africans challenge geographic, gender, sexual, lexical, and visual boundaries, as evidenced in the experiences of *'yan daudu*, Hausa men living in northern Nigeria who sexually desire other men, and in images from Zanele Muholi, a black South African lesbian activist, whose militant photography portrays queer Africans' desires and lives on the social margins (Baderoon 2011; Gaudio 2009).

On the African continent, queer African studies is focused in South Africa partly because queer politics has long infused the domestic political agenda. Led by the African National Congress (ANC), the postapartheid government's support for the sexual-orientation nondiscrimination clause in the 1994 constitution coincided with the expansion of queer studies in North America. LGBTI South Africans from different racial backgrounds involved with antiapartheid organizing lobbied ANC leaders in exile and in South Africa to back gay rights (Cock 2003). Geopolitical anxieties have surfaced in continental African LGBTI organizing, particularly in reaction to South Africa's "dominance" in a supranational imaginary that rewards pro-LGBTI rights stances (Currier 2012b: 150). Some African LGBTI activists actively seek to differentiate national gender and sexual diversity mobilization from strategies used by South African activists. Rejecting South African marriage-equality organizing, Lourence Misedah, a Kenyan LGBTI activist, stated, "We want Kenyans to see things in our context and know that we are Kenyans and not South Africans . . . then [Kenyans] will not see gay and lesbian rights as an imported thing" (Judge, Manion, and de Waal 2008: 306). Despite objections raised in pan-African LGBTI organizing, South Africa represents a liberated nation for African gender and sexual dissidents, including LGBTI refugees, a portrayal in tension with that of nations like Uganda, which the British Broadcasting Corporation (2011) depicted as "the world's worst place to be gay" in a documentary.

These examples of queer studies in the African academy and African/ist forays into queer studies rely on the operationalization of queerness as anchored in gender and sexual diversity. This operationalization suggests that queer and African studies have more in common than previously acknowledged, particularly in the twin provinces of agency and representation. As scholars have struggled over the definition of an authentic subject for African studies, queer studies approaches the possibility of a "queer subject" with unease (Butler 1993; Green 2002; Schramm 2008). Such slippery subjectivity and lack of a paradigmatic referent are important commonalities bridging African studies and queer studies. The unwieldy melding of these two turbulent field formations has engendered a salutary questioning of marginality, methodology, identity, subjectivity, and representation, queries that drive the antifoundationalist impulses of queer African studies.

African Queer Subjects: Crises in/of Representation

The critical conflation of these two disciplinary formations borne out of a radical skepticism toward Western taxonomies calls into question the political viability (and innocence) of antihegemonic and antiheteronormative discourses. Indeed, the margin and its own alleged commitment to giving voice to "others" has become the object of close scrutiny from scholars who, inspired by Gayatri Spivak's work, point out the academic tendency to co-opt, appropriate, and generate "margins" to bolster canonical fields of studies. Although African queer studies may allow for a productive stretching of institutional margins and boundaries, the subjects of difference, or subjects-as-difference, that queer African studies purports to represent run the risk of being further obscured by an endless game of differential representations that ultimately reinstate the supposed centrality of the white, Western, heterosexual self/body. Drawing from Rey Chow's (2002: 7) critique of poststructuralist attempts via liberal multiculturalism to undo the center by multiplying differences, margins, and intersections, Jasbir Puar (2007: 206) notes that "no matter how intersectional our models of subjectivity, no matter how attuned to locational politics of space, place, and scale, these formulations may still limit us if they presume the automatic primacy and singularity of the disciplinary subject and its identitarian interpellation."

Over the last decade, queer African studies has highlighted the importance of resisting "identitarian interpellation" (Puar 2007: 206). Although examples of alternative gender and sexual configurations in African cultures, otherwise traditionally viewed as bastions of sexual conservatism, have been used to bolster sweeping arguments about the global variety of sexual practices, such as the "cherry-picking obscure references" invoked by Epprecht (2008: 15), examples of "boy-wives" and woman-woman marriages illustrate the "potential to conceptualize sexual practices, intimacy, and sociality beyond the rubric of identity politics" (Gunkel 2013: 76) while pointing "to possibilities for alliances, sociality, and kinship, also within queer communities" (Murray and Roscoe 1998). African feminist scholars have "mapped the changing meanings of sex, gender, and embodiment during colonial modernity," and although their writing does not directly invoke "queer" formations, it "tracks how bodies gain and lose meaning over time, how sex and sexuality become attached to bodies as they move through space, how power circulates and shifts as it genders and ungenders" (Macharia 2015: 144).

If African studies as area studies problematizes the geopolitical place of African subjects whose national and ethnic identities are caught up in a messy network of global politics, then queer African studies further questions the location of queer African subjects who live and strategize in liminal spaces at the moving junction of visibility and invisibility. Following Chow's (2010) analysis of "visibility" via Foucault (1978) and Gilles Deleuze (1988), as a highly theoretical rather than empirical issue, queer African studies challenges both African studies' claim for clear continental mapping and queer studies' attempt to shed light on marginal subjects by articulating, albeit partially and imperfectly, the conditions of (im)possibility of their representation. Queer African studies can therefore be seen as the space in which the contours of cultural and sexual identities become questioned and blurred—a space that may allow for the forging of new forms of alliance, sociality, and kinship but also transcends limited assumptions about location, belonging, and identity. Along with Spivak's (1994: 70) warning about the dangers posed by an uncritical conflation between *Darstellung* ("'re-presentation' as in art, or philosophy") and *Vertretung* ("representation as 'speaking for,' as in politics"), the challenge here lies in representing queer African subjects without subjecting them to the panoptic control of an ethnocentric gaze.

Macharia (2014) challenges the potentially crippling gridlock of queer African studies by pointing out the brutal and costly risk of dissolution, disintegration, or erasure experienced by queer African subjects:

> How does one encounter oneself as both inhabitant and object of an archive, as the product/er of accident, coincidence, forgetting, recovery, erasure, reconstruction, and illegibility, the "dust" we term archive? And might it be useful to term this "encounter" a half-method, a satisfying trick that only partially assuages desire? A more honest, if less palatable, assessment might be that all methods are partial, Frankenstein assemblages held together by sweat and desire.

While being put under erasure, queer African subjects require new modes of reading and interpretation. As "a complex record of queer activity," notes Ann Cvetkovich (2003: 169–70), the archive requires "users, interpreters, and cultural historians to . . . piece together the jigsaw puzzle of queer history in the making." As Macharia (2014) suggests, queer African bodies can also been seen as productively subversive in their ever-shifting, haunting, and fragmentary (in)visibility, and this is precisely what archivization should attempt to document. Although the "archival turns" to "geopolitics in sexual studies," as Anjali Arondekar (2009: 12) argues, have led scholars to foreground "the analytical limits of the archive," "they continue to privilege the reading practices of recovery over all others." Alongside Arondekar's (ibid.: 21) archival work on sexuality in colonial India, we argue that similar archival work on same-sex sexuality in Africa "requires a theory of reading that moves away from the notion that discovering an object will somehow lead to a formulation of subjectivity—from the presumption that if one finds a body, one can recover a person." Macharia (2014) mentions the exhibition "Critically Queer" during the first day of a symposium at which he was supposed to discuss the *Queer African Reader* edited by Sokani Ekine and Hakima Abbas and which, he notes, derailed his speaking plans by exhibiting the "missing," "obscured," "exiled," and "impossible" subjects typically erased by "the fantasy of the known and knowable queer lining up to be counted and documented in a thousand NGO reports." He points out both the moving and painful challenge and the pleasure fostered by such queer visual representations—the residual by-products of discourses that fail to take them into account. The precariousness of such fleeting representations, however, precipitates the disintegration of abusive taxonomies. Rather than a "fabulous stranger" met on vacation, notes Macharia (2014), "queer" is "the smelly stranger you move away from in a shared bus," "whose presence disorganizes how we know, how we organize space" and who ultimately "undoes the fantasy of an infinitely elastic 'we.'"

In light of such complex or even murky representational challenges, queer African activists have been displaying incredible agility and resorting to inventiveness and creativity, to a kind of political bricolage that draws from new forms of technological productions and artifacts—the "instant archives" created by websites, social media, blogs, and YouTube videos—as well as from more traditional strategies of mobilization and intervention. Such political agility is attuned both to global networks of communication and to the local interstices and ellipses of everyday lives and realities, to the infinite variety and differences of a globalizing African continent that has been historically engaged in complex trans-Saharan, transatlantic, and transoceanic networks of communication and exchange, and whose multiple regional, cultural, and linguistic variations resist the missionary thrust of systematic discourses. In the 1998 documentary *Woubi Chéri* filmed in Côte d'Ivoire, Tatiana, a male-to-female *travesti*, says, "Without the right to be different, Africa is going nowhere." Barbara, another male-to-female *travesti*, also declares, "You have to be creative, live life like an artist. You can't always be down-to-earth. Tradition is fine, but you have to be in-between. I think that's what the third millennium will be all about . . . a mix of modern and traditional, different ways of life and sex."

Although queer theory can be described as a "traveling" or "nomadic" theory that benefits, in both its conceptualization and its lived experience, from its multiple variations and reformulations through time and space, the global hypervisibility allowed by new media representations must be questioned and closely scrutinized.[8] While fostering transnational networks of communication that escape regional or continental limitations, the discursive and visual instantaneity provided by these new media can also verge on a problematic form of uncritical showiness or spectacularity that, in turn, risks fostering further essentializing misrepresentations, both locally and globally. Such transnational networks might give the dangerously illusory impression that geopolitical locations have dissolved into a global space where the specific realities of social, cultural, and sexual locations have become irrelevant. Analyzing the increase over the last two decades of "online petitions and campaigns emerging from Europe and North America against homophobia in various African countries," Henriette Gunkel (2013: 77–78) aptly raises ethical concerns about this new, Western-based form of "global" online LGBTI solidarity, which also leads to "the hypervisibility of African queer bodies in online forums on hate crime" and produces armchair political tourism.[9] Alongside the hypertheorization of African queer bodies, the issues borne out of such virtual forms of representation and mobilization might also contribute to an abstraction of these bodies and their subjects, who become once again the focus of an objectifying and voyeuristic Western gaze, albeit allegedly benevolent and well-meaning. Moreover, the development of such global cybercollectivities can contribute to the underrating, underfunding, and disempowerment of local organizations whose much-needed engagement on the ground becomes obscured, flattened, or even deemed irrelevant on the global scale. African LGBTI activists use rights discourses innovatively, which upholds the observation that leading African studies scholars, such as Frederick Cooper (2012) and Mahmood Mamdani (2009), have made about how different forms of rights claims and justice can succeed in African nations.

At the confluence of two highly self-conscious theoretical areas, queer African studies therefore needs not only to call into question each field's respective limitations in a productively critical fashion but also, and against such hypertheorization, to pay attention to the complexity of queer African subjectivities and corporealities. While bodies, in a Foucauldian perspective, serve as historical surfaces on which the violence of politics gets inscribed, their materiality should not be seen as disposable or theoretically recuperable. Queer African studies needs to account for the shifting agility of resistant bodies, for their experience of intimacy and pleasure (dating, partying, romance, and fantasy) as well as for their strategic ways to fight pain and suffering (homophobia, discrimination, abuse, taunting, threats, and torture), which stems partly from African nations' economic marginalization.[10] In other words, queer African studies calls attention to the ethical weight of theory and, by bringing together African studies and queer studies, to the need for concrete intervention. Because it is positioned at the loaded intersection of area, race, and sexuality, of postcolonialism and queer theory, queer African studies, in all its complex theoretical ramifications, also and paradoxically points out the limits or liminality of theory and the need for discursive re-embodiment or, in Puar's (2005: 131) terms, for a renewed emphasis on "affective queerness" and corporealities. Our treatment of "corporeality" resists the fetishization of the African body that subtended European colonization and its phantasmic imprints on African sexualities. Instead, it describes dynamic sites of affective transaction between discourses and their material impact to account for the moving trajectories of bodies caught between material locations and theoretical dislocations, objective experiences and subjective representations. The unruliness of queer African bodies, shaped by sociocultural and political conditions as well as by others' fantasies and desires, ruptures the logic of academic discourses and thus illustrates Judith Halberstam's (2005: 5) contention that "the notion of a body-centered identity" can give way to "a model that locates sexual subjectivities within and between embodiment, place, and practice."

One way that queer African studies scholars have called for more dynamic transactions between theory and practice and for discursive creativity, nuances, and productive ambiguity is by turning to the political dimension and self-reflexive resourcefulness of aesthetics, which has been harnessed in the service of political interpretation. Focusing on two South African writers, Hoad (2007: 105) remarks that "pan-African aesthetic production" can be an "intellectual resource in the fight against both AIDS and racism." More generally, there has been an "aesthetic turn" in postcolonial studies over the last ten years that has fueled new productive directions in postcolonial studies (Su 2011: 65). Spivak (2003: 4–5) expresses her belief that "the politics of the production of knowledge in area studies (and also anthropology and the other 'human sciences') can be touched by a new Comparative Literature, whose hallmark remains a care for language and idiom." As Mbembe (2011: 117) further remarks, an "authentic human encounter" "must begin through reciprocal disorientation. This vital disorientation, in turn, requires the elaboration of forms of thought that are at once profoundly historical and philosophical, sociological, hermeneutical, and ethical—memory and antimemory, militant and antimilitant, political and antipolitical, and poetic." By destabilizing discursive categories, these resistant "forms of thought" can, in turn, generate a creative "vortex," "a turbulence that creates distance between different pedagogical territories" (Rosello 2003: 125).

Aesthetic models that creatively contextualize differences instead of distancing them are also able to bring us closer to bodies that, while being different and preoccupied with their specific challenges, experience pain, pleasure, and desires in very concrete ways. For instance, various critics have pointed out Chimamanda Ngozi Adichie's emphasis on her characters' sexuality by noting that the sexual content and references enhance her characters' concrete humanity, in both their suffering and their pleasure (Eromosele 2013: 104). Commenting on

Adichie's *Half of a Yellow Sun* (2006) and Aminatta Forna's *The Memory of Love* (2010), Zoe Norridge (2012: 30) remarks that in these novels "sex functions as the nexus through which the body is made present, a body that is then wounded, a physicality that is then used to explore painful experiences precisely because we are already conscious of the body as sensation." For Norridge (2012: 35, 36), such an "embodied form of reading," in turn, allows us to access "other complex systems of meaning" at both intimate and conceptual levels. Such "complex systems of meaning" can generate new analytic approaches to queer African subjects. In Macharia's (2015: 144) terms, they may allow us not only to probe how "gendered and sexed and sexualised bodies become invested with political significance" but also to reinstate "the very figure whose enfleshment matters" and who, too often, "has disappeared into a mass of acronyms and percentages." Aesthetic representations of queer Africans, whether in literature, art, or other visual representations, offer a productive alternative to "a mode of documentation that privileges the accumulation of injured and dead bodies over creating conditions of livability" (Macharia 2015: 145).

Emphasizing the link between sexuality and humanity suggests that queer African studies need not resort to the endless, and often paralyzing, self-referentiality of academic theories but can also draw from a wider philosophical discourse or reflection on alterity that, while being attuned to difference, does not deny the humanity of queer Africans engaged in the search for safety, love, and success all over the world. For Mbembe, "African identity does not exist as a substance. It is constituted, in varying forms, through a series of practices, notably *practices of the self*." The forms and idioms of African identity, Mbembe (2002: 272–73) asserts, are "mobile, reversible, and unstable. Given this element of play, they cannot be reduced to a purely biological order based on blood, race, or geography. . . . Only the disparate, and often intersecting, practices through which Africans *stylize* their conduct and life can account for the thickness of which the African present is made." As Jacques Derrida (1998: 26–27) reminds us, asserting the otherness of the same is not tantamount to celebrating multiplicity and differences but, rather, to questioning the homogeneity of the self by showing it as being intimately divided or "folded."[11] This does not mean that all differences are collapsed within one undifferentiated category; on the contrary, it is in this "fold" of difference within homogeneity that, according to Derrida (ibid.: 27), a delicate articulation between the particular story and the universal history—"this articulation between transcendental or ontological universality, and the exemplary or testimonial singularity of *martyred* existence," can happen. Human rights thus cannot rely on abstract notions of humanity or universalism but, rather, must be firmly rooted in a critical acknowledgment of both the tense and necessary relationship between democracy and difference(s). It is therefore also such a critical consciousness of both (the limitations of) global discourses and the material resistance of cultural differences that should inform queer African studies' own ethical engagement with human rights on the African continent and elsewhere, as it pertains to queer Africans' own "folded" conditions of existence or more generally, to use Mbembe's (2001: 15) terms, to "the African subject . . . focusing on him/herself, withdrawing, in the act and context of *displacement* and *entanglement.*"

Conclusion: Toward Queer African Reassemblages

The question remains about what practical and theoretical "models" are best suited to queer African studies, to their need for mobile, strategic intervention and their commitment to representing Africa, not as an ahistorical Western utopia, but as a dystopic space engaged in multiple continental and global changes. Queer African studies forces us to (re)invent theories attuned to concrete bodily realities, yet complex enough to account for the subtle subject positions of queer African subjects whose erasure, as we have shown, is particularly painful and costly. Simultaneously, these discursive models must reflect global representations, discourses, the mobility of capital, and the local realities and specificities of lived gender and sexual diversity that remain linked to economic hardship. Such (re)localization of African studies in general, and queer African studies in particular, is rendered even more important by the problematic national boundaries of African countries.

　　Queer African studies ought to re-form into renewed creative directions that draw from and go beyond intersectional perspectives. In particular, dynamic forms of intersectionality ("assemblages"), not only between African studies and queer studies but also between black queer studies and queer of color critiques, which have not adequately addressed the contributions of queer African studies, can be created to break away from the inevitable, crippling, and disempowering limits of representation and to account for the rhizomatic complexity of African genders and sexualities. Drawing from Deleuze and Félix Guattari's (1987) theory of assemblage, Puar (2005: 122), in particular, has challenged "queer theorizing that, despite (and perhaps because of) a commitment to an intersectional analytic, fails to interrogate the epistemological will to knowledge that invariably reproduces the disciplinary interests of the U.S. nation-state." Displacing queerness-as-identity and the both stabilizing and disciplinary effects of intersectionality itself, assemblages "allow us to attune to intensities, emotions, energies, affectivities, textures as they inhabit events, spatiality, and corporealities" (ibid.: 128). How-ever, Puar notes, it is important to recognize that assemblages, as futuristic as they might be, "allow for complicities of privilege and the production of new normativi-ties even as they cannot anticipate spaces and moments of resistance" (ibid.: 137). Such "Frankenstein assemblages," as Macharia (2014) terms them, "held together by sweat and desire," might after all be "a half-method, a satisfying trick that only partially assuages desire."

Even in African diasporic settings, there is no guarantee that gender and sexual dissidence—in its lived variety and in organized resistance to antiqueer impulses—is received as such. For instance, African art that represents gender heteroglossia and sexual dissidence can be interpreted as an unchanging "Afri-can" otherness, such that African queerness becomes immobilized as racialized alterity that never becomes part of African-descendant experiences. Reading the photography of Kiluanji Kia Henda, from Angola, Rachel Nelson (2013: 39, 40) uses the example of the 2008 photograph *Poderosa de Bom Jesus*, which features a "locally famous self-identified transvestite" wearing the garb associated with "Mumuila women in southwestern Angola," in a rural setting. When Kia Henda included the image in a show in Luanda, he wanted spectators to grapple with the combination of African cultural signifiers with elements of gender nonnormativ-ity, a factor associated with Western interference (Nelson 2013: 40). Kia Henda wanted the image to unsettle what viewers assumed to be "stable" signifiers of "African" identity. As part of an art show in São Paulo, Brazil, Kia Henda report-edly had to include information that the subject was a "transvestite" (Nelson 2013: 40). Brazilian viewers engaged with the photograph as another rendering of Afri-can authenticity represented by a female-bodied person. Yet Kia Henda was sur-prised to discover that when an Afro-Brazilian artist "reproduced the photograph as a painting," he meant the painting to serve as a celebration of stable African culture, instead of experimenting with the constructedness of African culture (Nelson 2013: 40). In this example, an image of African queerness intended by the African artist to upset binaries of African authenticity and Western artifice settles into a depiction of an immovable Africanness.

As illustrated by numerous writers, artists, and critics engaged in imagin-ing renewed *"practices of the* (queer African) *self"* (Mbembe 2002: 269), queer African agency and subjectivities can illustrate Chela Sandoval's (1991: 11–13) notion of "oppositional consciousness" or José Esteban Muñoz's (1999: 25) strat-egy of "disidentification." In turn, queer African studies can draw inspiration from the various "re-mappings" of Africa explored by Jean Comaroff and John Comaroff (2012), Charles Piot (2010), Frances Bodomo in the short film *Afronauts* (2014), and Octavia Butler (2000) in her Afro-futurist writings or, more generally, from Judith Halberstam's (2011) alternative bricolages in *The Queer Art of Failure*. In the Afro-optimism captured in some scholarly treatments of African economic, political, and social developments, theorists suggest viewing the recent economic recession gripping northern countries as an opportunity for African policymakers and thought leaders to "restructure their economies [and cultural imaginaries] away from the prying restraints of hegemonic powers preoccupied with their own recovery" (Zeleza 2009: 169). As queer studies and African studies engage in renewed transnational and cross-disciplinary transactions, the most productive parts of this encounter might lie in the moments and points of friction, dissonance, tension, and disarticulation between these two field formations, in these temporal and spatial instances of destabilization that render their *agencement* both fragile and temporary. It might be precisely in this brittle temporality, or rather in the folds of multiple entangled temporalities, that these field formations have the best chance of resisting "the repetitions of colonial epistemes" that are bound to "rework" themselves into even the most unruly and dissident discourses (Arondekar 2005: 250).

Notes

We thank Anjali Arondekar, Geeta Patel, *GLQ* anonymous reviewers, and faculty and graduate students in the University of Cincinnati's Department of Women's, Gender, and Sexuality Studies for their insightful comments and suggestions on this essay.

1. Although we focus on the emergence of "African studies" in US academia, our findings can be applied to European academia insofar as comparable geopolitical interests govern the treatment of "African studies" specifically in Britain and France. While postcolonial studies has flourished in the Anglo-American context, postcolonial studies has had a more limited impact in France where the field tends to be perceived, according to Pascal Blanchard (2010: 136), "as holding a strong ability to destabilize 'national unity' and the social body, thereby explaining the great difficulty today to work both on the effects of colonization in France and on postcolonial heritages."

2. Drawing from Michel Serres's (1991) *Le Tiers-instruit*, Mireille Rosello (2003: 124) notes that the attempt "to formulate a theoretical and historical model of 'Francophone studies' . . . always ends up in what Michel Serres calls the 'third' space, the middle of the river, the vortex that any migrant discovers after leaving the native land and before reaching the shore. The idea of 'Francophone studies' is not the name of a new border but a turbulence that creates distance between different pedagogical territories."

3. As Spivak (1993: ix) puts it, "As the margin or 'outside' enters an institution or teach-

ing machine, what *kind* of teaching machine it enters will determine its contours. Therefore the struggle continues, in different ways, after the infiltration."

4. Alternative genealogies of African studies and queer studies challenge each field's inadequacies, but still expose blind spots in the field formation of each. For instance, while examining W. E. B. DuBois's contribution to conceptualizing the African diaspora, Paul Gilroy (1993: 113) elucidates how limiting DuBois's visualization of "Africa" was. In his writings, "Africa emerged . . . as a mythic counterpart to modernity in the Americas—a moral symbol transmitted by exquisite objects seen fleetingly in the African collection at Fisk University but largely disappearing from DuBois's account, leaving an empty, aching space between his local and global manifestations of racial injustice."

5. For instance, African scholars dominate the vibrant field of African philosophy, motivated in large part to counter scientific racism and the deleterious effects of European colonialism on African societies (Eze 1998; Nzegwu 2006).

6. By *Africanist*, we mean scholars who are not African born but who specialize in African studies.

7. An exception is Delroy Constantine-Simms's (2000) edited volume, *The Greatest Taboo: Homosexuality in Black Communities.*

8. We borrow the notions of "traveling theory" and nomadic theory, respectively, from Edward Said (1983) and from Deleuze and Guattari's (1986) theory of nomadology.

9. We thank Anjali Arondekar and Geeta Patel for this phrasing.

10. Commenting on the historic and often violent *"embodiment* of the 'French race'"—"the intimate bodily practices which came to signify national and racial membership: the sexual acts of citizens and subjects, eugenically sound modes of heterosexual coupling, the affective labor of the domestic sphere, and a national narrative, formulated by reproduction, which envisioned France's past as well as its future"—Elisa Camiscioli (2009: 9) notes that "'embodiment' is also a useful analytical category because it is the antithesis of the *abstract individualism* upon which modern French political theory is based" (ibid.).

11. As Derrida (1983, 1998: 26–27) explains in *Dissemination* and reminds us in *Monolingualism*, "For it is in the form of a thinking of the unique, precisely, and not of the plural, as it was too often believed, that a thought of dissemination formerly introduced itself as a folding thought of the fold."

References

Achebe, Chinua. 2009. *The Education of a British-Protected Child: Essays.* New York: Knopf.

Adichie, Chimamanda Ngozi. 2006. *Half of a Yellow Sun.* New York: Knopf.

Afronauts. 2014. Directed by Frances Bodomo. www.afronautsfilm.com.

Amory, Deborah. 1997a. "African Studies as American Institution." In *Anthropological Locations: Boundaries and Grounds of a Field Science*, edited by Akhil Gupta and James Ferguson, 102–16. Berkeley: University of California Press.

———. 1997b. "'Homosexuality' in Africa: Issues and Debates." *Issue: A Journal of Opinion* 25, no. 1: 5–10.

Arondekar, Anjali. 2005. "Border/Line Sex: Queer Postcolonialities, or How Race Matters Outside the United States." *Interventions: The International Journal of Postcolonial Studies* 7, no. 2: 236–50.

———. 2009. *For the Record: On Sexuality and the Colonial Archive in India*. Durham, NC: Duke University Press.

Baderoon, Gabeba. 2011. "'Gender within Gender': Zanele Muholi's Images of Trans Being and Becoming." *Feminist Studies* 37, no. 2: 390–416.

Biruk, Crystal. 2014. "'Aid for Gays': The Moral and the Material in 'African Homophobia' in Post-2009 Malawi." *Journal of Modern African Studies* 52, no. 3: 447–73.

Blanchard, Pascal. 2010. "L'identité, l'historien et le passé colonial: Le trio impossible?" In *Je est un autre: Pour une identité-monde*, edited by Michel Le Bris and Jean Rouaud, with Nathalie Skowronek, 123–38. Paris: Gallimard.

Boellstorff, Tom. 2007. *A Coincidence of Desires: Anthropology, Queer Studies, Indonesia*. Durham, NC: Duke University Press.

British Broadcasting Corporation. 2011. "The World's Worst Place to Be Gay." www .youtube.com/watch?v=fV0tS6G8NNU.

Butler, Judith. 1993. "Critically Queer." *GLQ* 1, no. 1: 17–32.

Butler, Octavia E. 2000. *Lilith's Brood*. New York: Aspect/Warner Books.

Camiscioli, Elisa. 2009. *Reproducing the French Race: Immigration, Intimacy, and Embodiment in the Early Twentieth Century*. Durham, NC: Duke University Press.

Carter, Clare. 2013. "The Brutality of 'Corrective Rape.'" *New York Times*, June 27. www .nytimes.com/interactive/2013/07/26/opinion/26corrective-rape.html.

Chabal, Patrick. 2008. "On Reason and Afro-Pessimism." *Africa* 78, no. 4: 603–10.

Chow, Rey. 2002. *The Protestant Ethic and the Spirit of Capitalism*. New York: Columbia University Press.

———. 2010. "Postcolonial Visibilities: Questions Inspired by Deleuze's Method." In *Deleuze and the Postcolonial*, edited by Simone Bignall and Paul Patton, 62–77. Edinburgh: Edinburgh University Press.

Clarke, Douglas. 2013. "Twice Removed: African Invisibility in Western Queer Theory." In *Queer African Reader*, edited by Sokari Ekine and Hakima Abbas, 173–85. Dakar, Senegal: Pambazuka.

Cock, Jacklyn. 2003. "Engendering Gay and Lesbian Rights: The Equality Clause in the South African Constitution." *Women's Studies International Forum* 26, no. 1: 35–45.

Comaroff, Jean, and John L. Comaroff. 2012. *Theory from the South, or, How Euro-America Is Evolving toward Africa*. Boulder, CO: Paradigm.

Constantine-Simms, Delroy, ed. 2000. *The Greatest Taboo: Homosexuality in Black Communities*. Los Angeles: Alyson Books.

Cooper, Frederick. 2012. "Afterword: Social Rights and Human Rights in the Time of Decolonization." *Humanity: An International Journal of Human Rights, Humanitarianism, and Development* 3, no. 3: 473–92.

Corey-Boulet, Robbie. 2013. "Eric Ohena Lembembe, Gay Rights Activist, Tortured and Killed." *Huffington Post*, July 16. www.huffingtonpost.com/2013/07/16/eric-ohena -lembembe-killed-dead_n_3604460.html.

Currier, Ashley. 2012a. "The Aftermath of Decolonization: Gender and Sexual Dissidence in Postindependence Namibia." *Signs: Journal of Women in Culture and Society* 37, no. 2: 441–67.

———. 2012b. *Out in Africa: LGBT Organizing in Namibia and South Africa*. Minneapolis: University of Minnesota Press.

Cvetkovich, Ann. 2003. *An Archive of Feelings: Trauma, Sexuality, and Lesbian Public Cultures*. Durham, NC: Duke University Press.

Daily Observer. 2014. "'God Is Angry with Liberia.'" July 31. www.liberianobserver.com /news-religion/god-angry-liberia.

DeJong, Christina, and Eric Long. 2014. "The Death Penalty as Genocide: The Persecution of 'Homosexuals' in Uganda." In *Handbook of LGBT Communities, Crime, and Justice*, edited by Dana Peterson and Vanessa R. Panfil, 339–62. New York: Springer.

Deleuze, Gilles. 1988. *Foucault*. Translated and edited by Séan Hand. Minneapolis: University of Minnesota Press.

Deleuze, Gilles, and Félix Guattari. 1986. *Nomadology: The War Machine*. Translated by Brian Massumi. New York: Semiotext(e).

———. 1987. *A Thousand Plateaus: Capitalism and Schizophrenia*. Minneapolis: University of Minnesota Press.

Derrida, Jacques. 1983. *Dissemination*. Translated by Barbara Johnson. Chicago: University of Chicago Press.

———. 1998. *Monolingualism of the Other: or, The Prosthesis of Origin*. Translated by Patrick Mensah. Palo Alto, CA: Stanford University Press.

Dynes, Wayne. 1983. "Homosexuality in Sub-Saharan Africa: An Unnecessary Controversy." *Gay Books Bulletin* 9: 20–21.

Ekine, Sokari, and Hakima Abbas. 2013. Introduction. In *Queer African Reader*, edited by Sokari Ekine and Hakima Abbas, 1–8. Dakar, Senegal: Pambazuka.

Eng, David, Judith Halberstam, and José Esteban Muñoz. 2005. "What's Queer about Queer Studies Now?" *Social Text* 23, nos. 3–4: 1–17.

Epprecht, Marc. 2004. *Hungochani: The History of a Dissident Sexuality in Southern Africa*. Montreal: McGill-Queen's University Press.

———. 2008. *Heterosexual Africa? The History of an Idea from the Age of Exploration to the Age of AIDS*. Athens: Ohio University Press.

————. 2013. *Sexuality and Social Justice in Africa: Rethinking Homophobia and Forg-
    ing Resistance*. New York: Zed.

Eromosele, Ehijele Femi. 2013. "Sex and Sexuality in the Works of Chimamanda Ngozi
    Adichie." *Journal of Pan African Studies* 5, no. 9: 90–110.

Eze, Emmanuel Chukwudi, ed. 1998. *African Philosophy: An Anthology*. Malden, MA:
    Blackwell.

Feder, J. Lester. 2013. "Human Rights Campaign's Move into International Work Puts
    Global LGBT Advocates on Edge." *BuzzFeed*, November 5. www.buzzfeed.com
    /lesterfeder/human-rights-campaigns-move-into-international-work-puts
    -glo#1pt01xk.

Ferguson, Roderick A. 2004. *Aberrations in Black: Toward a Queer of Color Critique*.
    Minneapolis: University of Minnesota Press.

Forna, Aminatta. 2010. *The Memory of Love*. New York: Atlantic Monthly Press.

Foucault, Michel. 1978. *The History of Sexuality, Volume 1: An Introduction*. Translated
    by Robert Hurley. New York: Vintage.

Gaudio, Rudolf Pell. 2009. *Allah Made Us: Sexual Outlaws in an Islamic African City*.
    Malden, MA: Blackwell.

Gettleman, Jeffrey. 2011. "Remembering David Kato, a Gay Ugandan and a Marked
    Man." *New York Times*, January 30.

Gilroy, Paul. 1993. *The Black Atlantic: Modernity and Double Consciousness*. Cambridge,
    MA: Harvard University Press.

Green, Adam Isaiah. 2002. "Gay but Not Queer: Toward a Post-queer Study of Sexuality."
    Theory and Society 31, no. 4: 521–45.

Grewal, Inderpal, and Caren Kaplan. 2001. "Global Identities: Theorizing Transnational
    Studies of Sexuality." *GLQ* 7, no. 4: 663–79.

Grosz, Elizabeth. 1994. *Volatile Bodies: Toward a Corporeal Feminism*. Bloomington:
    Indiana University Press.

Gunkel, Henriette. 2010. *The Cultural Politics of Female Sexuality in South Africa*. New
    York: Routledge.

————. 2013. "Some Reflections on Postcolonial Homophobia, Local Interventions, and
    LGBTI Solidarity Online: The Politics of Global Petitions." *African Studies Review*
    56, no. 2: 67–81.

Halberstam, Judith. 1998. *Female Masculinity*. Durham, NC: Duke University Press.

————. 2005. *In a Queer Time and Place: Transgender Bodies, Subcultural Lives*. New
    York: New York University Press.

————. 2011. *The Queer Art of Failure*. Durham, NC: Duke University Press.

Harper, Philip Brian. 2005. "The Evidence of Felt Intuition: Minority Experience, Every-
    day Life, and Critical Speculative Knowledge." In *Black Queer Studies: A Critical
    Anthology*, edited by E. Patrick Johnson and Mae G. Henderson, 106–23. Durham,
    NC: Duke University Press.

Hemmings, Clare. 2007. "What's in a Name? Bisexuality, Transnational Sexuality Studies, and Western Colonial Legacies." *International Journal of Human Rights* 11, nos. 1–2: 13–32.

Hoad, Neville. 2007. *African Intimacies: Race, Homosexuality, and Globalization.* Minneapolis: University of Minnesota Press.

Hong, Grace Kyungwon, and Roderick A. Ferguson, eds. 2011. *Strange Affinities: The Gender and Sexual Politics of Comparative Racialization.* Durham, NC: Duke University Press.

Judge, Melanie, Anthony Manion, and Shaun de Waal. 2008. "'We First Need to Be Recognized': Activists Reflect on Same-Sex Marriage and LGBTI Rights in Africa." In *To Have and to Hold: The Making of Same-Sex Marriage in South Africa,* edited by Melanie Judge, Anthony Manion, and Shaun de Waal, 300–306. Johannesburg: Fanele.

Kendall, Kathryn Limakatso. 1999. "Women in Lesotho and the (Western) Construction of Homophobia." In *Female Desires: Same-Sex Relations and Transgender Practices across Cultures,* edited by Evelyn Blackwood and Saskia E. Wieringa, 157–78. New York: Columbia University Press.

Korang, Kwaku Larbi. 2006. "Useless Provocation or Meaningful Challenge? The 'Posts' versus African Studies." In *The Study of Africa, Volume 1: Disciplinary and Interdisciplinary Encounters,* edited by Paul Tiyambe Zeleza, 443–66. Dakar, Senegal: CODESRIA.

Livermon, Xavier. 2012. "Queer(y)ing Freedom: Black Queer Visibilities in Postapartheid South Africa." *GLQ* 18, nos. 2–3: 297–323.

Macharia, Keguro. 2014. "Archive and Method: Toward a Queer African Studies." *Gukira* 6. gukira.wordpress.com/2014/06/06/archive-method-toward-a-queer-african-studies/.

———. 2015. "Archive and Method in Queer African Studies." *Agenda* 22, no. 1: 140–46.

Mama, Amina. 1996. *Women's Studies and Studies of Women in Africa during the 1990s.* Dakar, Senegal: CODESRIA.

Mamdani, Mahmood. 2009. "Beware Human Rights Fundamentalism!" *Mail & Guardian,* March 20. mg.co.za/article/2009-03-20-beware-human-rights-fundamentalism.

Martin, Daniel. 2011. "Foreign Aid for Countries with Anti-gay Rights Records to Be Slashed, Pledges Cameron." *Daily Mail,* October 10. www.dailymail.co.uk/news/article-2047254/David-Cameron-Foreign-aid-cut-anti-gay-countries.html.

Martin, William G. 2011. "The Rise of African Studies (USA) and the Transnational Study of Africa." *African Studies Review* 54, no. 1: 59–83.

Massaquoi, Notisha. 2008. "The Continent as a Closet: The Making of an African Queer Theory." *Outliers* 1, no. 1: 50–60.

Mbembe, Achille. 2001. *On the Postcolony.* Berkeley: University of California Press.

———. 2002. "African Modes of Self-Writing." Translated by Steven Rendall. *Public Culture* 14, no. 1: 239–73.

———. 2011. "Provincializing France?" Translated by Janet Roitman. *Public Culture* 23, no. 1: 85–119.

Melber, Henning. 2005. "African Studies: Why, What for, and by Whom?" *Africa Spectrum* 40, no. 3: 369–76.

Mudimbe, V. Y. 1988. *The Invention of Africa: Gnosis, Philosophy, and the Order of Knowledge.* Bloomington: Indiana University Press.

Muñoz, José Esteban. 1999. *Disidentifications: Queers of Color and the Performance of Politics.* Minneapolis: University of Minnesota Press.

Munro, Brenna M. 2012. *South Africa and the Dream of Love to Come: Queer Sexuality and the Struggle for Freedom.* Minneapolis: University of Minnesota Press.

Murray, Stephen O., and Will Roscoe, eds. 1998. *Boy-Wives and Female Husbands: Studies of African Homosexualities.* New York: Palgrave Macmillan.

Nelson, Rachel. 2013. "(Mis)Seeing in/as Contemporary Art: Kiluanji Kia Henda and the AfroNauts." *Nka* 33: 38–45.

Norridge, Zoe. 2012. "Sex as Synecdoche: Intimate Languages of Violence in Chimamanda Ngozi Adichie's *Half of a Yellow Sun* and Aminatta Forna's *The Memory of Love.*" *Research in African Literatures* 43, no. 2: 18–39.

Nyanzi, Stella. 2014. "Queering Queer Africa." In *Reclaiming Afrikan: Queer Perspectives on Sexual and Gender Identities*, edited by Zethu Matebeni, 61–66. Athlone, South Africa: Modjaji Books.

Nyong'o, Tavia. 2012. "Queer Africa and the Fantasy of Virtual Participation." *Women's Studies Quarterly* 40, nos. 1–2: 40–63.

Nzegwu, Nkiru Uwechia. 2006. *Family Matters: Feminist Concepts in African Philosophy of Culture.* Albany: State University of New York Press.

Pierce, Steven. 2009. "Africa and 1968: Derepression, Libidinal Politics, and the Problem of Global Interpretation." In *Gender and Sexuality in 1968: Transformative Politics in the Cultural Imagination*, edited by Lessie Jo Frazier and Deborah Cohen, 131–44. New York: Palgrave Macmillan.

Pincheon, Bill Stanford. 2000. "An Ethnography of Silences: Race, (Homo)Sexualities, and a Discourse of Africa." *African Studies Review* 43, no. 3: 39–58.

Piot, Charles. 2010. *Nostalgia for the Future: West Africa after the Cold War.* Chicago: University of Chicago Press.

Puar, Jasbir. 2005. "Queer Times, Queer Assemblages." *Social Text* 23, nos. 3–4: 121–39.

———. 2007. *Terrorist Assemblages: Homonationalism in Queer Times.* Durham, NC: Duke University Press.

———. 2011. "'I Would Rather Be a Cyborg Than a Goddess': Intersectionality, Assemblage, and Affective Politics." *EIPCP.* eipcp.net/transversal/0811/puar/en.

Reddy, Vasu. 2000. "Institutionalizing Sexuality: Theorizing Queer in Post-apartheid South Africa." In *The Greatest Taboo: Homosexuality in Black Communities*, edited by Delroy Constantine-Simms, 163–84. Los Angeles: Alyson Books.

Rosello, Mireille. 2003. "Unhoming Francophone Studies: A House in the Middle of the Current." *Yale French Studies* 103: 123–32.

Said, Edward W. 1983. *The World, the Text, and the Critic*. Cambridge, MA: Harvard University Press.

Sandoval, Chela. 1991. "U.S. Third World Feminism: The Theory and Method of Oppositional Consciousness in the Postmodern World." *Genders* 10: 1–24.

Schramm, Katharina. 2008. "Leaving Area Studies Behind: The Challenge of Diasporic Connections in the Field of African Studies." *African and Black Diaspora: An International Journal* 1, nos. 1–2: 1–12.

Sedgwick, Eve Kosofsky. 1993. *Tendencies*. Durham, NC: Duke University Press.

Serres, Michel. 1991. *Le Tiers-instruit*. Paris: François Bourin.

Spivak, Gayatri Chakravorty. 1993. *Outside in the Teaching Machine*. New York: Routledge.

———. 1994. "Can the Subaltern Speak?" In *Colonial Discourse and Post-colonial Theory: A Reader*, edited by Patrick Williams and Laura Chrisman, 66–111. New York: Columbia University Press.

———. 2003. *Death of a Discipline*. New York: Columbia University Press.

Spivey, Sue E., and Christine M. Robinson. 2010. "Genocidal Intentions: Social Death and the Ex-gay Movement." *Genocide Studies and Prevention* 5, no. 1: 68–88.

Su, John. 2011. "Amitav Ghosh and the Aesthetic Turn in Postcolonial Studies." *Journal of Modern Literature* 34, no. 3: 65–86.

Swarr, Amanda Lock. 2012. *Sex in Transition: Remaking Gender and Race in South Africa*. Albany: State University of New York Press.

Thomann, Matthew. 2014. "The Price of Inclusion: Sexual Subjectivity, Violence, and the Nonprofit Industrial Complex in Abidjan, Côte d'Ivoire." PhD diss., American University.

Walcott, Rinaldo. 2012. "Outside in Black Studies: Reading from a Queer Place in the Diaspora." In *Queerly Canadian: An Introductory Reader in Sexuality Studies*, edited by Maureen FitzGerald and Scott Rayter, 23–34. Toronto: Women's Press.

Woubi Chéri. 1998. DVD. Directed by Philip Brooks and Laurent Bocahut. San Francisco: California Newsreel.

Woubshet, Dagmawi. 2010. "New World Alphabet." *Transition* 103: 118–21.

Zeleza, Paul Tiyambe. 2009. "What Happened to the African Renaissance? The Challenges of Development in the Twenty-First Century." *Comparative Studies of South Asia, Africa, and the Middle East* 29, no. 1: 155–70.

WORKING THE *MALECON*

Whiteness, Queer Respectability, and the Loss of Intimacy in Cuba

Karina Lissette Cespedes

After Love: Queer Intimacy and Erotic Economies in Post-Soviet Cuba
Noelle M. Stout
Durham, NC: Duke University Press, 2014. vii + 248 pp.

After Love stands out among recent ethnographies on Cuba's post-Soviet erotic economies. Particularly noteworthy is Noelle Stout's analysis of white- or light-skinned mixed-race families without connections to remittances from abroad. Their particular dependence on whiteness provides "a complementary perspective to studies on blackness and marginality in post-Soviet Cuba" (14). Stout's focus on anachronistic partnering among white Cubans and white tourists from the global north captures the differences between the economies of desire navigated by black Cubans and white Cubans. Additionally, the book provides a long-awaited analysis of the marginality of lesbians enduring post-Soviet economic restructuring, providing one of the few accounts of lesbian social networks in the anthropological literature.

 After Love engages three distinct households. The first is shared by white gay and lesbian siblings invested in gay respectability—households that incorporate tactical sex workers migrating into Havana in their extended social networks, but whose members argue that those who engage in tactical sex work are lazy and uninterested in "hard work." The second household is run by a white gay proprietor of a small business and his roommate/assistant, both using the services of *pingueros* (male sex workers servicing gay men), who lament the erosion of sincere emotional ties and the rise of relationships of convenience and economic dependency. These two households express lingering socialist ideals about work and love, and "believe . . . the loss of true affection [is] diagnostic of a dystopic future in which everyone [would] face . . . the challenges of daily life and state control alone" (39). Although the "loss of genuine love" has been a Cuban lament stretching back to the pre-Revolutionary era, Stout looks to these two households as diagnostic of the particularities of the contemporary post-Soviet "loss of love." These households proved deeply dependent on white gay social networks unsympathetic to structural disadvantages, and "despite their sensitivity to how job security rested on personal networks, lighter-skinned and white urban gays often ignored the reasons why some could remain within the boundaries of 'decent labor'" (78).

Stout's third household is exemplary of queer black Caribbean women operating outside the privileges of whiteness, hetero- and homonormativity, and the boundaries of "decent labor." Prizing elements of African American hip-hop culture, the women running the show in this central Havana household refused to define themselves as lesbian—instead using the term *moderna* (a creative adaptation of the term *modern*) to describe their sexual relationships with each other, their respective Cuban male lovers, and their tourist clients. The women Stout engages with in this household are exemplary of women of color outside white lesbian social networks; the women in the latter also "secured their living through relationships with foreign men . . . that departed from their 'true' homoerotic desires" (79), but unlike the *moderna* household, they disavowed their actions as *jineterismo* (tactical sex/hustling). These *modernas* who go to work on the *malecon* (Havana's famous seawall known to be a pickup site for hustlers) navigate queer enclaves as "fixers," providing services between male sex workers and clients—including opening their home as a space for African American gay tourists to engage in affective exchanges with black *pingueros*.

The book captures the underappreciated tensions between populations of color and those identifying as "whites," highlighting the discourses of racialized deviancy and laziness found in the tense and bitter codependencies between *pingueros* and white gay men, lesbian enclaves, discourses of gay respectability, and the advantages of white gay and lesbian social networks. Stout's attention to the interconnections between tactical sex, whiteness, and the rise of a respectable gay identity in Cuba makes this an important text in Cuban studies. Her attention to gay respectability suggests a shift in the racialization of sexual identities. As such, Stout's study suggests that terms like *jinetera* (women engaging in tactical sex) and *pinguero* have taken on heightened racial meaning, used to describe black participation in tourism from the poorer and less "cultured" provinces seen as parasitically attaching themselves to respectable white gay and lesbian enclaves. The racialization of these social categories suggests a transition from the discourses of *jineteras* as "heroes" reported in the 1990s, to white Cubans, themselves on the margins of sexuality, who "imagine *jineteras* as poorer, darker, and less educated than themselves" (78).

A noteworthy aspect of the book is Stout's attention to the perspective of tourists in gay/*pinguero* enclaves. Her account adds to the growing body of literature on *pingueros*, emerging out of anthropology and the turn toward critiquing the desires and motivations of white and nonwhite tourists from the global north.

However, the book does not address the black social networks that ensure survival for Afro-descendant populations. The mixed-race and black collaborators whom Stout engages appear to be just as disconnected from black social networks as they are from the white ones, with the exception of a growing interest and dependence on African American gay tourism and African American cultural forms—such as hip-hop. Stout's black and mulatto collaborators appear disconnected to a legacy of black intimate spaces of autonomy and black cultural resistance on the island. Also unexplored are the potential existence of black lesbian social networks, the interdependence between black Cuban gay men and *pingueros* from the provinces, and the relationship of these to regimes of whiteness. Additionally, Stout's focus on the rise of new class systems related to tourism relies on class categorizations that best operate within capitalism and are imprecise in Cuba's still mixed economy; as such, descriptions of her collaborators as "lower-middle class" or "middle-class" read as strained translations and simplifications of the complex social structuring of Cuba, which still includes socialist distinctions of status not found in the class system of North and South America.

Stout's attention to experiences of abandonment, betrayal, and disillusionment adds to the growing scholarship on Cuban sexual identities under neoliberalism and raises important question about populations in Cuba's economies of desire who have reached the outer limits of affective exchanges.

Karina Lissette Cespedes is associate professor in the Department of Ethnic Studies at Colorado State University.

DOI 10.1215/10642684-3428870

WILL STEELWORKERS JOIN THE FIGHT FOR LGBTQ CIVIL RIGHTS?

Elizabeth Lapovsky Kennedy

Steel Closets: Voices from Gay, Lesbian, and Transgender Steelworkers
Anne Balay
Chapel Hill: University of North Carolina Press, 2014. xi + 192 pp.

Steel Closets: Voices from Gay, Lesbian, and Transgender Steelworkers is a small gem of a book that poses the question, why aren't gay steelworkers actively interested in coming out in the mills? And the related questions: Why hasn't the expanding movement for gay civil rights affected the mills? Why don't gay, lesbian, and transgender steelworkers feel conditions are getting better, as Anne Balay amply documents that they don't? These are germane questions for a growing LGBTQ civil rights movement.

Living in northwest Indiana close to the giant steel mills, Balay became intrigued by how little information existed on queer steelworkers, particularly given her own experience of working as an auto mechanic in a male-dominated shop. She searched assiduously to find forty gay steelworkers—divided evenly between women and men—who were willing to tell their stories. But the book goes beyond the recovering of hidden voices. Balay approaches the material from a perspective grounded in contemporary LGBTQ scholarship; she analyzes the intersections of class, gender, and sex in the formation of identity and explores the dialectical relationship between desire and space.

Balay makes the steel mill come alive as a key shaper of the conditions of work and of gender and desire. The mill emerges as a behemoth, lumbering into the contemporary world, engulfing all who cross its path. Balay links the mill's physical isolation to its isolation from broader societal movements, through such things as the massive physical structure that workers enter through a gate, or the labor practice of the swing shift, which prevents workers from socializing with outsiders, or the practice of showering before leaving to wash the plant off one's body. This separation is reinforced by the overwhelmingly timeless quality of the mill, since many of the processes and therefore the building designs are over one hundred years old. Change does not seem to be on the agenda.

Balay is not arguing that nothing has changed; rather, she presents all the contradictions that shape the complexity of steelworkers' identities. All their stories (collected from 2009 to 2012) emphasize the need for secrecy and the real dangers in identifying as gay. The narrators recount the horrendous homophobia they faced on the job—physical violence, rape, firing, verbal abuse, and general graffiti such as "die faggot die." Only a few narrators were "out," and that was after enduring severe harassment and developing a strategy of joking that played with the stigma imposed by other workers.

To maintain secrecy, it was imperative for steelworkers to separate work and family, which has always been a challenge in the steel mill because the dangerous nature of the work requires close cooperation. Balay argues that recent technological changes have further blurred the division between public and private. Workers now have more free time during which they talk about their home life, sex, and drinking. Ironically, their stories show that this intimacy is always stressful for gay-identified workers, increasing isolation because the closeness cannot be realized without risking exposure.

Reminding the reader that the steelworker was/is the archetype of American masculinity, Balay gives the pleasures of gender a central role in her analysis, devoting a chapter each to female masculinity and male masculinity in the mills. All women narrators were masculine. They were aggressive, strong women who took pride in meeting the challenge of difficult work, liked holding their own when men tried to boss them, and liked joking with men. They disliked the homophobic and sexist treatment, yet at the same time most took pride in and even liked the job. These women told of terrible things that happened at the plant but in the very next sentence stated obvious pleasure in their competence and their ability to hang out with the men. Balay convincingly argues that women do this work not only for the money but also because it suits their temperament and gives them pleasure. For such women, the steel mills offer some freedom to express their personalities, and they temporarily thrive, particularly since they are not welcome in other jobs because of their masculinity.

Balay argues that "the mill produces masculinity just as it produces steel" (100). She captures the atmosphere by sharing a narrator's description of the mill as being surrounded "by a green haze of testosterone" (99). In a climate where the steelworker is no longer unambiguously associated with masculinity because of layoffs and cutbacks, she explores how masculinity is produced through embracing toughness, danger, and risk. Balay does an excellent job in revealing the hidden pleasures for men—some gay, most not—in this all-masculine environment. All the narrators describe the horseplay and ribald conversations between men and the quick hookups between men in the nooks and crannies of the mill. Narrators did not expect these kinds of connections, which were quite consistent with their sexual interests but profoundly hostile to their naming queer desire, since their partners identify as "normal" or "straight" men. Thus it is not at all in queer steelworkers' immediate interests to come out at work, as it would limit their sexual pleasures with other male workers.

Steel Closets strikes a helpful balance between stories of complicity with oppression and stories of resistance. The book by definition is about the oppressiveness of the mill, the way workers cope with secrecy, violence, and danger. At the same time, Balay relays stories of pleasure and reminds the reader that the oral histories themselves create imaginary communities of resistance. Capturing the contradictions and complexities of identity, the book lays the groundwork for wondering about the catalysts for change in the mills while preparing the reader to become better informed allies of queer blue-collar workers.

Elizabeth Lapovsky Kennedy is Professor Emeritus of Gender and Women's Studies at the University of Arizona.

DOI 10.1215/10642684-3428882

IDENTITY AT PLAY

Margaret Rhee

Gaming at the Edge: Sexuality and Gender at the Margins of Gamer Culture
Adrienne Shaw
Minneapolis: University of Minnesota Press, 2015. x + 304 pp.

In *Gaming at the Edge: Sexuality and Gender at the Margins of Gamer Culture*, Adrienne Shaw offers a grounded and provocative take on representation: "The industry, as well as scholars, must treat diversity as a goal in its own right, rather than an exception to the rule or the sole domain of those who are marginalized" (5). Through an accessible theoretical voice, Shaw astutely urges representation studies and media industries to revise their approach to gaming. Building on the foundational work of feminist, queer, communication, and critical race studies, her qualitative research methods present a new political and theoretical vision of representation in the digital age. Shaw focuses on digital games, although her theoretical framework engages with and applies to other types of media, and offers a groundbreaking emphasis on a new medium that has generated controversial discourse on the inclusion of women and LGBTQ representation. Her primary method involves "dozens of in-depth interviews with people who play digital games and are members of marginalized groups to parse the connected but distinct issues of identity, identification, and media representation" (7).

Shaw's monograph, grounded in audience reception study, thoroughly interrogates her research questions on representation through various methodologies. For example, in chapter 1, Shaw outlines the theoretical and methodological challenges of studying representation, and the benefits of ethnographic approaches to media study. She then offers an intriguing finding in chapter 2, where she argues that "although people may identify with characters because they identify as members of a specific group, this is not the only way they form connections with media texts" (9). In chapter 3, Shaw provides a fascinating view of ludic and narrative elements of video game play and the politics of avatars. In chapter 4, she discusses whether representation of marginalized groups is a priority to marginalized players, and she asserts that it is not a strong factor for the inclination to play. Finally, in the conclusion, Shaw furthers her argument by analyzing her research participants' response that it is "nice when it happens" that games include diverse characters. She develops her argument for changing future policies in the gaming industry and representational studies that do not burden marginalized players with the responsibility of representation.

Shaw's extensive research on gaming and the LGBT community began in 2007, and her study draws not only from audience reception but also from industry policies. The conclusion recounts her experience at an Electronic Arts (EA) and Human Rights Coalition mini-conference on LGBT issues. From this "diversity event," Shaw argues that designers should be cognizant of their own "default choices" and represent characters that are not just male, white, and heterosexual. The burden of representation should not fall on marginalized players, and Shaw turns to her participants' responses on diversity to illustrate this point. As Shaw explains, "In part, what the 'nice when it happens' theme signals is that players are not interested in carrying the responsibility for caring about representation" (226). This ambivalence, she claims, can be explained by the contemporary media landscape, which may give marginalized game players more access to diversity in media such as film and television. Moreover, she writes, "people often view video games as relatively trivial and, thus, in-game representation as inconsequential. What 'nice when it happens' indicates is that individuals push back against the attempt to locate responsibility for representation in the audience" (214).

Although Shaw offers important suggestions to media producers in their approaches to diversity, and qualifies her analysis of marginalized player responses of "nice when it happens" in terms of their potential "disempowerment" by lack of representation, her analysis could have been strengthened with further discussion of media activism. As Shaw writes: "When does difference make a difference in how members of marginalized groups interact with video games and other media? The identity politics–based approach to studying and demanding representation simply does not work" (8). While the participants in Shaw's study seem relatively unconcerned with media activism, Shaw, as a central voice in the study, presents a model of an activist-scholar who has taken on the burden of representation with important results. Along the lines of LGBTQ scholars and activists such as Vito Russo, Marlon Riggs, and Judy Sisneros, Shaw's voice clarifies how marginalized communities are enriched by engaged activism. While the burden, as Shaw astutely claims, should not lie with marginalized players, her critique of inclusionary politics may be strengthened without rejecting inclusionary policies. For example, her critique of SONY Online Entertainment's program GIRL: Gamers in Real Life (which advocates for more women as producers and consumers) suggests GIRL and other programs do not directly lead to nuanced representations of gender or sexuality. However, we can understand that programs such as GIRL may challenge the lack of inclusion of women working in the industry. *Gaming at the Edge*, however, provides an important intervention into the politics of representation: "How we represent media representation is as important as media representation itself" (215).

Margaret Rhee is a visiting assistant professor of women and gender studies at the University of Oregon.

DOI 10.1215/10642684-3428894

LOOKING FOR THE QUEER IN THE NATIVE

Mark Rifkin

The Queerness of Native American Literature
Lisa Tatonetti
Minneapolis: University of Minnesota Press, 2014. xxii + 278 pp.

In *The Queerness of Native American Literature*, Lisa Tatonetti sets out to illustrate that "the field of Native literature was always already queer" (xii). She does
so through a range of strategies, attending to magazines and printed ephemera,
novels, films, and poetry. More than simply locating forms of queer self-expression,
in the sense of texts generated by subjects who might be identified as "queer," the
book seeks to suggest that *queerness* (meaning here challenges to normative modes
of sexuality and gender) proliferates in and through forms of Native cultural production from the 1970s onward. The reason for this time span is less causal than
(counter)canonical. As Tatonetti observes, the period after the publication in 1968
of N. Scott Momaday's Pulitzer Prize–winning novel *House Made of Dawn* has
come to be known, following a phrase coined by Kenneth Lincoln, as the Native
American literary renaissance, and the book aims to inhabit this rubric in order to
refunction it, proposing that we might productively rethink how we approach contemporary Native writing and visual culture by attending to its heretofore under-
examined queer traces and trajectories. Doing so aims to track "unruly articulations of queer relationships in now-canonical Native literature" (ix).

At one point, Tatonetti quotes Leslie McCall's observation that "different methodologies produce different kinds of substantive knowledge" (144), and
Tatonetti's own methodology might be characterized as one of accretion and jux-
taposition. Each chapter builds up a range of interpretive objects either to make
particular histories visible or to trace representational itineraries across a particular genre or author's oeuvre. The first chapter establishes a genealogy of "queer
Native literatures" by surveying writing from the 1970s onward for examples of
the copresence of Native voices and queer topics in gay magazines, Native texts
in anthologies of various kinds (including *This Bridge Called My Back*), drama,
fiction, poetry, and scholarship. The next chapter turns to the poetry of Maurice

Kenny. It foregrounds his largely overlooked published writing in non-Native magazines (particularly *Fag Rag*) in ways that center "urbanity, sex, and the overlapping nature of oppressions," providing queer mappings that fall out of "heteronormative framing[s] of the Native American literary renaissance and Red Power era" (36). Chapter 3 turns to the work of Louise Erdrich, providing a sweeping analysis of appearances of female masculinity, homoeroticism, and other deviations from "the primacy and supposed normalcy of heteroromance" in her many novels (84); Tatonetti shows that "Erdrich represents lesbian, gay, bisexual, transgender, transsexual, intersex, queer and Two-Spirit (LGBTIQ2) identities as part of the everyday fabric of Native communities" (68). In chapter 4, Tatonetti moves from text to film, addressing how *Big Eden*, *Johnny Greyeyes*, and *The Business of Fancydancing* all "segregate Indigeneity from queer sexuality by relegating queerness entirely to off-reservation spaces" in ways that suggest that nonnormative desire must be separated out from questions of sovereignty and Native territoriality (123). The final chapter takes up the writings of Janice Gould, exploring Gould's representation of her relation to her people's history and lands across her poetry collections and essays as examples of "Indigenous assemblage" and "queer diaspora": "Gould's depictions of family demonstrate that Indigenous ties are not fixed, linear maps strictly bounded by and confined to mission, reserve, or reservation geographies but are instead breathing, *active* entities capable of transformation and continuance" (147). Tatonetti's own process of assemblage and apposition works to make clear the scope and significance of varied queer presences throughout Native cultural production from the 1970s onward.

In this vein, though, I wonder about the amount of work she asks *queer* to do here. The term clearly extends beyond identities based on homoerotic object choice or nondominant forms of gender expression, opening onto the ways a wide range of Native texts challenge (hetero)normalization. However, to suggest that Native self-representations writ large are and have been "always already queer" seems to shift from employing intellectual strategies in queer studies to designating Indigenous artistic production as expressive of an immanent "queer" intent/orientation. While Tatonetti addresses how non-Natives have seized on Native histories and social practices to validate their own belonging as settlers, the book is not as fastidious as it might be in marking how categorizing things Native as "queer" can repeat rather than displace this problem. The question of the extent to which "queer" is deemed a useful rubric by Native authors, filmmakers, and people more broadly (as well as the variety of responses to that question) could have been posed more explicitly. In addition, the book often gestures toward disjunctions between indigeneity and queerness, such as in the straightness of the reservation in the films she discusses, in the fact that in many of Erdrich's novels those characters that are nonnormative in terms of their sexuality or gender expression are white, and in the fact that Kenny's self-consciously Native and explicitly homoerotic poems appear in different venues. This tension seems to me worthy of further exploration. How do we approach these examples, even stagings, of nonrelation? Are they solely evidence of the force of normativity or phobia? What difference does naming forms of desire, pleasure, gender expression, embodiment, family formation, homemaking, and so forth as "queer" make to how they mean in relation to other social forms and formations? How do we interpret the putative failure to be "queer," in whatever that term might designate?

The strength of Tatonetti's study lies in its collating of authors, texts, moments, relations that might be conceptualized as "queer." Doing so helps make available a rich archive for contesting heteronormative presumptions, including the de facto imagination that things "queer" are a relatively new addition to Native letters and cultural life. I am less certain, however, about the implications of employing "queer" as a primary category in which to situate the possibilities for Indigenous self-determination and Native flourishing.

Mark Rifkin is director of the Women's and Gender Studies Program and professor of English at the University of North Carolina at Greensboro.

DOI 10.1215/10642684-3428906

RIDDING ONESELF OF MAD MASTERS

Tom Roach

Thoughts and Things
Leo Bersani
Chicago: University of Chicago Press, 2015. xv + 120 pp.

"As it is," spews the tempestuous Birkin in D. H. Lawrence's *Women in Love*, "what you want is pornography—looking at yourself in mirrors, watching your naked animal actions in mirrors, so that you can have it all in your conscious-ness, make it all mental." Arguing against the will to conceptualize *Eros*, a will that at root is a lust for power, and in favor of an immanent sensuality untainted by psychology, Birkin and his creator resonate throughout Leo Bersani's new col-lection of essays, *Thoughts and Things*. If in the past Marcel Proust has been Bersani's most frequent literary guide through the nine circles of the sexual psyche (he appears here alongside René Descartes and Sigmund Freud in essay-title-of-the-year contender "'Ardent Masturbation'"), Lawrence seems the spectral chap-erone—the unconscious?—of Bersani's output since 2004's *Forms of Being*, per-haps even since the stunning final essay of 1995's *Homos*, "The Gay Outlaw." In other words, if Bersani via Proust once worked to "make it all mental," as Birkin would have it, his more recent ontological and, in chapter 5 of the new volume, cosmological explorations of sensuality and relationality might best be designated Lawrentian.

This, then, is neither the Bersani who, so the story goes, inaugurated the antisocial turn in queer studies, nor is it the Bersani celebrated for his meticulous psychoanalytic investigations of sexual desire and its discontents. The intellectual rigor remains brilliantly on display, and one can certainly find traces here of the sex-induced self-shattering and phantasmic ego dissolution the author championed in his seminal "Is the Rectum a Grave?" However, the Freudian interpretative frame-work that once buttressed these concepts seems itself to have imploded. Despite an engaged reckoning with Freud throughout—chapter 4, for example, begins with dream analysis and proceeds to an assertion that the Freudian self is in fact not divided but an incongruous, nonidentical unity—this volume on the whole could indicate that Bersani is simply through with talking about sex. Or, to put it more precisely, flipped and reversed: through with talking about sex, Bersani simply *is*. As the essays collectively develop the author's signature concepts concerning connectedness amid estrangement, difference within sameness, and self-divestiture in the face of a seductive and voracious narcissism, one gleans in Bersani's style and tone an "at-homeness" even in the most *unheimlich* of environments—notably the cosmos. Unlike earlier essays such as "Against Monogamy" and "Sociability and Cruising" in which queer sex plays a key role in realizing a nonviolent ethics, here we find an ecstatic yet humbled self emerging in decidedly nonsexual characters and circumstances: in Carol White, protagonist of Todd Haynes's *Safe* (chapter 2), and even in the disorienting relationship the author has with his own thought and work (the antipreface, "Against Prefaces?"). Might this turning away from sex be the inevitable result of maturity? Might it be for Bersani a new form of post-Freudian, post-Proustian freedom? Recall the wise words of the wizened Cephalus, one of Socrates's first interlocutors in Plato's *Republic*: "When the desires cease to strain and finally relax, then what Sophocles says comes to pass in every way; it is possible to be rid of very many mad masters." For Bersani, the maddest of masters is the ego and perhaps only when one is through with sex—that is, through with affording sex both the power of individuation and the status of a self-hermeneutic—that our ontological porosity, our solidarity with world-being, becomes sensible.

But to be through with sex one must first endure it, experience it, and experiment with its potential. To be rid of mad masters one must know them intimately and confront their folly head-on. This is to say, everything Bersani was not afraid to ask about sex in the past suffuses each page of *Thoughts and Things*. These essays are not merely the culmination of his previous inquiries into antirelational sexuality and impersonal intimacy, however; they are openings to dazzlingly new lines of thought. For at least a decade Bersani has been detailing the psychic benefits of encounters with strangers (anonymous sex) and strangeness (aesthetic subjectivation), and now he is able to articulate convincingly an anti-intersubjective ethical schema that prompts a genuine respect for difference. The self propelled by and through these ethics—an exogenous self, neither subject nor object, neither thought nor thing—is not so much born as affirmed, its "placedness" in the world primordial, but all too often obscured. If previous masters Freud and Proust taught Bersani much about sex and the self, perhaps it will take Lawrence to illuminate a sensuality that seethes beneath, between, and through thoughts and things, a sensuality pulsating with ecological rhythms that sync the self to the world. Given

Bersani's fearless, unpredictable, and thrillingly disconcerting intellectual trajectory to date, we should all look forward to seeing if and how he grapples with this master.

Tom Roach is associate professor of literary and cultural studies and coordinator of women, gender, and sexuality studies at Bryant University.

DOI 10.1215/10642684-3428918

About the Contributors

Anjali Arondekar is associate professor of feminist studies at the University of California, Santa Cruz. Her research engages the poetics and politics of sexuality, colonialism, and historiography, with a focus on South Asia. She is the author of *For the Record: On Sexuality and the Colonial Archive in India* (2009), winner of the Alan Bray Memorial Book Award for best book in lesbian, gay, or queer studies in literature and cultural studies (Modern Language Association, 2010). Her current book project, "Abundance: On Sexuality and Historiography," grows out of her interest in the figurations of sexuality, ethics, and collectivity in colonial British and Portuguese India.

Ashley Currier is associate professor of women's, gender, and sexuality studies at the University of Cincinnati. She is the author of *Out in Africa: LGBT Organizing in Namibia and South Africa* (2012). Her current work focuses on the politicization of homosexuality in Malawi and the transnational dynamics of LGBT rights promotion in Côte d'Ivoire and Liberia.

Aliyah Khan is assistant professor in the Department of English, the Department of Afroamerican and African Studies, and the Arab and Muslim Studies Program at the University of Michigan, Ann Arbor. Her current research and writing focus on indigeneity, sexuality, and Islamic creolization in the contemporary Caribbean and its diasporas.

Keguro Macharia is from Nairobi, Kenya.

Thérèse Migraine-George is a professor of romance languages and literatures and women's, gender, and sexuality studies at the University of Cincinnati. She is the author of *African Women and Representation: From Performance to Politics* (2008), *From Francophonie to World Literature in French: Ethics, Poetics, and Politics* (2013), two novels, and a book of essays.

Maya Mikdashi is a Mellon Postdoc at the Institute for Research on Women and the Department of Women and Gender Studies at Rutgers University, and the author of the forthcoming book *Sex and Sectarianism: Secularism, Secularity and War in Contemporary Lebanon*. She has worked on documentary and narrative film projects, and cofounded *Jadaliyya*, an e-zine centered on critical approaches to studying the transnational Middle East.

Geeta Patel is associate professor in the Department of Middle Eastern and South Asian Languages and Cultures and the Women, Gender & Sexuality Program at the University of Virginia. The author of *Lyrical Movements, Historical Haunt-ings: On Gender, Colonialism, and Desire in Miraji's Urdu Poetry* (2002), she has two forthcoming books: *Techno-Intimacy* and *Billboard Fantasies*. She has pub-lished academic and popular pieces on poetry and on capital and is coediting an issue of *Society and Business Review on Islamic Capital* and writing a manuscript titled "The Poetics of Finance," on pensions, insurance, credit, debt, poetics, and promises.

Jasbir K. Puar is associate professor of women's and gender studies at Rutgers Uni-versity. She is the author of *Terrorist Assemblages: Homonationalism in Queer Times* (2007), winner of the Cultural Studies Book Award from the Association for Asian American Studies. Her edited volumes include a special issue of *GLQ*, coed-ited volumes of *Society and Space*, *Social Text*, and *Women's Studies Quarterly*. Her forthcoming monograph, "States of Debility and Capacity" (2017), will appear in a new series, ANIMA, which she coedits with Mel Chen.

Lucinda Ramberg is assistant professor in anthropology and feminist, gender, and sexuality studies at Cornell University. Her first book, *Given to the Goddess: South Indian Devadasis and the Sexuality of Religion* (2014) was awarded the 2015 Clif-ford Geertz Prize in the anthropology of religion, the first Michelle Rosaldo Prize for a first book in feminist anthropology, and the 2015 Ruth Benedict Prize from the Association for Queer Anthropology. She is currently at work on a book proj-ect titled "We Were Always Buddhist: Dalit Conversion and Sexual Modernity in South India."

Neferti X. M. Tadiar is the author of *Things Fall Away: Philippine Historical Experi-ence and the Makings of Globalization* (2009) and *Fantasy-Production: Sexual Economies and Other Philippine Consequences for the New World Order* (2004). She is professor of women's, gender, and sexuality studies at Barnard College, Columbia University, and coeditor of the journal *Social Text*. Her current book project is titled "Remaindered Life."

Diana Taylor is University Professor and professor of performance studies and Span-ish at New York University. She is the author of five books including the award-winning *The Archive and the Repertoire* (2003) and *Performance* (2016). She is the recipient of the Guggenheim Fellowship and the ACLS Digital Innovation Fellowship, and recently became vice president of the Modern Language Association (MLA) and will be president in 2017. She is founding director of the Hemispheric Institute of Performance and Politics.

Ronaldo V. Wilson is associate professor of poetry, fiction, and literature in the literature department at the University of California, Santa Cruz. He is the author of *Narrative of the Life of the Brown Boy and the White Man* (2008), winner of the 2007 Cave Canem Prize, and *Poems of the Black Object* (2009), winner of the Thom Gunn Award for Gay Poetry and the Asian American Literary Award in Poetry in 2010. His latest books are *Farther Traveler: Poetry, Prose, Other* (2015) and *Lucy 72* (2015).

DOI 10.1215/10642684-3428930

CLEARING THE GROUND: C. P. Cavafy
POETRY AND PROSE, 1902–1911
Translations and Essay by Martin McKinsey

CLEARING THE GROUND illuminates a crucial decade of Cavafy's artistic development, marked at one end by a period of personal crisis and near creative stasis, at the other by the poetic force of the celebrated "Ithaca." The years in between are held together by the "Unpublished Notes on Poetics and Ethics."

Part private confession, part public pronouncement, part journal entry, and philosophical *pensée*, these notes were recorded between 1902 and 1911. In some of them, according to the eminent critic G. P. Savidis, Cavafy attempted to formulate "thoughts and feelings never before uttered" in his own language — in certain cases, in any language.

The full body of the notes is correlated in this volume with the poetry Cavafy was writing contemporaneously — in particular the startling "hidden poems" begun in 1904. What emerges is a striking narrative of artistic and personal becoming.

The afterward by Martin McKinsey examines Cavafy's sexuality and accompanying pressures in historical context and suggests the part they may have played in his poetic breakthrough.

• • •

I scanned Cavafy availed by 15 pundits of translation and criticism; only now I begin to discern this poet to be a man as I would be, a man whose diversified fulfillments and consummations were to be held within one apprehension, the which, I now discern, he had achieved.
Thank you, Martin McKinsey. —Richard Howard

It strikes me as a must for anyone interested in modern poetry, queer studies, or (as I am most) how a poet discovers the courage and conviction to make a lasting mark in language. —Joshua Weiner

An important contribution to primary and secondary bibliographies of modern gay letters.
—Josiah Blackmore

The notes put each poem in a new light. —Thomas W. Laqueur

 a press for literary translation

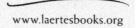 www.laertesbooks.org

   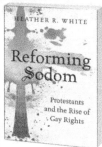

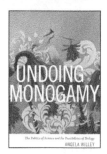

Undoing Monogamy
The Politics of Science and the Possibilities
of Biology
ANGELA WILLEY
9 illustrations, paper, $23.95

*"Undoing Monogamy is a highly generative book for
anyone interested in feminist science studies, cultural
studies of sexuality, and especially new materialism."*
— **Jennifer Terry**

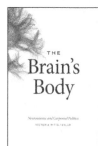

The Brain's Body
Neuroscience and Corporeal Politics
VICTORIA PITTS-TAYLOR
paper, $22.95

*"An exciting book, The Brain's Body adds wonderful new
dimensions to the fruitful but still limited conversation
between neuroscience and feminism."*
— **Rebecca M. Jordan-Young**

Biocultural Creatures
Toward a New Theory of the Human
SAMANTHA FROST
paper, $22.95

*"Samantha Frost offers a clear, accessible, and
theoretically invigorated exploration of the life sciences,
demonstrating the need for a new theory of the human."*
— **Susan Merrill Squier**

Obstruction
NICK SALVATO
19 illustrations, paper, $24.95

*"Joining gorgeous readings to new critical vocabularies
and startling insights, Obstruction rewards the close and
slow reader... it creates paradigms that, once absorbed,
become difficult to think without."* — **Jack Halberstam**

The Feminist Bookstore Movement
Lesbian Antiracism and Feminist Accountability
KRISTEN HOGAN
34 illustrations, paper, $24.95

"*The Feminist Bookstore Movement should be required reading for any feminist who appreciates a good book.*"
— *AnaLouise Keating*

Blacktino Queer Performance
**PATRICK E. JOHNSON &
RAMÓN H. RIVERA-SERVERA**
23 illustrations, paper, $34.95

"*[A]n essential volume for all concerned with performance and its theory. Its pages bristle with smart and unexpected discoveries arranged with fresh expertise.*" — *Thomas F. DeFrantz*

Ingenious Citizenship
Recrafting Democracy for Social Change
CHARLES T. LEE
paper, $25.95

"*A refreshing take on forms of liberal complicity.... Timely and smart. A convincing account.*" — *Jasbir K. Puar*

Light in the Dark/Luz en lo Oscuro
Rewriting Identity, Spirituality, Reality
GLORIA E. ANZALDÚA
Post-Contemporary Interventions
10 illustrations, paper, $23.95

"*It is such a pleasure to see this book at last; it makes her legacy vivid when it is most needed.*" — *Donna Haraway*

Queer Marxism in Two Chinas
PETRUS LIU
2 illustrations, paper, $23.95

"*In this quite stunning book, Petrus Liu offers a new intervention into gender and sexuality studies.*"
— *Judith Butler*

DUKE UNIVERSITY PRESS

presents a new series:

ANIMA
edited by Mel Y. Chen and Jasbir K. Puar

Cultivating projects that enact transdisciplinarity through the deployment of feral methods and rogue genres, ANIMA reimagines that which animates or enlivens a thing, opening up the study of "life" in all its definitional, philosophical, cultural, and political complexities. Books in this series bring together queer theory, postcolonial studies, critical race scholarship, and disability theory to foreground the oft-occluded import of race and sex in the fields of posthumanist theory, new materialisms, vitalism, media theory, animal studies, and object-oriented ontologies. ANIMA emphasizes how life, vitality, and animatedness reside beyond what is conventionally and humanistically known.

Bioinsecurities
Disease Interventions, Empire, and the
Government of Species
NEEL AHUJA
16 illustrations, paper, $24.95

"Bioinsecurities is impressive for the scope of its vision and its meticulous attention to detail and nuance."
— *Priscilla Wald*

Forthcoming:

Animate Planet
Making Visceral Sense of Living in a High-Tech Ecologically Damaged World
KATH WESTON
24 illustrations, paper, $24.95

DUKE
UNIVERSITY PRESS

dukeupress.edu | 888-651-0122 | 🐦 @DUKEpress

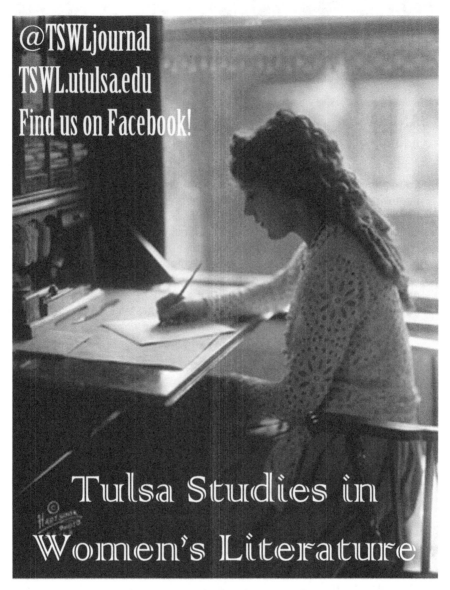

@TSWLjournal
TSWL.utulsa.edu
Find us on Facebook!

Tulsa Studies in
Women's Literature

A journal dedicated to
scholarship on women's
literature of all
nationalities and time periods

Subscribe now for Spring 2016 Vol. 35 No. 1

Printed and bound by CPI Group (UK) Ltd, Croydon, CR0 4YY

13/04/2025

14656484-0002